Quality: Sustaining Customer Service

The Sunday Times 'Business Skills' series currently comprises books on total quality management, personal skills and leadership skills.

This first class series has received a warm welcome from readers and critics alike: the opinion of Christopher Lorenz of the *Financial Times*, for example, is that it is 'excellent . . . well worth reading'. It is designed to build into an essential management library of authoritative and handsomely produced books. Each one, providing a definitive standalone summary of best business theory and practice in its field, is also carefully co-ordinated to complement *The Sunday Times* 'Business Skills' video training package of the same name produced by Taylor Made Films.

BOOKS IN THE SERIES:

QUALITY: TOTAL CUSTOMER SERVICE
Lynda King Taylor
ISBN 0712698434

QUALITY: MEASURING AND MONITORING
Tony Bendell, John Kelly, Ted Merry, Fraser Sims
ISBN 071265514X (P)

QUALITY: ACHIEVING EXCELLENCE
Edgar Wille
ISBN 0712698639

QUALITY: CHANGE THROUGH TEAMWORK
**Rani Chaudhry-Lawton, Richard Lawton, Karen Murphy,
Angela Terry**
ISBN 0712698337

EFFECTIVE MEETINGS
Phil Hodgson, Jane Hodgson
ISBN 0712698736

TIME MANAGEMENT
Martin Scott
ISBN 0712698531

SUCCESSFUL PRESENTATIONS
Carole McKenzie
ISBN 071265691X (P)

LEADERSHIP: THE ART OF DELEGATION
David Oates
ISBN 0712656510 (P)

LEADERSHIP: THE ART OF MOTIVATION
Nick Thornely and Dan Lees
ISBN 0712656464 (P)

Quality: Sustaining Customer Service

by

Lynda King Taylor

C
CENTURY
BUSINESS

First published in the UK 1993
by Century Business
An imprint of Random House UK Ltd
20 Vauxhall Bridge Road, London SW1V 2SA

Random House Australia (Pty) Ltd
20 Alfred Street, Milsons Point
Sydney, NSW 2061, Australia

Random House New Zealand Ltd
18 Poland Road, Glenfield
Auckland 10, New Zealand

Random House South Africa (Pty) Ltd
PO Box 337, Bergvlei, South Africa

Set in Bembo by SX Composing Ltd, Rayleigh, Essex
Printed and bound in Great Britain by Mackays of Chatham PLC, Kent

A catalogue record for this book is available from the British Library.

ISBN 0-7126-5519-0

Contents

Acknowledgements

This book is dedicated to those who made it possible. I have written two books in one year for the *Sunday Times* Business Skills Series and to achieve this required support and skill, not to mention style and a sense of humour, from those who surround me.

First, my thanks to the team who help me give birth to my words and produce a book with all pain, patience, paternalism and passion. The support team includes Lucy Spencer and her crew at Computer Training Agency in Hatfield. They have now worked with me on two treatise and at all times have shown a dedication beyond the call of duty. I have been shown sustained customer service by Lucy, Sam, Marian, Kurston, Jenny, Jackie, Rachel, Sarah, Debby and John, who alone knew where the apostrophe went! In keeping with all excellence organisations, they have not only served me – the customer – with personal and professional prowess, they have been fun, and made a tough task and target all the more tolerable and tenable. I also thank Alan and Sean for their editorial energy and particularly acknowledge both Susan West and Elizabeth Hennessy at Century Business who are the most supportive and spirited publishers I have worked alongside. Authors can be notoriously fickle and finical, and they managed me magnificently! Thank you.

Thanks go to my 'Mystery Shoppers' team who are required to reap research to reinforce the author's 'gut' reactions. Colleagues such as Annie Redmile at The Communications Team, Christopher Hope at Convergent Communications and Rod Fountain at Westoning House all in London. Along with David Dowse of Royal Crescent PR in Cheltenham they provided prompt, profound proficiency, not to mention pleasure!

Then there are the team who live *in* the book – the organisations I have worked alongside. Quite simply, without them there would be no book. Their strive and stealth, courage and commitment are commendable. Too many to mention by name, I sincerely thank you all for allowing me to be part of your journey. In addition, may I thank both Neil Garnett of Texaco UK and Chief Inspector Tony Brooking of the Metropolitan Police Service who were very supportive with logistics and kept me in the right direction within their organisations when deadlines were demanding. They, plus the Scottish Tourist Board, in keeping with so many others in the case study companies, were always at the end of a telephone, and gave me quality customer service for which I am most grateful.

Finally, there are those who live *with* the book. They are my fondest friends who have given energy, empathy, enthusiasm and unerring understanding. I dedicate my book to you all – and especially to my mum.

Thank you all so very, very much.

Lynda King Taylor
London – 1993

Foreword

Whilst many UK organisations admit customer service is essential, research for this book reveals that a significant number have instigated programmes with a flurry of activity but without lasting success. The main problem is sustaining a focus on customers after the initial enthusiasm wanes.

The organisations studied in this book have been selected as examples where the focus on customers has become a way of life, or where a customer–centred emphasis is being developed in the boardroom and below in a culture that has been highly cynical about such endeavours.

Many of the organisations featured realise that it is individuals in the market place who pay their wages and allowed them to operate or survive at all. All truly understand the value of satisfied customers, and by constantly reviewing, and continually improving, customer service, they not only identify and meet customers' needs and expectations, but often exceed them. Other organisations are still selling that truth to their internal customer – the staff. Achieving service excellence is a continuing journey, not a destination. Survival is of course not guaranteed, although failure in sustaining customer service is terminal. For the organisations in my latest *Sunday Times* Business Skills Series title, sustaining customer service in the 1990s is not merely an option – quite simply they believe there is no alternative. Too many organisations believe they offer what the customer wants without ever asking them, and too few have grasped that the essentials of customer service are providing products and services to meet the customer's wants, needs and expectations. The trouble with sustaining customer services is that all too often companies set their standards by some criteria other than those the customer themselves would like to see in action.

The studies also highlight that customers exist inside the organisation as well as externally. Staff need to understand the value of working with one another and management must have a constant visibility. Too few organisations in my research had regular team briefings to discuss opportunities for improving service both within the organisation and outside, or to discuss whether customers' needs were being anticipated, met, exceeded and sustained.

Many staff I met admitted that they would not even recognise their boss, as they seldom saw him or her 'walking the job'. This, however, is a constant in many of the organisations portrayed in this book – management regularly being seen on the shop floor, or at the kerb, mixing with their staff as well as with their external customers. Organisations become flatter, teams get built and trust supersedes checking and control. All the case studies illustrate that the entire organisation must be geared up for superior customer service – it should never be given only lip service nor be simply a PR exercise. Readers will discover, as they travel across the studies, this is easier for some organisations than others.

Service today has become a vital element in the battle for the hearts, minds, money and support of the customer and general public. As such, a truly excellent service organisation 'inverts the tri-angle', with the customer at the top of the matrix and management becoming a servant to those at the sharp end who directly interface with the customer. Few UK organisations are built to satisfy the needs of the customer, but are rather more geared to boardroom bureaucracy and executive ego. BR – InterCity, the NHS, the Metropolitan Police and the financial companies immediately spring to mind from those in this book. But, because they are clearly on a learning-curve of cultural change, they are worthy of inclusion, if for no other rationale or reason than their honesty in exposing the dilemmas they face in their determination to improve and sustain customer service.

This book brings out the constants and consistencies on which executives insist in the quest for optimum customer service. These include a strong listening brief, towards staff and customers. Organisations throughout the studies restate and live their corporate values. The shared values in the organisation create a philosophy, a way 'we do things around here'. Beliefs drive behaviour which affect attitudes to customer service. The organisations check that existing values, aims policies and principles are consistent with core corporate commitments. When they are not, they rethink, restate, rekindle and reinforce new values, and involve everyone in understanding and living them. They then find practical ways through which they can implement corporate values. What executives *do* is what counts, and not what they say. The best add the spice of passion, potency, excitement, energy and enthusiasm to an intellectual and professional commitment to customer service.

Organisations in this book listen. What makes staff and customers happy and unhappy? What are their future wants and needs? How can the organisation retain them as customers, staff and supporters. Still listening, they ask what gets in the way of their staff delivering excellent quality and service, and seek to learn the truth. By doing this they discover ways to empower their front-line staff through more authority, information and a flattened organisation structure. Recruitment, training and staff recognition are a key to success, as are the essentials of listening and action on staff feedback. Team building becomes the norm as trust replaces control. For this they make a major investment in training. Customer service professionalism, self-confidence, caring and commitment require high levels of knowledge, skills and motivation. Training has a crucial contribution to make in all the areas covered in this book. It is often costly, but the price is not as high as the cost of ignorance.

Organisations check out their competitors – when they have them. But even the police appreciate that there could be alternatives. Companies in this book visit the opposition, use their services, learn from them, and are totally open-minded about them. After all, competitors who retain customers must be doing something right. More important, many organisations surprise and outwit the competition by being trend setters and innovators, which not only satisfies customer needs, but anticipates future ones.

Organisations in this book become flatter as they clear out bureaucratic dead-wood. Bureaucracy is a cancer and so is cynicism. It is always costly, and always inimical to good customer service. Tough targets can therefore be set, such as 20 per cent fewer reports for rules' sake, 20 per cent fewer meetings for meetings' sake. Challenges are made to every procedure and process system and only a minimum survive. The constant focus is on core business and competencies. Close partnership is pursued only with those suppliers who come on board the customer service way of life. Creative information technology is used to manage the new, sometimes complex, relationships with customers.

Measurement drives service performance, and all the organisations portrayed place great importance on this at the most senior level, usually in the boardroom. Customer questionnaires, user groups, consultative teams, forums and clinics become a way of life, as are personal visits between the organisations and its customers, freephone facilities, helplines, complaint and comment card analysis. All the studies reveal the problems of sustaining customer service over a long period of time, and the need for management to lead the way by agreeing and monitoring realistic long-term standards for every important aspect of quality and service. The key lesson is that customer satisfaction should be measured with the same dedication given to financial analysis, remuneration and reward.

The studies in the book speak for themselves. All the organisations covered in this book, in their attempt to sustain customer service, have had to remake themselves; some are turning themselves inside out. But all are committed to improving their actual product and service, the way it is presented, produced and served, to both their internal and external customers, and their after-sales service and support.

I am very grateful to all the organisations for their time, patience and wealth of wisdom and honesty in contributing to this book. My thanks to you all for working with me, and allowing me to share your experiences for the benefit of others. My best wishes for your journey to service exellence – and sustaining it. You all deserve to win.

Lynda King Taylor
London – 1993

1. Texaco Europe

'I have heard of a man who had a mind to sell his house, and therefore carried a piece of brick in his pocket, which he showed as a pattern to encourage purchasers.'

Jonathan Swift (1667–1745)

The Texas Company was formed in the USA in 1902, the name Texaco coming from the company's cable address. Texaco arrived in the UK in 1916, but petrol sales were low on the list of priorities at the time. The brand name Regent was used to market the company's petrol, a name that an older generation will remember. Texaco, as a trade name, replaced Regent in the late 1960s. Today, Texaco is Britain's fourth largest petrol retailer and ranks among the top ten North Sea operators.

Texaco are consistently striving for initiatives through which they can capture the hearts and minds of their employees for the customer service ethos. In the boardroom it's all about sustaining the 'discretionary' effort that employees give Texaco. That is the effort they need not give to the company to preclude being fired, i.e. doing that bit more than the minimal amount necessary to perform their jobs. In the view of Glenn Tilton, Chairman of Texaco UK, customer service is not something that the company can decree and then expect to succeed in achieving for long. Rather, it is the employee who has to give customer service willingly. 'For customer service to be sustained the employee has to be convinced that service is something worth giving to the customer, and that it is part of the contract that the employee has by implication – an implied contract

Figure 1.1 Some Texaco Facts and Figures

- Texaco was involved in the drilling of the first oil well in the UK sector of the North Sea in 1964.
- The first petrol in the UK refined from North sea oil was sold by Texaco in 1975.
- The first shops to appear on service station forecourts were pioneered by Texaco in the 1980s.
- The first company in the UK to make unleaded petrol available at all its main service stations was Texaco in July 1989.
- Texaco supplies nearly 1,300 service station outlets throughout the country.
- Every day Texaco sells nearly 9 million litres of petrol (approx. 2 million gallons) and 900,000 litres of diesel (approx. 190,000 gallons).
- In 1991 Texaco's sales of petrol and diesel in the UK totalled 3,500 million litres (770 million gallons).
- A busy Texaco service station will serve 4,000 customers a week.
- James Hunt won the 1976 Formula One world championship driving a Texaco-sponsored McLaren.
- Throughout the 1970s Texaco sponsored the indestructible world motorcycling champion Barry Sheene.
- The first Texaco TV ad, featuring James Hunt with classic comedians Morecambe and Wise, appeared in 1977. It was voted the most memorable commercial of the year.
- One of the longest running sponsorships in the world is Texaco's support for radio broadcasts from the Metropolitan Opera in New York, going strong for over 50 years.
- Since 1984 the company has sponsored the Texaco Trophy one-day international cricket series.
- Other notable Texaco sponsorships and partnerships include London City Ballet, Young Musician of Wales Competition, Texaco Theatre School, London and South East Division Rugby, Texaco Ladies' Challenger Tennis Tournaments.
- Texaco is a major Olympics sponsor, supporting national teams in 39 countries around the world, including the UK.
- The company has been a major private sector partner of the Department of Transport in road safety campaigns, with its award-winning 'Children Should Be Seen and Not Hurt' programmes.
- To celebrate the company's 75th anniversary in the UK, Texaco employees raised over £300,000 for the National Children's Home (NCH) charity. The entire Board of Directors of Texaco Ltd rose to the challenge by hauling a 14-ton road tanker 75 yards at London's Canary Wharf to raise over £25,000 for the NCH.

between the employee and all of our customers.' Glenn Tilton gives an example of such discretionary effort. On one of his regular shop floor walkabouts he stopped and talked to a young girl who had been with Texaco for six months in their Customer Care Division at Swindon. She had the job of picking up the telephone and dealing with customer complaints all day long.

> In my wisdom I said 'this must be a very frustrating and difficult job for you, and we appreciate your doing it'. She looked at me and said, 'Mr Tilton, why would you think that it is frustrating and difficult?'. I replied, 'Well, sitting here answering the phone and, by definition, dealing with people who are unhappy, you presumably have a frustrating and difficult time.' She said 'On the contrary, I have an opportunity to solve a problem and to turn an unhappy person into a happy person with every ring of the phone. I cannot imagine anything more rewarding and I love my work.' I said to myself that I should not have made such an assumption. What seemed to me, as I approached her, to be drudgery was clearly a mistaken impression on my part. I underestimated the power of that young spirit to turn her job into a challenge and into very positive work.

Part of the Texaco customer service ethos, says Glenn Tilton, is capitalising

> on that hidden spirit we get from integrating our ethos into everybody's approach to their work. This is what differentiates Texaco as a company. Once we get that differentiation integrated into our corporate personality I would challenge any company to try to replicate it. I believe that the differentiation of our corporate personality in that context, involving a special commitment to quality and customer service, is the most beneficial competitive advantage we can create.

There is no doubt that Texaco's customer service drive comes from the boardroom. For the 'more than a few' in the organisation who have not got the service message, Glenn Tilton warns: 'Our strategy is to isolate them. We subject them to peer pressure, and

3

make them conspicuous by their difference from the majority. If they continue to be different from the majority I convey to them that they had better seek employment elsewhere.'

What Texaco feel they must do is to embrace the logic of pulling together into a common thread various initiatives that at first seemed to be separate, distinct and disparate. For example, a reaffirmed commitment to quality and customer service, direct from the boardroom to the forecourt, is enshrined in Texaco's 'Our Service Promise' brochure, which has Tilton's photograph on it and is given to the customer at every service station. 'That is what I would like to see memorialised', says Tilton.

The market place must know that we, in Texaco management, understand and fervently believe in the association between our relationship with our employees and their relationship with our customers. It is about valuing yourself and your self-esteem – all back to that lesson that girl taught me at Swindon.

It is worth remembering that he would not have learned that lesson if he had not been there in Swindon at the coal-face. In excellence organisations, such visible commitment from the boardroom, serving those who directly interface with the customer, is a constant. It is also hard work. As Glenn Tilton indicates, there is no room for waverers. In this and other studies in this book, opinion concurs that everyone must come on board and make real commitment.

THE VALUE PROPOSITION IN SUSTAINING CUSTOMER SERVICE

In customer service the vital task is the removal of company rhetoric and its replacement with action, especially since customer service can become a broadly used term to cover a multitude of things. If a company is not careful, it becomes so commonplace that familiarity really does breed contempt. What an organisation must insure against is claiming to provide customer service without actually making sure the customer believes that to be the case. It is easy to carry out surveys which endorse what you are doing as an organisation, but you may focus on such a small populace that you are not getting to the real meat of the subject. As an organisation you must be able to assess customer service delivery for all those people who do not say anything about your service.

Quality – such as the quest for BS 5750 – has often been the hook on which organisations have hung their hat to achieve success. Alas, I have seen all too often companies that have created the façade, whilst the structure inside is wanting. John Darnley is General Manager Sales and Marketing for Texaco UK. Every time you see anything to do with Texaco, in one brand form or another, it is his responsibility. His overall brief is to ensure that whatever class of market Texaco operate within there exists a 'superior value alternative' versus the competition, although he also has to be attentive to profit targets. As he explains, 'As an organisation, we must establish who are our targeted customers, what is their requirement for doing business with us. That's what Texaco have to deliver – the "value proposition".'

Achieving that objective with a non-differentiated product like a litre of petrol is tough. Texaco believe that although they operate in a commodity-type market place, they can give their brand a differentiated position. They tackle that, with their design, their System 2000 sites, major retail training programmes and so on. Any Texaco service station that has been built in the last five years will typically conform to a retail image standard Texaco call System 2000, with a recognisable colour scheme and a consistent image which is an attempt to differentiate in order to sustain customer service.

As John Darnley says,

System 2000 is quite simply everything. Everything we do is an attempt to say to Mr or Mrs Customer, 'Given that you have an equal buying opportunity we can meet your requirement better if you come to Texaco. The value that you receive, less the price you pay, is more valuable to you than a competitive alternative'. If the customer lined all these points up at the end of a cul-de-sac, i.e. with Shell, Esso or Texaco, we know that we can deliver better value. It's at that point that we believe we are giving customer service and can meet the value proposition.

Texaco know they are in business competing with others and are in a game of inches, not miles, with all the variety of customers they have got to be able to target to stay ahead in business.

Figure 1.2 Texaco's Mission: Our Mission

To create a continuous improvement process which unites Texaco Ltd in its commitment to a quality culture and focuses our efforts to meet or exceed customers' expectations by:

Inspired leadership.
Employee participation.
Teamwork.

'It is not always easy to say that we are all things to all people', says John Darnley.

We have to establish who are target customers, and having done that, we have to establish what they want in that experience with Texaco, less the price they have to pay, I'm sorry to keep coming back to that, but that is what it is all about. Ultimately, the choice that you make to go to a restaurant calculates the benefits less the price, i.e. the value you get from it. Texaco must do that successfully, building the brand and creating the customer service which is inherent in delivering the 'value proposition'. If you measure it, it gets done. Quality of service has, to a degree, to be driven by the result. We have got to see quality as a way of achieving a successful business, and sustaining customer service is clearly the ultimate test.

How this objective is being achieved within Texaco is covered in this chapter with reference to two of their operations, Texaco (Ireland) and Texaco UK Upstream. Texaco's Communication Charter is also reviewed, as an approach to sustaining customer service through improved staff communication. (For text, see Appendix 1.1.)

TEXACO COMMUNICATION CHARTER FOR SUSTAINING CUSTOMER SERVICE

Texaco's Communication Charter is a key component in the company's drive for total quality service. It establishes new guidelines for good communications, greater staff participation and for all employees to be better informed about the company and their role in it. Texaco believe this is essential if the organisation is to sustain internal and external customer service. For a company which considered itself to be well above average in staff communications, the results of a 1990 Texaco worldwide survey into staff attitudes proved both illuminating and disturbing. This 'vision and values' survey cast doubts on the effectiveness of communications throughout the company, with a lack of good practice being seen as a major block to improving quality and service. Comparing the Texaco UK survey results with those of Texaco Europe and Texaco overall, the UK scored lowest in this communication category. In particular, UK staff questioned the effectiveness of communication within the company and whether Texaco lived up to the principle of good communication.

The results certainly caused Texaco to stop and think, because staff felt they were not involved in the communication process, something fundamental to sustaining customer service. Glenn Tilton, Chairman of Texaco UK, immediately established a number of 'action teams' to tackle key problem areas arising from the survey. The issue of communication was naturally top priority. A communication team, consisting of senior managers from a wide cross-section of job functions, was briefed to investigate the problem areas.

First, what were the problems? Although the survey results seemed clear enough, was it that UK staff were simply more demanding then their colleagues around the world? Or was it perhaps that the UK company's culture and style gave the impression of poor communication? Equally important, what could the small communications team actually do to effect meaningful and measurable improvements within the company? It was essential the team did not focus too quickly on one particular issue but rather on the whole arena. Consequently, the problem–solving technique known as FADE ('focus, analyse, develop and execute') was employed from the start.

The 'focus' phase started with extensive brainstorming sessions from which key words and phrases began to emerge fairly consistently. These words were introduced into the 'problem statement' and subsequent 'priority objective' which eventually achieved team consensus. **Problem Statement**: Texaco currently lacks effective and participative communication. This inhibits the cultural change which is needed to achieve excellence. **Priority Objective**: This team will identify and implement participative communication processes which will enhance individual and group contribution and commitment to the successful achievement of shared goals.

From Texaco's early work sessions it was clear that, to ensure success, the solution could not simply come from within the group. They had to put participative communication into practice. Explains Neil Garnett, Manager of Corporate Communications at Texaco UK:

> This meant that the next stage, 'analysis', required extensive contribution from staff to determine those communications problems common throughout the organisation. However, rather than send out yet another paper questionnaire, which might or might not get completed and returned, we wanted to make the process as two-way and participative as possible. Thus a series of focus group meetings were proposed. Over 200 staff, about 10 per cent of the workforce, from all sites and across all grades, were randomly selected to form some twenty groups which communication team members would take turns in running. By this time we also had been smitten by the participation bug. To ensure a high degree of reply comparability, a uniform programme was designed which allowed staff the freedom to express personal concerns and

communication problems, but which was so structured that responses could be analysed according to common trends, opinions and ideas.

Attendance at these focus groups was entirely voluntary, and confidentiality was strictly guaranteed. The meetings sparked great interest, and very few invitees did not attend. Each group was scheduled to last about three and a half hours, and Neil Garnett says that most overran. 'Once discussions were under way, input from staff was wholehearted and most groups ran an hour over, with one or two lasting more than five hours! Discussions included identification of information needs and sources for day-to-day activities, the kinds of meetings attended and their effectiveness, and the effect on communication of different management styles. With over 200 individuals, the range of opinion was wide, but some of the comments were: "While overall communication is relatively good . . . it is in middle management where communication most often breaks down." Similarly: "The aims of Texaco are praiseworthy but the execution of the aims fall short; the breakdown appears to be at mid-management level." '

Several common subjects clearly emerged which formed the building blocks for development of Texaco's proposals. Garnett admits the 'development' stage was potentially the most difficult.

Staff involved in the focus groups had given us their full support and a wealth of ideas. As a team we were conscious that in order to get all staff to 'buy into' the final solution, it had to reflect as much as possible of what their colleagues contributed. There were other potentially conflicting issues. We had enough material to fill two volumes of Encyclopaedia Britannica, *but we did not want to produce a weighty tome staff would never read. The final result had to be brief, straightforward and simple. Also the solution would need to cover individual, work group and cultural communication problems. Which approach would allow us to put these three essentially distinct areas together into one package?*

The Charter simply emerged from team discussions. In a year of meetings and debates this was almost the first time there was immediate and unanimous acceptance of a suggestion. It was felt to be absolutely right.

> *The number of Charter points was finally reduced to 14. In addition, to give the document some 'teeth', minimum standards were included. So, for example, when the Charter referred to employees getting regular informal feedback from their supervisor in addition to their annual performance assessment, the minimum standard beefed this up by stipulating at least once per month and at the conclusion of a major task. We could have produced a much thicker document, but we felt it was important to condense our recommendations into a brief, easily understood publication like the Charter. As a last check, the 200-plus individuals who had participated in the focus group meetings were sent a copy of the draft Charter for their comments. Their reaction was more than encouraging. Over 95 per cent of the responses were positive. We had cleared the last hurdle – almost!*

Finally, Texaco had the 'execution' phase, which had to be striking to ensure maximum impact. A visually strong new design was created with a range of brochures, posters and special trainers' packs. The communication of the Charter was a two stage process in line with the participative spirit of the project. All staff were sent their own copy, with a covering letter from Roger Columb, Texaco's Managing Director. Departmental managers held meetings with their staff to review Charter concepts and the implications for their work teams. In effect, they took on the role of departmental trainers. To prepare them for this role, a special briefing meeting was called, attended by Glenn Tilton, to review all aspects of the Charter and its contents.

Texaco's Communication Charter is an ongoing project, involving regular monitoring and spot checks. Sample surveys are also undertaken to determine whether all staff have participated in departmental briefings and whether they are comfortable with, and understand, the contents. A Charter approach may seem a bit 'twee' but it has been ideally suited to Texaco's needs, and they believe it has been the most appropriate approach. As Neil Garnett says, 'If everyone accepts it, uses it and builds it into their day to day activities, we will see tremendous benefits to our internal communication.'

The original communication team leader, Jim Rowalt, General Manager – Producing Operations, endorses these comments.

> *If we can address and improve our performance across all the 14 areas in the Charter then the company will be a more communicative animal. People have said they want to understand more about their individual roles within the organisation and they want more inter-reaction with other members of the company. They wanted to feel part of the whole and to have a more participative, two-way style of communications. The Charter lays down a set of principles for everyone to follow. It is not a prescriptive set of procedures, but we are backing the Charter with actions that will monitor and measure its success.*

Roger Colomb agrees:

> *I constantly urge people to read the Charter and to operate its principles. Only if we accept and include them in our everyday working routines will we be able to create a more open, participative and enjoyable working environment which is essential for sustaining quality and service excellence.*

Ultimately, every Texaco employee has the right to bring a breach of the Charter to the appropriate Managing Director or department head for resolution. From my conversations with Texaco staff it was clear that some are looking forward to taking the company up on that offer!

TEXACO (IRELAND)

The opening quotation for the Texaco study came from Jonathan Swift who graduated from Trinity College Dublin in 1686. The essence of one of his greatest books, *Gulliver's Travels*, is a study of the human capacity for self-deception. Texaco (Ireland), in discussing their customer service culture, openly admit that it was partly self-deception on the loyalty of their customers that caused them as an organisation to change. Texaco have 450 service stations in Ireland, and there are 128 Texaco (Ireland) staff. They do not have any service station staff on their own payroll, as they all work for the licensees or independent dealers who operate the 450 sites. There are approximately 700,000 motorists on Ireland's roads and Texaco have 125,000 motorists continuously doing business with them.

In 1989 Texaco (Ireland) had a successful promotion, similar in operation to Texaco UK's Star collection. In the late 1980s there was an upward movement in oil price on the open market in Rotterdam. This should have been reflected in Ireland but the Government decided they did not want price increases, and also stopped all promotions and giveaways. With their margins cut, Texaco (Ireland) had to reorganise themselves and align their operating costs with the margins. In so doing it became a considerably leaner and fitter company, certainly in terms of manpower. As Vincent O'Brien, Managing Director of Texaco (Ireland), says 'What we did as managers was sit down and say "Okay, when we do emerge out of this rationalisation, numerically and in shape and size we will be a different company. But do we not also need to be a different company in terms of our total culture?"'

This was the first time Texaco (Ireland) started talking about change and the 'total culture'. O'Brien believes change is a condition common to all living things – everyone has changed since yesterday. It is not change that causes concern – it is the pace of change. Some people are motivated by it, others are threatened by it, but no one can avoid it. In Texaco (Ireland) they believe that understanding change, and the necessity for it, makes it easier to accept; wanting change and being motivated by it makes it a very positive driving force towards the achievement of their objectives.

A pertinent episode was the elimination of promotional stamps and tokens. Something had to replace these incentives, as customers had been getting added value through such gifts. 'We knew we must give the customer something to differentiate us from the competition', says Vincent O'Brien, 'so we replaced the promotions with a whole customer care programme at our retail service stations. It was giving the customer something different.' Recalling the ending of promotions, O'Brien says, 'It was rather like putting the lid back on the cookie jar and seeing the flies start to go away! How do we hold on to our customer base when we are no longer entitled to give them freebies, samples, tokens or gifts?'

In effect, Texaco (Ireland) discovered they had been deceiving themselves; there was very low brand loyalty from their customers. To the vast majority of people, petrol is petrol. A lot of customers had chosen the company as a result of their promotions, and therefore had a loyalty to those rather than to the Texaco brand. In view of this misguided (some would say) loyalty, Texaco (Ireland) re-thought through their business. Says O'Brien, 'I believe there is a niche market out there for our people by giving the best service in the business and providing the customer with value for money, not only in reality but also in perception.'

Where then do Texaco (Ireland) stand in that perception, and what do they have to do to justify in the minds of the public that they took the right decision when they decided to do business with Texaco? To answer that question, Texaco (Ireland) believes that three other questions need to be asked: 1. Why do people do business with Texaco? 2. Why should people do business with Texaco? 3. Why do people do business with my competitors? As indicated earlier in this study, Texaco use the word differentiation, rather than competition. How then do they differentiate themselves from their competitors and how can that differentiation give them a sustainable competitive advantage?

WHO IS THE CUSTOMER? WHAT DOES HE OR SHE WANT?

Competitive advantage is the only certain way Texaco (Ireland) can preserve adequate margins in the long term. Throughout Texaco the company undertake market research and ask the motorist what priorities they have when it comes to selecting the service station where they do business. There is a long list of possible factors: easy entrance and exit, shop, nice staff, canopy, car wash, self-service, full service, prices, and so on. The company analyse these in the hope that a competitive advantage can be obtained through knowing what attracts the customer to a service station, and conversely what can drive the customer away. However, Texaco also know that Esso, Shell, BP and the rest are all looking at similar survey data and probably drawing the same conclusions. Occasionally, Texaco, or indeed their competitors, may come up with a new product or additive and that will create competition. With advances in technology, however, it does not take long for the competition to catch up. Therefore, when products and facilities are perceived to be the same, where is Texaco's sustainable competitive advantage, their permanent differentiation?

To Vincent O'Brien it is people:

> *It is our people who are our own sustainable competitive advantage. It is they who must continuously change to meet market needs and shifts and, above all, recognise it is only themselves that can delight the customer. Of course, Texaco (Ireland) have helped to train their people, and will continue to do so throughout the 1990s. But only they can deliver.*

This is obviously the case, as the research threw up the simple fact that the biggest single reason why customers did *not* shop with Texaco Ireland was unhelpful staff. 'It was quite obvious', says O'Brien, 'that what we needed at our service stations were friendly, helpful, quality forecourt staff. Therefore we needed to take that message of quality and service to everyone through organising and running various training sessions for our retailers and our retailers' staff.'

According to Jim Keane, Manager Retail Sales at Texaco (Ireland):

> *As a result of this test bed, our feedback clearly indicated that we were on the right track as our efforts were received with positive enthusiasm. Market surveys carried out over a period also confirmed the trend.*

Vincent O'Brien gave me the job of creating a team drawn from field personnel, to prepare a Sales Representative presentation for our retailers on the concept of Quality and Customer Care. This team project culminated with a road show presentation to selected retailers, complemented by TV advertising. In visits to 155 retailers at seven venues nationwide, we listened, listened, listened, and actioned the feedback.

By the end of 1989 Texaco (Ireland) had got their message across to their 155 top retailers, who pump 65 per cent of their total retail volume. Texaco had also trained on behalf of those retailers some 275 of their front line troops. They started with the retailers themselves on the basis that customer care has to be driven from the top down. Vincent O'Brien says:

It's no good if the retailer himself does not actually believe in the whole concept. Having brought them on board, as indicated, we started training the retailer's staff. Coupled with that, we produced a television commercial which really to this day states what Texaco stands for, 'Say hello to Texaco. We're putting service back into service stations'. The TV advertisement highlighted that Texaco (Ireland) was not just dealing with product quality but also the quality of our forecourt service and equipment.

'PUTTING THE SERVICE BACK INTO SERVICE STATION'

Texaco (Ireland) felt it was important to go to the public by making a TV statement. That was a deliberate part of their strategy. Says O'Brien:

It put a tremendous responsibility on the retailer to respond to, and deliver, the advertisement's statement. I believe that was the right way to do it. You can train, and train, for ever and a day, but it doesn't matter whether you are playing cricket or football, you really have to go and play the match before you know what it is all about. That is what we said to our retailers. We were obviously a little bit concerned about over-promising but in actual fact we had very few negative feedbacks from it at all. At the end of the day I ask our retailers the simple question 'What business are we in?' The answer to that is, as I've already endorsed, 'We are in the people business'. That really is our business – it is about satisfying people. Of course, you must be sure you have got things technically right – you have got to get the quality of your products right – but if you get all of those things right, and do not get the people side of your business right, you really knock it all on the head.

Figure 1.3   Texaco (Ireland) Retail Mission Statement

Quality and customer care will form the basis of developing Texaco Retail into a customer–driven profitable enterprise. The effort will come from within with heavy emphasis on the importance of ongoing training both for staff and retailers. There is a New Vision for Texaco (Ireland):

- A Company that is constantly changing in its determination to serve its customers better and improve its operating efficiency.
- A Company of well trained professionals dedicated to serving their customer.
- A Company that respects its customers and is respected by them.
- A Company that is both admired and feared by its competitors.
- A Company that the rest of the industry strives to imitate but when they do they find that we have moved to a higher plateau.
- A Company that welcomes the question 'why' from its employees and customers.

Today, Texaco are constantly reinforcing the customer service message. As Jim Keane says:

We are forever searching and looking for fresh opportunities to become more successful and profitable than ever before. Customer service management is all about giving added value in today's competitive environment. You may ask how can you provide added value without incurring additional cost? Part of the solution is to go back to basics — service with a smile, and it pays. Our research shows that retailers known for customer satisfaction often out-perform their competitors. It's basically 'Good money from good service'. The quest for the best customer service is enshrined in our guiding principles of vision and value (see Figure 1.3). To achieve our vision and value we must listen to our customer. What his or her needs and wants are. In other words, constantly get feedback and then make some co-ordinating sense from it.

Vincent O'Brien recognises the importance of the customer and is constantly seeking out ways to satisfy their needs. Traditionally he got this information through the normal company channels, up through the system. Today, he is always 'walking the job'; and in his quest for excellence he decided to approach the customer directly through his questionnaire 'Say Hello to Texaco'. He actions the responses from customers very quickly, and the questionnaire is designed to allow for responses which can be easily co-ordinated and actioned, such as the provision of puncture repair and window-wiping services. The important aspect of this survey is that responses go straight to O'Brien 'post paid' and he sees them all.

REINFORCING THE CUSTOMER SERVICE MESSAGE

The surveys are, of course, essential, but they mean nothing in sustaining customer service if the people side of the business is not right. Vincent O'Brien is the first to admit, however, that 'getting the people side right' is not always easy. Texaco (Ireland) have had to achieve consistency right across all their sites, and that can be difficult when stations are independent or licensees. Usually, the company are having to influence people who are not on their staff payroll. Sustaining the 'quality customer service' ethos requires a constant reinforcement, and this Texaco (Ireland) do through a whole series of meetings, going out on the road talking to the retailers, explaining to them the advantages of the service message. How do Texaco (Ireland) define the customer? They appreciate that it is not just the motorist or the retailer. Rather, 'customer' goes beyond that and includes, for example, the person working alongside another staff member waiting for their input in order to be able to move forward, i.e. the internal customer. Not only the representative but also the switchboard operator or the order clerk – everyone has a customer. As Vincent O'Brien says, 'Each evening, as staff head for home, I hope they ask themselves the question "Have I served my customer?".' To achieve this, O'Brien believes that the kind of people Texaco (Ireland) should employ are:

- People who operate with a team spirit.
- People who support one another.
- People who compete with one another in the achievement of their objectives.
- People who question the way things are done and yet accept and co-operate with the higher decision even when it differs from their own personal opinion.
- People who reach out for responsibility beyond their brief.
- People who add value to the company.

The kind of people they believe they do *not* need are:

- People who have a problem for every solution rather than a solution for every problem.
- People who discourage others by their actions or lack of actions.
- People who find reasons for not doing things instead of finding reasons for doing things.
- People whose only answer when they fail to meet their objectives is to hope that everyone else fails too.

Managing Customer-Centred Change

All of this means changes in attitude, behaviour and stance. Vincent O'Brien admits that whilst all people have to live through change, and change is a constant, some people feel threatened by it. Such people must have support through the change process demanded by a customer service culture.

> *You will find that you will have a small number of people who find it extremely difficult to come on board. What you essentially have to do is to continue to walk with them. What you try to ensure is that their reluctance is not blocking a group of other people from coming on board. That is something you really have to think twice about. You have to make sure that all the key players are with you. I know you would like to have 100 per cent running with change, but that is unrealistic. A large proportion of people will come on board pretty automatically, but you have to really watch for that approximate 15 per cent who may not necessarily be in the opposed camp, but may well be in the neutral camp.*

Interestingly, this 15 per cent figure is one quoted by many organisations covered in this book: 10 per cent definitely not wishing to commit to the service ethos, and 5 per cent who may be 'neutral' but are probably only paying lip-service to the concept. This is why the constant boardroom reinforcement message is so vital.

Texaco (Ireland) discovered that those people who had most difficulty in accepting change were not those at the sharp end of the business; more often it was those in middle management. In any company living through internal cultural change there has to be a greater degree of empowerment for people down the line. In consequence, it is the middle management group who see their roles and responsibility diminishing, and to whom a lot of explanation is due. O'Brien emphasises:

> *In fact, the empowerment of their people to act and be responsible, and to carry out and make decisions at a lower level than before, does not*

diminish their roles and responsibilities; rather, it encourages them to bring themselves and their people forward. It's not necessarily to do with age, more the length of time some managers have been in the game. Often the middle management level see themselves as the meat in the sandwich. The top executive in the boardroom is pushing hard for cultural change and the new quality customer-centred organisation. However, you have a lot of people on the shop floor saying 'This feels good, this looks as if it is going to let me get on with my job', but there is this group in the middle who are asking 'Where do we fit into all of this?'. They are the group you really have to work hard on, because at the end of the day you really must bring those people along with you.

Texaco (Ireland) have been particularly concerned, therefore, to ensure that middle managers participate in comprehensive training programmes. They have, for example, all attended customer care and quality programmes, and have all been on continuous improvement courses. Although this is time-consuming, training of the type illustrated throughout this book is essential for the successful management of change. This is why organisations in this book, all of whom are facing similar challenges, place such emphasis on high quality external training and development programmes. They can be costly, but is there any alternative?

Another way of dealing with those who are reluctant to change is through peer pressure. The objective of any change, particularly to a customer-centred organisation, is to win over the majority. If a company can do that successfully, then those people who are reluctant to come on board would not be negative in a blocking sense, because they would see their companions and peers moving forward. They can then be carried forward with the tide, to a degree. If an organisation can get enough people on board, no-one really wants to be the odd person out. Vincent O'Brien believes that few in an organisation are overtly hostile to what the board are trying to achieve. However, there can be certain managers who say they are committed to sustaining customer service but in reality are 'yes' men.

When this arises, you have got to talk to their subordinates. You can always sense, when talking to people one level below a particular employee, whether that person is on board or not. It need not necessarily be something specific they say, but you can usually see the frustration that these people feel when they are not getting sufficient green lights from their boss.

What this requires is another constant in excellence organisations – 'management by walkabout'. This means visibility on the part of the Chief Executive and the senior management team: getting out and about, and being seen. Through this approach it becomes quite natural for managers to be talking to subordinates along the lines indicated by Vincent O'Brien.

QUANTIFYING SERVICE ENERGIES

The challenge at Texaco (Ireland) now is to sustain their customer service image. This requires continual training and monitoring. Their next stage is a more structured monitoring system, that is, better ways to measure what they have been doing. They do not know what is happening on the ground in terms of actually quantifying and measuring their customer service energies, whether in terms of quarterly, monthly or half-yearly snapshots to see whether Texaco (Ireland) are moving forward or remaining static. They have begun a whole new series of market research which is trying to test, 'Are they as good as they think they are?'. Although they are four years down the road from starting their customer care programme, and training all their retail staff, the question must be, given the investment they have put in, 'Is it really registering to the extent they would have hoped and expected?' Also, 'Are there any new ideas out there in the market place?' Often an organisation can become so focused on one particular aspect of customer care that it misses out on other progressive efforts. Texaco (Ireland) will still use the 'mystery motorist' input gained from their survey sources, but in much future research they will organise group discussions. They have found that a most effective way of measuring performance is to bring a group of 15-20 people together with market researchers in different centres around Ireland for several hours of discussions. Trying to do a sample on one service station can be tricky: motorists who pull into a service station are usually in a hurry to get out, and certainly don't want to answer a lot of questions.

In the discussion group approach, Texaco do not know where the participating individuals do actually buy their petrol from, so they are, in effect, sampling the average motorist to establish proper benchmarks from which they will launch any new initiatives. Every service station by its very nature is different. Some are big, with maybe 48 nozzles; some are small, with two pumps outside a public house or a general store. What Texaco (Ireland) are saying is that customer service should be appropriate for the particular location. In some cases customer service may be nothing other than 'Good morning' and a smile. However, they are trying to achieve consistent degrees of courtesy and friendliness across all their 450 service stations. As O'Brien says:

> *That is the key issue. When you go into a Texaco station anywhere in Ireland it should be friendly, it should be warm, it should be welcoming. It should not make any difference if it is our biggest site or one of the small two-pump stations; you should get the same degree of warmth, friendliness and total customer service.*

CUSTOMER SERVICE AT TWO TEXACO STATIONS

John Cuddihy, who runs the Texaco (Ireland) service station at Douglas Road in Cork, says:

> *The customer is, without doubt, the most important person here. Without customers we will not grow and prosper; it is, after all, our customers who dictate how busy we become. If our customers like the service they are getting, they will come back. If they don't like it, they will go elsewehere. Customers are funny – they do not say much about bad service or complain but, in the end, they win. They just don't come*

back. Here, customer service is a priority. All you have to do is remember Texaco's slogan 'We are putting the service back into the service station'.

John Cuddihy believes that 'a smile can go a long way' but that his staff must appreciate just who a customer is:

- A customer is not dependent on us, we are dependent on them.
- A customer is who we are here for.
- A customer is not an interruption.
- A customer is doing us a favour by speaking to us and giving us an opportunity to serve them.

Figure 1.4   Douglas Road Customer Service Code

At the Douglas Road station customer service is summed up in the word 'Texaco': **T** – Talk to your customer. **E** – Excellence – give them excellent service. **X** – Xpress your gratitude for their custom. **A** – Accuracy – the ability to observe your customers' needs. **C** – Courtesy – the ability to be obliging and polite. **O** – Offer them every service available to you (oil, water check, windscreen services).

'You'll never see anyone here argue with a customer', promises John Cuddihy. 'They know they may well win the argument, but, much more likely, they will lose the customer. We have always to ask ourselves, with every customer, why they passed our competitors and came into Texaco, and realise that service is part of the answer.' Cuddihy has put a complaints and compliments box in his service station shop and welcomes complaints from customers.

Once we get a complaint we have an opportunity to find a solution and satisfy the customer, our ultimate aim. It is widely known that every dissatisfied customer will tell ten other potential customers about the bad service they have received. It is not always easy to treat every customer as special, but we can try. It is very difficult for us to say we will be perfect, but if we improve a little every day we will be coming nearer to perfection in sustaining customer service, which is what we want.

Another excellent Texaco (Ireland) example I saw was the Ballydowd service station, run by Vincent Callan. He points out that Ballydowd has succeeded in developing a 'one-stop location' which caters for all customer needs and adds, 'Every customer who passes through our station is always made to feel good and is handled in a professional manner.' Three major examples of this approach are worth citing:

Customer Complaints

Vincent Callan feels that any customer complaint can also be looked on as an opportunity to turn a bad customer experience into a long-term customer friendship. 'We have bent over backwards to solve any problems that have arisen, and smothered the customer with kindness. The benefit of this is that we very rarely lose a customer and also that good news spreads quickly.'

Forecourt Service

Ballydowd have a complete forecourt service running from 7am to 11pm with adequate staff to make the service effective. Customers can have their cars filled with petrol, checked for oil and water, vacuumed and also have the car washed without delay. Says Callan, 'I believe this had a major effect on the high level of lady drivers now using the station. I would attribute 15 per cent of present business volume to the level of service being offered.'

Customer Information Centre

This is located just inside the front doors of the Ballydowd shop and offers a telephone, fax, photo-copier, map and tourist information. 'This has been very successful' notes Callan: 'It is in regular use at all times during the day, and we only charge 75p to send a one-page fax, half the cost in Dublin.'

Focus on Service Strengths

Customer service in Texaco (Ireland) is continually reviewed, improved and sustained. Jim Keane's team still exists and it is constantly involved with:

- recognising training needs
- implementing training programmes
- ensuring a uniformity of purpose
- establishing direction and keeping the programme on course
- conducting site audits
- ensuring the support package is improved upon

The team's objective is to redefine the mundane and make their redefinitions happen on the ground. Emphasis on the training and development programme endorses this support. Says Keane:

In the 1990s we must differentiate ourselves from our competitors by ensuring that doing business with Texaco is the best experience a customer could imagine. We are confident we have the ability to do this better than the competition because we have the people with the commitment and the know-how to motivate both the front-line people and our retailers through our on-going customer care programme. We believe from our experiences over the last two years that our future focus lies very much with our retailers. So, our mission is quite simply to promote quality customer care through our retailers.

Texaco (Ireland) field sales managers and their teams are now selecting receptive retailers to champion their cause. They are training these retailers in 'service station customer care management'. Says Jim Keane,

We now have a customer-driven network of stations which set a high-level benchmark of standards and quality service. They are at the frontiers of modern service station retailing and the envy of the industry. But we must constantly strive to reinforce the message – we simply

cannot afford to be complacent. Our customer care goal is quite simply, the 'moment of truth', when the customer, having made his or her first contact with us, leaves our place of business a happy customer.

Vincent O'Brien continues:

We have now reduced our costs, increased our efficiency and are generating earnings. All of this has to be sustained, and in order to do this we must continue to innovate, to be flexible and to focus on our strengths while eliminating any weakness.

When O'Brien says 'innovate', he means that the company must shape trends, not react to them.

Opportunities are out there in the market place – trends need to be shaped and Texaco (Ireland) must do it. Our representatives know they must be order makers not order takers. Being 'flexible' means being responsive to the needs of the customer – remembering that the system does not dictate, the customer does. You can shape a trend which meets customer needs and yet permits you to operate efficiently.' And he adds: 'I believe that in the people business, which we are all in, it is people who make the difference. People are our differentiation. It is the entire team that make Texaco and its retailers the best in the business.

TEXACO UK UPSTREAM

During 1992 Texaco reorganised the whole of their upstream operation, in order to grow the business significantly. What that required was a different perspective for the future on what people would do, their work and the kinds of references they would have to work to if Texaco were to make these new developments happen.

In essence, the reorganising of Texaco UK Upstream is a study of sustaining customer service internally. For the uninitiated, this upstream operation is responsible for the drilling and discovery of underground hydrocarbon deposits, their appraisal and, if there are sufficient quantities, engineering a development scenario for recovery. That might mean building a platform and putting in place equipment such as pipelines to take the discovery to market.

During 1991 Texaco made four or five discoveries which were evaluated as being big enough to do something with. However, the UK company did not have a component of its business that specialised in developing a new field. They had components that could make discoveries, and they had components that could produce from existing discoveries very efficiently. But they lacked the capacity for developing upstream assets. In the North Sea, Texaco have one of the best portfolios of upstream assets in their entire worldwide operation. What they needed was an organisation for the 1990s that allowed them to exploit this asset base. Their activities have always taken place in the context of a changing environment but in recent years the pace of these changes has accelerated. Had they continued to maintain the status quo, they would have fallen behind competitors who were better able to respond to change.

REORGANISATION OF TEXACO'S UPSTREAM OPERATIONS

The nature of the work in the North Sea and upstream does not facilitate gradual transition when reorganisation becomes necessary. The opportunity to do new things has a cost and time window, and it is imperative to do them as soon as realistically possible. One thing was clear: the old organisation did not have the structure to make the developments happen. Texaco therefore embarked upon a review of the organisational structure of their upstream business, anticipating that its conclusions would have far-reaching implications for the way in which they carried out their business in the years ahead. Their aim therefore was to develop a flexible organisation which could respond quickly to changing business needs.

By creating business units and multi-disciplinary teams to undertake specific objectives, the company aimed to achieve a flexible structure which would sustain competitive edge and customer service. Bob Solberg, Managing Director of Texaco UK Upstream (later Deputy Chairman, Texaco UK), explained:

> *In order to make this new organisation perform efficiently we needed to work together in an atmosphere of mutual support and co-operation to ensure a quality performance. We are endeavouring to change the corporate culture and this could not be done overnight. We have to succeed if Texaco UK Upstream is to achieve its strategic goals and build a long-term future. However, we also remembered that everyone is someone else's customer in our operation, so we developed the new organisation structure together.*

The defined objectives of the reorganisation were geared to business goals and customer needs, and the change process was managed in a participative style. Explains Solberg:

> *We took 27 people from across the organisation and gave them a six-week time horizon to do a study. We highlighted what we were trying to accomplish as a strategy for the business, and we asked them, with their knowledge of the organisation, what would be the most appropriate shape and style that the organisation could take, and what would be the lowest level of staffing that was sufficient. These 27 people were all in the original organisation, from different levels and from both our locations, Aberdeen and London. They did not produce the strategy. You have to know what you are trying to do before you build the organisation to do it. So they started as a team with the strategy known, and were asked 'If you had to do this, what is the best service style for the organisation to have? How quickly could Texaco get that new organisation up and running, and how efficiently could you staff it while providing the best service to our customer?*

The members of the team were removed from their other operations and given this assignment exclusively. An important consideration is that whenever Texaco undertake these participative projects they use a Texaco employee from another location who is skilled at 'facilitating' such an organisational steer. This is the 'facilitator', who develops a menu, a time agenda, the rules on how items should be considered and how the team should be organised, at least initially. The facilitator does not develop any rules about what the study group or project team can undertake, think about or propose, but he does give the team discipline on how they should relate to each other and how quickly they have to try to reach conclusions. The use of external facilitators in this fashion is a norm in many excellence organisations, their selection and training is discussed in other studies in this book.

As Bob Solberg explains:

This study group were not senior management. Senior management did gather on another team comprising six people, including myself, and the team of 27 worked for the team of six. They were our customers. We acted as a unit which they were employed by. They would bring their findings to us and we would help sort them out, agree or disagree with, as the case may be. But, periodically on the really tough issues the two teams would have to get together and work through explanations of the strategy.

Interestingly, one of the items that the Texaco team of 27 had the most misunderstanding about was the role of management in a customer–centred environment: what do the managers do? Bob Solberg had asked them to consider levels of supervision. As a guideline he suggested a flatter management structure of three or four levels at the outside, but what the team of 27 kept wanting was more levels of management.

When the two teams came together and worked it through, it became more of a misunderstanding between us about what managers do. As a result of working together we were able to agree a new understanding of the role of management. The first ingredient is that of 'management monitor', responsible for producing different results from the organisation. That is a big part of managers' responsibility, although it should only constitute about a third of their time. The rest of what managers do is to look after the assignment of resources. They ensure the organisation has the proper resources of both money and human beings.

Hopefully, the Texaco Communication Charter mentioned earlier will aid the above type of discussion, and also help avoid, in any future Texaco reorganisations, some of the confusions that occurred with the upstream one. Texaco's implementation plan began early 1992 and everything was completed by August of that year. But problems were already rearing their heads after two to three months. A pressing issue was obvious: large numbers of individuals had little or no understanding of the rationale for the reorganisation.

ENSURING EVERYONE UNDERSTANDS THE CULTURE

When Texaco UK Upstream announced their new customer-centred structure, they were very careful to contact every individual employee with an explanation of what the board were trying to achieve. They published a book that gave all of the logic for the reorganisation, then travelled to make presentations to all affected staff about what Texaco were asking individuals to participate in. They named the new management, and redistributed people through the new organisation.

It took several weeks to do all this communicating. About two months later, in the third month of the new organisation, Bob Solberg gathered together every manager in the new organisation, about 25 people. They went to a retreat for a week and worked on three things: team building, which was really getting to know one another better; strategy and strategic measures for the future; and communication. At the start of the communication part of this week of retreat, there was a facilitator who asked people to talk about the new organisation. What became painfully obvious to Solberg was that not everyone understood why Texaco UK Upstream had been reorganised. Doubters existed, even in the management team. The discussion and activities were interrupted as everyone re-reviewed the reasons why Texaco had started the reorganisation.

This continual reinforcement message is a vital component when engineering any major change. Says Solberg:

> *We discovered, within an hour of listening to people discussing why we did this – and remember these were senior people giving directions to the people around them every day – that in some cases they were saying things that missed the focus point entirely and were not even accurate. What that showed me was that, in all organisations, if you do not talk to people all the time, and constantly reinforce your message, individuals will make up reasons for their own point of view. Then you do not have a co-ordinated working unit. I guess there's a lesson to be learned from that, which is the importance of confirming and reconfirming, of communicating in many forms what it is you are trying to do and how you are doing it.*

All this meant two things. One was that everyone explored in much greater depth, with Solberg and with one other, the wisdom of the customer–centred reorganisation. They had to come to grips with it, understand it, agree with it. Second, they were obliged to agree a structured and consistent message which they could take home for distribution to their staff. It was essential everyone had a true understanding of the message, rather than the confusion which had been apparent. Obviously, various groups in the organisation will continue to have different priorities, missions and strategies. But at least now they will not have greatly varying perspectives as regards the rationale of reorganising Texaco's upstream business.

SUSTAINING THE SERVICE PARTNERSHIP

Living with the reorganised business, and being customers of one another, has been a brave new world for Texaco Upstream to come to terms with. To Solberg, however:

> *That's where we are going to reap the best benefits. It's very clear that*

the different units have taken this issue on board and endeavour very seriously to give better service and to do things in a more co-operative way. It's also had far-reaching implications outside the company in our dealings with government regulators and with our partners. It is beginning to be a very prominent behaviour spiral, and we see that our partners, for example, are now reacting to this and trying to emulate our customer-centred approach and activities.

The reorganisation has yielded internal and cultural spin–offs for Texaco. The company used to have an organisation that had drilling and production in the same unit. Before the reorganisation there was constant irritation between the two disciplines, but separating them has made an improvement, in that each unit now has an identity of its own. Managers from these businesses now agree that separating them into discrete units and asking them to work together are the two key parts of the reorganisation which have proved to be valuable and worthwhile. Bob Solberg gives an example of this when talking about 'reducing turfism' in Texaco Upstream.

Turfism arose where drillers and producers working in the same unit differed on the solution to a problem, and would fight for the authority and resources to solve that situation. That problem could still exist in the new organisation, but not to the same degree. It is one of the dangers we have to watch for. We have to be sure that somebody who has production in their assignment does not say to the driller 'You can never come and work in our oilfield, we will handle everything inside of this field, because it's ours to manage'. What we have had to do is debate, teach and fight for, as management's responsibility, the objective of minimising turf wars and developing customer/supplier relationships. We are all in business together, and what you have to do is make people responsible for discrete pieces of work and then ask them to work together. This way, you really are building the team and giving everyone a specific task for which they have a responsibility.

To Texaco, customer service is the lifeblood of their upstream changes, and quality has been written into the heart of their reorganisation, with its success dependent upon teamwork within and between departments. Individuals are being given greater responsibilty for their own jobs, autonomy is being pushed down the line. Again this flatter hierarchy and pro-active autonomy is a constant in excellence organisations. Bob Solberg is convinced that sustaining quality customer service is 'building relationships and managing people. It is about a way of behaving. The challenge is to construct new behaviour in managers. A key element is to encourage individuals at all levels to make decisions within their professional competence. The appropriate level of authority to carry out these decisions will be granted and managers will be expected to develop staff, manage business results and lead our quality customer–centred process. We have deliberately staffed the organisation lean so that departments are incapable of being self–sufficient, forcing them to be dependent upon other departments and to work with them as customers.'

Roger Colomb, the Managing Director of Texaco UK, sums it all up:

Quite simply, to survive in the UK as a successful oil company we have to differentiate, and really create, a competitive advantage through superior quality service. That goes hand in hand with the flattening of the organisation, taking out layers of people who were in management positions but basically who acted as post offices where they moved propositions up the company or down as the case may be. You must flatten the structure and get a more proactive, positive organisation where people feel they have got the authority to deal with the problems that their job says they have to deal with. This is a continuing revolution that we have started. Being a customer service-centred organisation, and sustaining it, is not a one day 'sheep dip' cosmetic as I think some companies have tried. It is going to be a slow, evolving revolution and Texaco are ready for that, believe me, otherwise we would not be in business.

APPENDIX 1.1

THE TEXACO CHARTER

1. Every employee shall practice and promote open, honest and timely communication, and time to communicate will be given equal priority with other task matters.
   Minimum standard – to be tested by regular sampling within work units.
2. All managers and supervisors will receive training and be judged on their annual performance assessment.
   Minimum standard – all managers and supervisors to attend communications course.
3. All employees will discuss, agree and record with their manager/supervisor clear and measurable work objectives and have the right to request and receive an annual individual discussion on career development with their immediate supervisor.
   Minimum standard – at least once per month and at the conclusion of a major task.
5. Managers/supervisors will be accessible to their staff and will regularly visit those people under their supervision.
   Minimum standard – to be included in the agreed work objectives of all managers/supervisors.
6. Employees will be encouraged, wherever practical, to visit locations and to meet people with whom they have regular business contact.
   Minimum standard – one per month with communications as a permanent agenda item.
7. Regular participative meetings of work groups will be held.
   Minimum standard – one per month with communications as a permanent agenda item.
8. All meetings will be conducted to "Quality" standards and principles.
   Minimum standard – adherence to be reviewed by all attendees at the end of each meeting.

9. Employees will be regularly informed of corporate goals and results and have the opportunity to attend an annual face-to-face meeting with senior executives.
   Minimum standard – goals and results, twice per year.

10. Department induction training will be given to all new staff to help their understanding of their department and its place within the organisation.
    Minimum standard – familiarisation training within the department within two months.

11. Electronic mail is to be the standard and preferred form of written communication and made accessible to all staff.
    Minimum standard – all employees should have access to a terminal and receive sufficient training to achieve competence.

12. Updated organisational charts/telephone directories and key departmental contact persons/points will be accessible to all.
    Minimum standard – updated quarterly.

13. Company wide communications will be distributed according to standards developed by Public and Government Affairs Department.
    Minimum standard – company wide communications should only take place after consultation with Public and Government Affairs.

14. **Every employee has the right to bring a breach of this Charter to the appropriate Managing Director/ Department Head for resolution.**

2. Sutcliffe Catering Group

'I must follow the people, am I not their leader.'

Benjamin Disraeli (1804–1881)

Sutcliffe Catering Group cater to nearly one million people in the UK every day. Provided mainly at people's place of work, the service ranges from the boardroom to the shop floor, and increasingly to other sectors such as school refectories, hospital wards, police canteens, military bases, leisure centres and travel termini. Imagine for a moment one million meal occasions every day, satisfying a range of tastes and expectations which could extend from the chairman's suite in a merchant bank to the needs of a seven-year-old in school. The company employs 22,000 people in 2,000 locations, and in 1992 generated a turnover of £370m. Its operations are mainly in the UK at the moment but extend virtually from Land's End to John o'Groats, and, at the end of 1992, began operating in Eire. Sutcliffe Catering Group must satisfy two masters:

- Customer A, who is actually the consumer of the food.
- Customer B, often referred to as the client, who is the employer of customer A and who invariably finances the service.

Says James D. Stirling Gallacher, who was Chairman of Sutcliffe Services Group over the last four years:

In some instances at least, the wishes of customer A and customer B are diametrically opposed in defining what they want. The one is wanting 'the top brick of the chimney'; the other is anxious to minimise the cost. Sutcliffe's challenge is to satisfy both aspirations at the same time.

Sutcliffe Catering was featured extensively in my first book in this series. This study revisits the company to assess its policy for sustaining customer service. Says Stirling Gallacher:

Sutcliffe's consistent objective is to satisfy the needs of our existing customers to the point where they remain our customers and, with their recommendation, and our sales and marketing efforts, they help us gain new customers. When one considers it, the qualities required to make Sutcliffe customers' aspirations a reality are mirrored by the attributes of the favoured or ideal restaurant that you or I would choose for those special private, or even business, occasions.

Such an establishment would certainly have:

- A quality of product that could be consistently relied upon and which was prepared and served in clean and comfortable conditions.
- Highly professional and welcoming staff.
- Sufficient numbers of staff to cope with customer needs, however varied.
- Staff continuity, ensuring that regular guests were recognised and individual tastes anticipated.
- Service flexible enough to cope with customers' idiosyncrasies.
- A management presence always in evidence and, when required, readily available.
- Value-for-money prices.

'Like the customers in that restaurant type', notes Stirling Gallacher, 'Sutcliffe's customers are looking for a service that is given by bright enthusiastic people who take a pride and pleasure in serving others and who are responsive to special requirements, using their own style and common sense. For this to occur means an investment in Sutcliffe people, particularly through their training.'

Of course, food is at the core of customer service in any successful catering business. Whether the meal is five-star Michelin standard or a primary school lunch, it must be enjoyable, nutritious and good value for money. However, the first important feature of Sutcliffe's customer service approach is the importance they give to local identity and autonomy. As Stirling Gallacher explains:

Of all the services performed for the benefit of you or me, catering for our varying palates must be among the most personal any of us experience. It follows, therefore, that the larger the organisation, the harder it is to convey the impression and indeed the reality of personal service. To highlight size in the context of strength, universality and even permanence is a plus in most instances, but to carelessly equate size with personal service is death! While accepting that we in Sutcliffe are big and getting bigger, I assure you we are working twice as hard to maintain our individual touch. You won't find Sutcliffe boasting of its size.

In order to maintain a close personal service Sutcliffe Catering is run as a decentralised organisation with eight autonomous regional companies, including a specialist schools catering company (Fairfield). Each regional management structure, with its own managing director, is free-standing and capable of operating separately or in conjunction with its fellows, according to what is required. Sutcliffe's contact with clients becomes even closer through area operating networks, plus specialist activities in schools, airport and shipboard services, and hospitals. There are certain constants, for example:

- They apply strict rules as to how many customers are placed in the care of their directors and area management. This ensures that routine monitoring visits are made to customers and that there is sufficient flexibility to allow a proper response to emergencies should these arise. And they breathe into this type of devolved structure a high degree of autonomy.

- They achieve local identity by having local people looking after their local clients and customers. They have enough people, with enough time, to look after the customer.
- They achieve speed and flexibility of response by placing the decision maker close to the point of service, where he or she is likely to understand the problem better than someone who does not have the measure of the local situation.
- They achieve a visible management presence which can respond, if required, to customer problems, their special requirements or, as vital just be seen to be about.

PEOPLE – THE MOST VALUABLE ELEMENT IN CUSTOMER SERVICE

'We in Sutcliffe Catering' says Stirling Gallacher 'see people as our greatest asset because we mainly work in another man's house. We do not employ capital assets to anything like the extent other businesses do. People are our most valuable asset, and as such require to be treated with respect.' Another feature of the company's approach to customer service which relates to the people they employ is that, like the favoured restaurant, Sutcliffe want customers to recognise that the staff and management are readily available. Their philosophy in regard to personnel, from director to the most junior member of staff, is set out in a published statement, which says: 'It is our duty as a company to allow every person within the company an opportunity to fulfil his or her potential and to make the maximum possible contribution to the achievement of quality.'

Stirling Gallacher explains,

To attract the best people we must pay the best. While our basic salaries rank among the most attractive in the industry, we also invest heavily in incentives based upon results. The results we reward most are mainly geared to sustainable growth – we are not interested in one-year profit miracles. Our business is all about securing a customer, satisfying him and keeping him, and that is the corner-stone of our incentive scheme. Our philosophy in terms of remuneration is not philanthropic. It is designed to help us maintain continuity of service as an essential ingredient of our customer service package. Just like the ideal restaurant, continuity of staff is very important in our business. We have to select our people very carefully because, without a foundation of sound staff, we cannot invest a sensible degree of autonomy on those people.

Sutcliffe want their customers to recognise them for quality of service. To this end they recruit a 'Sutcliffe type' who personifies their service concept by being:

- Totally dedicated to personal service and comfortable in that role.
- Proud and jealous of their reputation and achievement but never satisfied.
- Confident and able to operate without rigid rules, but respectful of the rules that do exist.
- Sensitive in anticipating, and being responsive and flexible in fulfilling, a customer's needs.
- Enthusiastic about technology, but viewing it as the servant of personal service, never its substitute or its master.

Sutcliffe also endeavour to encourage originality and flair in their staff. While Sutcliffe regional companies are constantly upgrading their core business of looking after people at work, they are also encouraged to develop through their own individual entrepreneurial flair. This encouragement even extends to the conception and development of activities which can 'grow to free-standing activities in their own right.' For instance:

- Automatic Vending, which until ten years ago was a division of Sutcliffe Catering, is now a vibrant, fast-developing international company in its own right, with its own management.
- Sutcliffe Design, which was set up as the company's own design resource, allowing Sutcliffe caterers to have a direct input into the shape of the facilities they will be operating.

For Sutcliffe, today's needs call for periods of more formal training because young people need to progress faster. Their training investment and strategy take into account the needs of 22,000 people in 2,000 separate locations. By virtue of numbers and spread, the most demanding of their training responsibilities involve the food service staff. In this grade, Sutcliffe have some 21,000-plus personnel at unit level nationwide. Their training programmes involve a wide range of skills induction and education, including health and safety, self-assessment, customer relations, food craft and food handling. The training needs of this vast raft of employees are serviced by 52 mobile instructors and 1,500 on-the-job trainers. To demonstrate their commitment to investing in people and customer service through training, Sutcliffe are:

- Spending on training at the rate of 5 per cent of their catering income (in 1992).
- Providing financial and other resources to some 35 craft colleges and universities in the UK.
- Employing 400 graduates throughout their activities.
- Meeting BS 5750 in one of their functions and actively pursuing accreditation for all their regional businesses.
- The first catering company to gain the National Training Award for the complete spectrum of their training activity.
- The managerial backer of 'Springboard', the catering industry's Careers Centre in London.

THE CUSTOMER PARTNERSHIP

All this commitment is directed to one end – fulfilling Sutcliffe's obligations in the customer partnership. As Stirling Gallacher states:

Our philosophy is 'If we look after our customers they will look after us', and they do. It is not surprising therefore that every year a fair proportion of our new business is referred to us by our existing customers. On the few occasions we lose a customer we treat this, whatever the reason, as our failure and set about correcting the weakness.

In common with most service organisations, Sutcliffe has formal contractual undertakings with its clients. Formal contracts are necessary because there has to be a record of what responsibilities each of the parties accept in regard to the undertaking. However, although important, the contract is not what Sutcliffe believes keeps a customer partnership together. The word 'partnership' means 'sharing' and Sutcliffe see 'the spirit of sharing' as the golden thread which keeps successful partnerships intact through their inevitable ups and downs. In their customer relationships, Sutcliffe's endeavours are directed to:

- Establishing from the outset a clear understanding of the customer's aims, objectives and standards. To achieve this understanding they are prepared to listen, and listen again, to what the customer wants.
- Regular and meaningful dialogue with the customer. It is incumbent on Sutcliffe, as the caterer, to be proactive in this relationship and to come up with innovative ideas which constantly address economics and improve service.
- Maintaining an 'open book' approach so that the customer has confidence in the caterer's financial stewardship, and can see how the monies are spent.
- Local management on each site carrying out a Quality Self-Assessment Programme four times a year to evaluate the standard of service. Clients are encouraged to participate in this exercise at least twice in the year.

James D. Stirling Gallacher has been 40 years in the industry and he has never known two customers to have identical requirements. Every customer's needs have to be approached on an indiviudal basis. Sutcliffe's aim is to be seen as an extension of the client's own management team rather than as an outsider – an approach which has resulted in the company winning awards such as Kodak's prestigious Quality First Certificate. As Stirling Gallacher says,

In a service business like ours, formal, binding contracts, important as

they may be, can never be the basis of lasting relationships. It is the trust, respect and fair-mindedness of the customers, coupled with consistently dedicated professional and honest service by the caterer, which binds the parties and guarantees sustained customer loyalty.

CONTINUOUS COMMITMENT TO SERVICE FROM THE BOARDROOM

To help achieve sustained customer loyalty, the Sutcliffe Catering Group Management Board meet six times a year to review quality of service issues. The commitment to customer service starts here, in the boardroom. Don Davenport is the Group Managing Director of Sutcliffe Catering Group. He says:

The whole aspect of quality of service is number one on that agenda, and it's number one on each of the regional company agendas for their own meetings. What we're trying to do is simply to discuss and measure everything that we are doing in order to get a very positive handle on what's good and bad about us, and how we are matching what our customers want.

Sutcliffe spend most of their time at these meetings looking at ways they can create forms of competitive advantage. They constantly review comparisons, information and research about competitors and the market in general, to keep them up to date with trends affecting them as a company. Says Davenport,

We really try and home in on what people are actually looking for. What we try to do is redefine exactly where we are and where the real hot spots are. In that group meeting we probably talk more about what our customers want than any other issue.

On the basis of all this information, the important action for Davenport is to spread the message through the organisation. As he says,

The more, for example, I can get out to more places and meet with our

people, the more pure that message is going to be. What I try to do is not just allow the normal communication style of word of mouth, or pieces of paper, to go down through our companies. I'm probably out of my office four days a week, and I get right down to the grassroots. Myself, and others of course, constantly go out from the boardroom and preach the service gospel. Now staff test this. If they feel it actually works, and it's got credibility then certainly it will be picked up and they will run with it.

Don Davenport admits that there must be a system which measures how well staff are doing.

You cannot just go out from the boardroom and put some customer service programmes in and think that it's actually happening. One programme that we've put in, which has really caught staff imagination, is our Quality Self-Assessment idea. Here, they self-assess how good they are. This starts to involve them in looking at a measurement by which, at every quarter of the year, they can judge whether they have got better at improved quality and total customer service.

Sutcliffe Catering have several kinds of performance measurement. For example, if they lose a client, someone from Head Office phones that client to find out why the contract was lost. If Sutcliffe were bad at something, what was it? In this way, they measure a quality loss. Many organisations spend a lot of time measuring how good, bad or indifferent they are, but this means nothing unless an organisation has commitment from the board and the ability to drive the philosophy through. What is the point of measuring or discovering what your customers want if you cannot then provide the goods?

'That's obviously true', says Don Davenport. 'I think an important point is that for years companies used to have "gut" instincts about things. My "gut" instinct tells me that we should be giving superior customer service. But you must have the comparisons, research, feedback and forms of measurement which enable you to say "This is what's really happening out there to us. Now what shall we do about it?" '

In 1992 his team received some feedback from their market surveys to the effect that clients felt they would like to deal with more mature people at the front-end of the business. Over the years, the industry has tended to recruit fairly young people, mainly because they can be paid less. Sutcliffe learnt that, amid the economic strains of the early 1990s, their clients wanted to deal with more mature people, who better understood their business. As a result of this, the company have steadily worked toward having older and more mature people at the General Manager level, increasing the typical age from 25 to 32-35. This new approach has given Sutcliffe an advantage over competitors.

Figure 2.1   Sutcliffe Mission Statement and Philosophy

MISSION STATEMENT
We aim to further enhance our position as the UK's leading contract caterer for the quality of its products and services. We will do this by forming a unique 'quality partnership' with our clients, our customers, our staff and our suppliers. We shall continue to encourage our regional companies to grow their business through the use of their entrepreneurial flair, their strong local identities and their ability to innovate.

PHILOSOPHY
Our actions will at all times reflect our key values. We believe in freedom with responsibility, in strong leadership and in flexibility, above all, we believe it is our duty as a Company to allow every person within it the opportunity to fulfil his or her potential and to make the maximum possible contribution to the achievement of quality.

THE SERVICE CULTURE

As an excellence organisation, Sutcliffe reinforce a number of points brought out elsewhere in the studies in this book. First, in the boardroom, they make a statement of how they want to be perceived, and what they want their image to be in the marketplace. That way the directors can take an autocratic stance as regards the customer service mission. As Davenport says, 'The boardroom must establish how it wishes the company to be perceived, and should stick with it through thick and thin.' He explains a second key point:

'Having set down your service mission, you must have a tremendous sense of purpose to keep on and on, pushing the message down the line. OK, you can have the discipline process you go through to achieve a quality standard, but achieving that does not actually make the meal better or sustain customer service. You're asking all your people, at all levels, to be exactly the same, to be out there in front, creating the enthusiasm for the mission. Where it will fall down is when you ask managers to take on a kind of vision that just does not fit right.'

To achieve their customer service mission, Sutcliffe believe in straight, old-fashioned leadership. Executives see their role as being to create the desired culture, taking the staff with them by sheer enthusiasm. There is no room for sitting behind a desk and forcing paper down the system. Important here, as Don Davenport illustrates, is to get people to pass on information.

People won't always tell you what's going on. They don't want to go to a sort of super-boss and suggest 'Well, if you don't mind me saying so, how we did x wasn't very clever because of this, that and the other'; or, 'Can I ask you why you're doing y, because I think it's really dumb?' In a customer-centred organisation, part of the culture is to get people feeling they can just talk to you, at whatever level you are, and feel they are making a contribution to the business. If you're out and about, and someone says 'I'm really disappointed because this, that and the other happens, and a lot of us are worried', then the next day you not only go back with something but you also do something about it.

A remarkable achievement of Sutcliffe managers, given the size of their whole business, is that their customers feel that Sutcliffe Catering are still small and personal. Why do they perceive that?

Sutcliffe spend a lot of their managerial time thinking about 'What are we doing as an organisation that big companies do? And if we were small, how would we approach it?' Aware that small companies do things differently from large companies, Sutcliffe consciously aim at achieving the style of a small business. A good example is contract insurance for clients. Insurance costs went through the roof in 1992 – 60 per cent up against 1991. In a big company you would most probably write a standard letter to your client or customer saying in effect, 'Next month, because of rising insurance costs, you must pay more, and you must sign.' But if a company only had 20 contracts, this would never happen. The owner would be going round those customers saying 'Just thought I'd pop in to explain the difficulties with insurance cover, and sadly we are going to be asking you to increase your insurance costs' etc. But why cannot the former be more like the latter? In Sutcliffe, they do just that, and indeed dealt with that insurance increase as if they were a small business. Part of the outcome is that their customers perceive this organisation of 22,000 staff as being small and beautiful.

SUSTAINING SERVICE THROUGH QUALITY AUDITS AND ASSESSMENT

To Sutcliffe Catering, sustaining customer service means more than providing high standards of food and catering. It is an attitude that all employees of the company are encouraged to bring to everything they do. Chris Page is Sutcliffe's Quality Services Director and he says quite simply, 'Quality is the responsibility of the individual.' In 1992 Sutcliffe undertook a comprehensive review of its entire operation to identify areas where it could improve its service to clients. In keeping with all excellence organisations this has resulted in a flattening of the organisational hierarchy. For example, one of the facts to emerge was that the roles of Area Supervisor and Area Manager were confusing clients. As a result, Sutcliffe undertook a complete reappraisal of its line management structure and introduced a number of key changes aimed at eliminating this confusion. Explains Chris Page:

We have now focused responsibility for all operational matters solely on our Area Managers. This means that the client has direct contact with only one executive. The streamlining of the structure has paved the way for our new team of Quality Services Managers to report directly to their Operations Director. One of the main responsibilities now in Sutcliffe Catering is carrying out regular audits to assess how closely the Company's performance matches the client's expectations.

Six principal areas are examined closely with each client: menu planning and food production; merchandising; customer relations and service standards; staff training; hygiene, health and safety; and finance and administration. Says Chris Page, 'Most of the Quality Services Managers have previously been Area Managers with responsibility for some 30–40 contracts. They therefore have the authority and experience to ensure that quality and service measures are practical and implemented.'

Another responsibility of the Quality Services Managers is to address the issue of BS 5750, and Sutcliffe have done pioneering work with the British Standards Institute to devise accreditation guidelines acceptable to the hotel and catering industry. Sutcliffe's aim is to introduce common systems throughout their organisation. With almost 2,000 contracts spread over eight different regional companies, this is a major task. For each customer the emphasis remains on flexibility, with the contract tailored to individual requirements. But beyond this, Sutcliffe also has to ensure that there are common procedures for every Catering Manager as far as this is consistent with flexibility and not increasing the administrative burden.

The Quality Services Manager's new job is effectively to help the Area and Catering Managers to focus on those service matters that can be improved, and to give constructive advice on how this can be better done. They are also responsible for administering and monitoring Sutcliffe's Quality Self-Assessment Programme mentioned earlier. Brian Clark is the Managing Director of Sutcliffe Catering Scotland and he endorses the importance of the organisation's Quality Self-Assessment Programme. This is geared primarily to Catering Managers and acts as a reminder that they should monitor all the important aspects of the business. The Catering Manager in Sutcliffe needs to be fairly expert in a wide range of fields, from industrial relations to hygiene, from food production to health safety and customer relations. Says Brian Clark:

Being such a broad field it is likely that in the normal course of events they will not check everything satisfactorily. What the Quality Self-Assessment Programme does is to ensure they do check everything against pre-determined criteria. This ensures we accomplish all the objectives on a particular contract and that it is up to a high standard on a regular basis. The Area Managers in the Company use this system as a means of assessing their own managers: it is like a mini appraisal on a

---

Figure 2.2 Performance Questions asked by Sutcliffe Catering

How much time do you spend talking to your customers during service times and understanding and responding to their needs? How well briefed are your serving staff on: the daily menu, use of servery equipment and utensils, portion control?

Given the facilities provided for you, how well laid out and creatively presented are: the service counter, the dining area and table decorations, other services areas, customer flow and clearing systems?

How skilled are your staff in promoting the sale of food items?

How well do your staff handle customer complaints/problems?

To what extent do your staff project a friendly professional image? To what extent do your staff conform with company standards in respect of: uniforms and uniform cleanliness, use of name badges, use of safety shoes, wearing of jewellery, make-up etc? How interesting and imaginative is your use of professionally prepared point of sale material to help complement and support your food and beverage sales? To what extent do you make use of special days/promotions to create interest in the restaurant, stimulate sales and improve customer loyalty?

---

quarterly basis. They are assessing the Catering Managers and in the same way the Catering Managers are assessing their staff. In effect it encourages a good dialogue on the quality of the service being delivered and also the quality of a particular Catering Manager.

It is considered an important part of the Catering Manager's job to spend sufficient time each day talking to customers to ascertain their degree of satisfaction with the service and also to build relationships with them. Customers who have not necessarily enjoyed their meal or some aspect of the service of the meal will often leave the dining room without giving any feedback to the catering staff and are potentially lost customers. In talking regularly with customers, the Catering Manager makes every effort to create an open and friendly atmosphere which encourages both critical and complimentary feedback. Like other Sutcliffe Catering Managers, Andrew Horsburgh (who looks after Compaq, the computer giant, at Erskine) has to make an assessment as to how he is performing. A number of questions are raised relating to customer relations and service standards, with scores ranging from 0–5 (see Figure 2.2).

Self-assessment is asking 'How well am I doing in this particular area? Am I achieving company standards and if so to what extent?' Andrew Horsburgh will gauge himself on such questions, and then his Area Manager, Frank McCabe, will sit down with him and say 'Well Andrew, I notice that you have not rated yourself very highly on this occasion on customer relations. Can we just talk about that and what actions you are proposing to take?' There would then be an action plan in which Horsburgh would be required to set out what he is proposing to do about improving the situation in areas where he has given himself low marks. Andrew Horsburgh says:

The multiple choice questions are easy to use. The questions asked cover the commitments Sutcliffe make to our clients and customers. When I complete the assessment I can use a summary page to compare ratings for each key area of my performance – this against my previous assessments – and then see areas where I can improve.

This is an exciting development in sustaining customer service. What is impressive is that the Sutcliffe Scotland environment allows this self-development to be actively encouraged. As Brian Clark says, 'It's about creating an environment where people in the business feel comfortable about being self-analytical about their own performance. It's about creating the right sort of relationships for doing business. It really encourages people to analyse what they are doing and be self-critical without feeling under threat by doing so.'

Another part of the Quality Self Assessment Programme is the Sutcliffe Guide to Catering Standards. This aims to give the Catering Manager a clear explanation of what is meant by the questions contained in the Quality Self-Assessment Programme. These 'self-catering' assessments are completed at each Sutcliffe operation at least once every quarter. From each self-assessment the Catering Manager is able to build an 'action plan' of the areas which have been identified for development, or improvement, and these points are then formally discussed with the Sutcliffe client at a quarterly review meeting. Throughout the programme Sutcliffe actively encourage clients such as BP Grangemouth and Compaq Scotland to be involved. Alex McDougall, Site Service Manager at Compaq Erskine, explains:

> As a company we believe that communication is the keystone in maintaining and improving our quality and service standards. To this end the communication links between Compaq Scotland and Sutcliffe Catering are extensive. Each week, for example, the Catering Manager has an hourly appointed meeting with myself on quality issues to ensure the smooth running of the service and each month the Area Manager has a meeting with me to discuss, and assess, the services the catering department are giving to us and to the customers. There is also a formal review of services and financial performance on a quarterly basis.

Don Davenport, Group Managing Director of Sutcliffe Catering, emphasises this partnership approach to sustaining and improving service standards:

We are continually improving what we do. We must. We need to further enhance our position as the UK's leading contract caterer for the quality of its products and services, and we do this by forming a unique 'quality partnership' with our clients, our customers, our staff and our suppliers. . . . Above all, we believe it is our duty as a company to allow every person within it the opportunity to fulfil his or her potential and to make the maximum possible contribution to the achievement of quality of service, and to sustain it. This is really what the Quality Self-Assessment Programme is all about.

UNDERSTANDING YOUR CUSTOMERS' NEEDS

It is Sutcliffe's prime objective to provide the highest possible standards of food and service within the policy and financial targets agreed with their clients. Every person within the company plays an important part in the drive for quality, and it is vital that every individual knows, understands and carries out procedures which enable Sutcliffe to achieve their objectives. Brian Clark endorses the value of business training for all his managers:

It is very easy for people in this business to have an hour's conversation with their clients about the catering service, and little else. If they do that, they are coming from a totally different standpoint than if they had gained a thorough appreciation of the customer's whole business and looked at it from the customer's point of view. What we are trying to do is train our managers to understand about business, to read and to talk about their clients, so that they really know how the catering service relates to that.'

WINNING OVER YOUR CUSTOMER

Perhaps the last word should be from those who are the consumers of the Sutcliffe product. Area Manager Stuart Keogh has BP Refinery and BP Chemicals, Grangemouth, under his wing as major clients. The two contracts were awarded jointly and were opened at very short notice in May 1992. Sutcliffe Scotland installed their own experienced management team, consisting of Keogh as Area Manager and a Catering Manager for each site, plus a Food Production Manager for both locations. The team spent considerable time introducing themselves to customers and gaining their views on the services. As a result, the layout of food and garnishing have been substantially changed to improve its appeal, and healthy eating options introduced. A central plank of the new contract is for closer consultation between Sutcliffe and BP staff as users, and particularly with the canteen committee. Chris Short, BP Refinery's senior Occupational Health Nursing Officer, uses the restaurant regularly, and currently has a healthy eating campaign in operation. She says that since Sutcliffe took over 'even those dishes not specifically identified as for healthy eating are healthier than before.' Other BP employees are positive about the service provided by Sutcliffe. Within four months, patronage levels had increased by 11 per cent at BP Chemicals and by 20 per cent at BP Refinery. There is no doubt among the customers that Sutcliffe is the leading contract caterer for quality – a reputation gained because of the company's products, services and people. And Sutcliffe never stop trying to improve. They believe that every single member of the organisation can make a positive contribution to the achievement of quality, and can make a difference to their reputation. As Area Manager Frank McCabe in Scotland says:

Of course, different customers want different things, but ultimately customer satisfaction is the most important part of my job and of all our work. Our customers pay our wages, and we want our contract to be renewed. Anyone in Sutcliffe will tell you that our customer always comes first. At the end of the day, we are all ambassadors for our company. Is there an alternative?

3. Simon-Eurolift, Eire

'Seek not to understand that you may believe, but believe that you may understand.'

Saint Augustine

By 1987 a company in Ireland called Eurolift had become a European market leader in the design and manufacture of small truck and trailer-mounted access platforms – used for a variety of purposes in construction, industrial maintenance and utilities. The company's niche in this rapidly growing market was essentially the plant hire sector. However, quality and customer service were not primary considerations at that time: orders were pouring in, and the main concern was to build machines and get them out of the door as fast as possible. In 1987 Simon Access acquired the company, which became Simon-Eurolift. This acquisition was part of Simon's strategic growth plan, in that Eurolift fitted the criteria for companies joining their rapidly growing global organisation; they had leadership in their product sector as well as geographical dominance.

Joining the Simon organisation was a watershed in many ways. Says Tom O'Driscoll, Managing Director of Simon-Eurolift:

The first, and perhaps most radical, of the ensuing changes, was the adoption of a new culture. The most visible manifestation of this change was in the clear mission statement and business definition which Simon Access brought to us. This definition, developed by the Managing Director of Simon Access, John Barker, places the emphasis firmly on the customer. (See Figure 3.1.)

Figure 3.1 Simon Access Business Definition and Mission Statement

BUSINESS DEFINITION

Simon Access is the world's leading supplier of specialist access equipment that provides a safe and cost-effective method of positioning people and materials to work at height.

MISSION STATEMENT

Simon Access is committed to world leadership in access markets by providing its customers with fully-supported, cost-effective and innovative access solutions, with special emphasis on quality and performance. Through an aggressive policy of new product development selective acquisition and distributor development, Simon Access will exploit the benefits of group synergy in design, engineering, manufacturing and marketing worldwide, while retaining flexibility for quick response to customer needs.

Instead of Simon-Eurolift setting their objectives in terms of 'building the most machines', the new mission statement required them to concentrate on providing their customers with 'fully-supported, cost-effective and innovative access solutions, with special emphasis on quality and performance'. The implications of this emphasis have been enormous, and all the subsequent changes in culture and practice at Simon-Eurolift, including their achievement of ISO 9001, the international quality standard, can be directly related to the statement.

As with any major organisational change, there was resistance to be overcome and not least in the boardroom. The advantages of joining a global organisation were clear enough – research and development resources, financial stability, marketing expertise and so on. For some, however, the cultural change was too difficult to assimilate, and changes were necessary at senior level before real progress could be made. The attitude of the sceptics could probably be summed up as 'We're doing very well, orders are good . . . Why should we change?' However, a brief glimpse over the horizon would have shown enormous difficulties building up in the marketplace, including poor quality, late delivery and complacency.

It was becoming abundantly obvious that being customer-led was no longer a choice but rather a matter of survival, and that heads had to be extracted from the sand.

When Tom O'Driscoll became General Manager in March 1991, he took over an organisation which had to change its whole way of being. In keeping with all service-oriented organisations covered in this book, this has meant gaining commitment from everyone. They also had to go into a 'control mode' in developing systems which would eventually allow for flexibility within the organisation.

CREATING CUSTOMER AWARENESS

From a cultural point of view, the board of Simon-Eurolift Ireland had to tackle the situation in two ways. First, it was necessary to create awareness, of both the internal and the external activities surrounding the organisation. Second, there had to be participation by everybody. That meant getting people more involved in what customers wanted. To achieve this, customers' previous problems were highlighted to all the staff. Joining Simon Access forced Eurolift to face up to its shortcomings. One immediate result was an increase in orders through a global distribution network, particularly in the German market. Simon-Eurolift were rapidly to discover that quality standards in that country were very high, and that to compete they would need to make some radical improvements. As Tom O'Driscoll explains:

> In pre-Simon days Eurolift were 64 per cent dependent on the Scandinavian market and there was a very good relationship which had built up between people. As a result, mistakes that had been made were understood and passed over, because of the personal relationships that people enjoyed. After Simon took us over, although our customer base increased, we had to start again. People were not as forgiving of our mistakes, because we were only at that stage beginning a relationship with them. I had to explain to everyone in our company that it was with these new customers that we had to get it right, otherwise the orders would not continue to come in.

Things came to a head very shortly after Tom O'Driscoll became General Manager. A consignment of Simon-Eurolift machines had recently been delivered to a major customer in Germany, MVS. By coincidence, John Barker, the Managing Director of Simon Access, was visiting MVS. He saw the machines and was very unhappy with the quality of paint finish; so he ordered that they should be returned immediately for corrective action in Cork. This episode proved to be the catalyst for a series of changes which continue to sustain Simon-Eurolift's quality and customer service. O'Driscoll explains:

There is nothing like the possibility of losing a major customer to focus the mind and facilitate change! One of the first moves we made was to ensure that everyone at the plant was aware of the gravity of the problem. We got everyone together and explained the situation in clear and compelling terms. We were talking about survival – of the company and all its employees. Nobody was left in any doubt that to secure the future of their own job, each had to commit to a policy of continuous quality and customer service improvement. The problem with the German customer may have been a paint-shop one, but it was important that everyone realised that becoming truly customer-focused involved everyone in our company.

Reinforcing the Message

Simon–Eurolift used their shop–floor bulletin board to maximum advantage. Instead of highlighting the positive points, they displayed all the customer complaints they had received, and made all shop-floor personnel aware of the problems. This reinforcement message continues to this day. To ensure that customer service is sustained, Tom O'Driscoll addresses the workforce on a regular basis with regard to the costs to the company of such product mistakes. As he says:

People are only too aware, especially in Ireland, that companies are not willing to stay very long in a country like ours, when profitability and performance have been eroded fairly quickly. That is very much a reality to people; it is not something they feel 'won't happen to us'. They know that if we do not get it right our company is not going to survive.

Another awareness and appreciation approach adopted by Simon-Eurolift has been to take various shop-floor staff to meet and talk with customers and distributors. For example, in the case of MVS, the company took staff, including the charge hand in the paint shop, to Germany to witness at first hand what the problems were. As the charge hand was directly responsible for the poor-quality paint job, he personally met the customer and 'lived through' the complaints experience.

Simon-Eurolift recognised from the beginning that participation would be the key to success. Starting at a simple level, they first ensured that every department in the factory was clearly defined in physical terms – where its work began and ended, and who worked within it. They then published a number of criteria by which every department would be assessed each month for 'housekeeping'. The criteria are simple ones – general tidiness, efficient filing etc. They publish all the scores, and ensure that every departament displays the results on notice boards. This competitive spirit has generated a strong feeling of pride throughout the plant, and the 'housekeeping' philosophy has had far-reaching effects. In addition to the pride factor, there is also a very visible improvement in how the factory looks. What has, in effect, been created is a miniature 'internal market' where departments vie with one other to achieve ever-higher levels of excellence. Clearly this requires careful management to ensure that the competition created remains on a friendly level, but there's no doubting the pride of staff when visitors are shown around the factory. In fact, the Simon-Eurolift plant is one of the cleanest I have ever visited.

BRINGING SUPPLIERS ON BOARD THE SERVICE PARTNERSHIP

The concept of 'partnership' is at the heart of any customer service organisation, and must extend to the supplier if any real success is to be achieved. Often the first thing a supplier will see, when quality standards are raised, is a sudden increase in goods inward rejections. Without good communications, this will create difficulties. Companies travelling the road towards a customer service culture need to explain what they are doing and, crucially, why this will be good for the supplier in the long term. Says Tom O'Driscoll:

> After all, if we go out of business, that supplier to us will lose a customer. To stay in business, we must work together to raise quality and service standards – it's as simple as that. Ultimately, with suppliers the position is the same as with staff; those that cannot adapt will not survive. We found we had to deal with each supplier in isolation to determine the problems they were having with regard to understanding our business. It was very obvious that in the past they had been treated as the person who had sent us goods and that was it. Nobody ever asked them what their capabilities were as to how they, or we, could make improvements. . . . What has been constructive is our 'partnership programme'. For example, our purchasing manager will go to each of the suppliers with a corporate team – maybe an engineer, possibly someone from manufacturing, another from finance, different people from different departments. They determine what the capabilities of that supplier are so that we can build and better sustain partnership service. Previously, a supplier may have been visited by the people from purchasing, for that was their job. We didn't have all the various people visiting one supplier. Now we do, and this is, again, part of an 'awareness' process for both sides: first for the suppliers, who now have a greater feel for our company, but second, also an awareness for the people within Simon-Eurolift itself as to what constraints our suppliers may actually work under.

SUSTAINING CUSTOMER RELATIONSHIPS

Simon-Eurolift believe that dialogue is the key to better understanding. As Tom O'Driscoll says, 'It's quite amazing the number of businesses which fail to take even the simplest of steps. What does our customer want from us? Why not ask?'

From my own observations, within Simon Access as a whole, there is a strong policy of involving their customers in product development from the earliest stage. Simon-Eurolift wholeheartedly endorse this approach. It has been vital for them to increase their dialogue with customers, and, at the same time, ensure that communication permeates throughout the entire factory. When customers visit, they are encouraged to talk to everyone – the shop floor, the receptionist, the design shop, everyone. All their people know that the customer is the one who pays the wages. Notice boards in reception and on the shop floor welcome visitors by name. Simultaneously, Simon-Eurolift have taken measures to ensure that as many people as possible get out and about to see customers and suppliers, and indeed to assess competitors. This exercise has involved sending mixed groups of staff to major exhibitions – a considerable investment in terms of time and money but one which is paying benefits unobtainable in any other way.

Says O'Driscoll,

There are benefits which are often less easy to define. For example, by entrusting people with the company's reputation, they tend to respond to that trust, and rise to meet higher expectations of them. Building trust must however start from honesty. This is a tough one, and can entail a great deal of soul-searching. How many companies are prepared to admit that they have got things wrong in the past? Some of the people responsible for those mistakes may still be with our company. However, the person that cannot make a mistake is not human, and the company that cannot admit one will not be seen as human either.

There were a few staff in Simon-Eurolift who were unable to assimilate the culture shock and adapt to the organisational changes. Says Tom O'Driscoll, 'We took every care to explain, to communicate why change has been necessary, and the great majority of our people have responded to this. Those that did not are no longer with us. This is a price that a company which is committed to total customer service must be prepared to pay. Like any organisation or society, the survival of the majority (in this case the company itself) must always take precedence over the resistance of a few.'

When Eurolift became Simon-Eurolift there was a great deal of work to be done in terms of the visual expression of the change of culture. For example, they adopted the Simon Access logo wholeheartedly, and took pains to explain to everyone what it stood for. As John Barker, their Managing Director, said at the time,

We are in a global business, serving a variety of customers worldwide. Our customers need to know they can meet all their access needs from just one supplier – wherever they are. By implementing a new corporate identity, we have signalled our unique level of global integration and commitment to continued growth.

Of course, as Tom O'Driscoll points out,

A logo on its own is simply a graphic device. Its real meaning is in what it stands for, and everyone at Simon-Eurolift is in no doubt – and believes – that this means the highest levels of quality and customer services. It's like wearing your heart on your sleeve. A visitor to our factory will see the logo everywhere, from reception to workshop machines and overalls – it is a constant reminder to everyone of the standards we aspire to sustain customer service.

In many factories I visit I find photo-displays of products, usually in gleaming new condition, intended to show how good the company is. Simon-Eurolift have taken a different approach. They have a bulletin board, sited where every employee will see it regularly, and, as indicated earlier, their display features their mistakes – photographs of machines and components which have gone wrong, or do not fit properly, or have some other defect. Says Tom O'Driscoll:

By being open about our mistakes we can indeed turn them into opportunities. This notice board is a constant reminder to us of what happens to customer relationships and product quality when our

attention slips. It is a very useful tool in helping us avoid the great danger for a customer-service-based company – complacency.

In another bold initiative, Simon–Eurolift have reduced the number of quality control inspectors on their production lines, the aim being to hand responsibility back to each individual staff member. Initially, the shop-floor reaction was that management were being rather stupid. After all, if Simon–Eurolift were trying to increase quality, why take quality inspectors out? This put a premium on effective communication, as Tom O'Driscoll explains:

We have to make sure each person is aware of what is expected of them, and they have to act as their own quality inspector. Also, you get a flatter management structure, which is another essential component in customer service. What we discovered is more enthusiasm to find out what is actually going on, with much more of a willingness to ask questions, and to get it right first time. And this from the sharp front end of the business.

During 1993 one of Simon–Eurolift's priorities is to increase flexibility within the company. To do that, the 'awareness' programme between a supplier and the internal point of view is being intensified. O'Driscoll explains:

What I would want to see within our organisation is, for example, when somebody orders a machine that we can produce it to a much faster delivery time than we are doing at present. That means our suppliers have to be in tune with our demands, and the capabilities of the shop floor have to be there. It's the customer chain, all the people have to be in tune with what we can do. Everything has to be in place and happen correctly. We simply cannot afford to have bad components, we cannot afford late deliveries, we can not afford somebody being out of step. The only way we are going to achieve that, is to 'buy' people into our philosophy through educating our workers and our suppliers.

Simon–Eurolift are actively working on this at the moment.

They have 'customer quality circles' across the workforce, and these have helped to change the corporate culture by making people more aware of the need to improve product reliability and service. As Tom O'Driscoll explains:

> We say to these groups of workers 'come up with ideas that first of all are within your own control, and, secondly, those that are outside of your control. As a management team we will take care of the problems outside of your control, but it is up to you to produce ideas on how to improve issues within your own control.' This is 'ownership'. We are going to adopt the same philosophy with our outside suppliers, the issues they can manage themselves, that they can improve, and those problems and aspects we can help them with through our own input. It is imperative that we all work together in the chain if customer service is to be sustained in Simon-Eurolift, and significantly so.'

4. The Pindar Group and AlphaGraphics

'Progress – man's distinctive mark alone.'

Robert Browning (1812–1889)

As a number of the studies in this book, such as the Texaco story, show, service becomes a crucial differentiator in a marketplace where customers have difficulty distinguishing products in any other way. What has been noticed in the research for this book is that in 'excellence organisations' management itself becomes a service. The role of management in the service organisation is to enhance the culture, set expectations of quality, provide a motivating climate, furnish the necessary resources, help solve problems, and make sure high quality job performance and service pays off. The chief executives of the organisations in this book not only believe this thesis, they live it. This is what they mean by 'moments of truth' – those brief instances of time in every customer contact that decide whether the customer forms a favourable impression or not. Most of these moments involve price, quality or service, and the way the information is delivered.

Managing service means having as many 'moments of truth' as possible. Most of us will forgive mistakes, even quite serious ones, if there is someone who tells us what is happening and makes an effort to put things right. In sustaining any customer service, organisations striving towards excellence are, at the very least, honest by nature. Managing these honest 'moments of truth' is the essence of service management. Unless leadership and inspiration are present, mediocrity tends to reinforce itself. Outstanding service requires focused energy which transcends slogans.

In all the organisations in this book, including the Pindar Group, managers rise to their responsibilities as leaders, and articulate the concept of service in such a style that employees find it believable, feasible, worthwhile and rewarding.

The Pindar Group of companies began as a small printer over 150 years ago. Since then they've grown considerably in status and reputation, and are now one of the largest and most respected privately-owned UK companies, providing communications through printing and other media. Today the Pindar Group operate from seven principal sites across the UK, with more than 700 staff.

An important part of the operation is their successful franchise chain, AlphaGraphics Printshops of the Future, the concept of which Pindar franchises from a US company. Their substantial growth in recent years is the direct result of seeds sown in the mid-1960s, when Tom Pindar pioneered the early application of computer-based phototypesetting technology. During the 1980s their reputation for innovation and service was instrumental in helping to win many significant typesetting and text-handling contracts, including all the UK Yellow Pages telephone directories, the complete revision of the Oxford English Dictionary and database creation from millions of pages of patent applications for the European Patent Office. The advent of desk-top typesetting and colour reproduction technologies have been embraced by the Pindar Group. Since the mid-1980s they have also offered system design, integration and training facilities for customers wishing to bring aspects of their print production in-house.

Business format franchising is where the originator of a proven business concept (the franchiser) allows others (the franchisees) to operate a business identical in format in return for initial and on-going fees. The Pindar franchising business concept is to market, through distinctive, high-volume retail centres, a broad range of quick-turnaround printing, electronic graphics and related services by the most advanced proven technology, with the emphasis on customer service and value. This is done through Pindar's AlphaGraphics Printshops of the Future operation, which has over 300 locations worldwide. AlphaGraphics Printshops do business in the extremely competitive instant printing market. In the UK they currently have 16 stores with a total of 150 employees, supported by a small head office staff based in Scarborough, Yorkshire.

For AlphaGraphics to grow and offer increasing opportunity to owners, managers and employees, they must be better than their competitors at the job of serving customers. They must have what Paul O'Sullivan, their Managing Director, calls an 'obsession with customer service'. Andrew Pindar is the Chief Executive of the Pindar Group and he knows that customer service has to be an ethos, a way of life, across the Group as a whole, from the board down. Everyone in the group believes that to survive and prosper in a service economy requires product differentiation, and that an effective service company must show evidence that it has something special to offer. They appreciate that service is not tangible, and that its value depends upon the personal experience of the customer. They also know that the organisation exists to serve the needs of the people who are serving the customer.

'For customer service to work, you must commit in the boardroom', says Andrew Pindar:

> In the light of experience, our cultural change initiative stumbled due to me gaining insufficient commitment from the board and line managers. I would suggest that any company initiative which involves the changing of habits requires a united understanding which must be gained. Failure to achieve that, in advance of the launch of any initiative, will compromise the impact, no matter how good the initial idea has been.

Pindar believes that before launching into any company-wide customer service culture, you have to spend many months preparing the ground. Only in exceptional circumstances do you find people being immediately open and receptive to change. Vital ingredients – such as team building, demonstratively participative management, and an unwavering commitment from the board and line managers –

must form the foundation for sustaining customer service. No matter how functionally skilled managers might be, if they cannot embrace the new way forward, then there can be no place for them in the organisation. There are only three certainties about customer loyalty: it is circumstantial, fragile and fleeting. The customer wants and expects service to be suitable and selfless all of the time. For the Pindar Group the conflict between cost benefits and the provision of customer service simply does not exist. As Andrew Pindar emphatically states,

Without excellent customer service, one is committing the organisation to a downward spiral of lost sales and cost prices. There is no conflict. To succeed, the organisation has to fully understand what customer service really means. It's not just a smile. Excellence in both personal and material service are imperative for success. People who count the cost and endeavour to measure the benefit reveal their cynicism. That cynicism will guarantee that the initiative will falter.

CREATING THE CUSTOMER SERVICE CULTURE

Throughout the Pindar Group they drill into their managers the need to be concerned with service image. This involves factors such as goodwill, credibility, honesty, ethics, reputation, trust, consistency, quality and integrity. As a practical matter, image could be defined as, 'a managed perception on the part of the customer of the way the company does business'. Excellence organisations manage that customer's perception by managing those 'moments of truth' mentioned earlier.

Getting everyone to commit to the customer service ethos has been vital for all the organisations in this book. The Pindar Group ran a Putting People First series of training programmes, run by outside experts which helped to change the organisation dramatically. Over 400 people, divided into groups of 50, came together for two very full days. Each session involved a full cross-section of people from all Pindar sites, which helped to break down barriers. There was a reinforcement stage a year later, Keeping People First, which was run as a company conference to good effect. Andrew Pindar says:

> *You can never do too much constant review and forms of high involvement, for the dark side is always there. We had to make it happen. Creating the environment is essential if every employee is to improve their customer service internally and externally. A large part of our Putting People First programme focused on the way we react to each other, the way our behaviour is read by others and the impact a negative attitude and approach have on our work and home lives. The facilitator used role-playing as a way of exposing different body language and verbal styles. I am sure that right up until this time most of our executive thought that any lessons to be learned would be for the 'troops'. However, it was fascinating to see the results being as revealing and relevant to those more senior people, in their interactions with others, as they were to anyone in the organisation.*

The 'culture' course was intensive, covering both the business side of the group as well as aspects of becoming a customer service company. Major emphasis in the two-day programme was placed on inter-personal and human relationships, ranging through body language, communication, transactional analysis, motivation, positive and negative 'stroking', and so on. For most employees the course was the first outward sign of the board's intention to effect change throughout the business. Management structures had begun to change to reflect the desire for a flatter structure but this was not immediately clear or obvious to all employees in their various plants. Organising the two-day course for all employees was a clear signal that participation was going to be encouraged, and that management were prepared to listen and to work with the workforce.

It's worth mentioning here that there was much fear. The time-honoured conventional management style for a traditional print plant was of course under threat. That provided the management with a challenge, as much as it did the workforce, although they perhaps did not see it that way at first. Pockets of suspicion existed on both sides of the fence, which the Pindar Group were trying to pull down in everyone's interest. Says Pindar:

> *Somewhat to our surprise we had strong feedback that people wanted to improve their level of internal and external service but felt constrained by a number of real or perceived barriers, all of which had been allowed to grow either deliberately or unwittingly by supervisors and managers.*

It was therefore important to steer the understanding of the customer service ethos and its process throughout the organisation, and to convert the cynics. For this, the choice and role of facilitators and 'mission champions' were vital. Says Andrew Pindar, 'We were tempted to pick as our 'champions' those in the organisation who are always positive. In fact, we did choose one or two people of that nature; however, the true 'champions' were those people who commanded peer group respect and who were listened to much more readily. Their objectivity was never in question.' (Readers' Attention is drawn to both the Board Products (Eastern) study, later in this book, where the selection and training of facilitators is considered in more detail.)

The Pindar Group also found, as a result of the training programme, that they had raised the level of expectation between departments, between functions, and often perhaps just between people. As Andrew Pindar says:

> *People throughout the company were stopping each other and saying 'This isn't good enough'. This also led to managers being criticised openly by their teams. Of course, they had always been criticised, but usually in clandestine groups in or out of the work environment, with the clear danger of current or potential customers overhearing. This created another set of problems, for it revealed a management style of 'unlistening autocracy', caused in the main through insufficient training and development of supervisors and managers.*

THE SERVICE SYSTEM

In their drive to become a customer-focused organisation, the Pindar Group believed early successes were needed. They endeavoured to achieve better customer service through higher employee involvement, a change in company name, house style and their overall external image. They also adopted team briefing as their principle means of internal communications. Says Andrew Pindar:

> *With hindsight, I think we should have placed much more emphasis on addressing some fundamental attitude issues where there was an obvious lack of understanding of the company's function and purpose. Even greater success could have been achieved if we had paid more attention to that hard foundation building, rather than doing the easy and somewhat superficial things such as house style and image.*

In looking at external service, the Pindar Group took an increasing number of production staff to their customers' premises to increase their understanding. Similarly, Pindar ran 'open days' in their factories, with invitations to visit going to those working elsewhere in the Group. Of significance was the number of people who chose to visit their own factory and to spend time looking at the production process before or after the one on which they worked. The Group also went out of their way to introduce customers to as many people as possible during factory visits. One practical thing they were able to do was to issue everybody with name badges, as they were to learn from staff feedback at team briefings that one of the principal reasons that salespeople, or others conducting factory tours, had been reluctant to involve employees on the shop floor was because they felt embarrassed at forgetting people's names.

Externally, the Group started to expect far more from suppliers (another constant throughout this book), with quite a number falling by the wayside as Pindar's judgement criteria shifted. But of greatest importance, says Andrew Pindar,

> *was the clear delight of our external customers, who noticed our new*

customer service approach and attitude. They rarely had found a large British printing company prepared to invest in all of its people. The results of this 'excellence' approach have been, over three years, a 20 per cent increase in sales and a 25 per cent increase in profit. Our sales costs dropped by 3 per cent, as we found ourselves holding on to customers for much longer. Selling itself became easier, with potential customers telling us they could 'feel' that we were different.

At this stage it is worth reviewing how the Pindar Group do an important part of their business through the AlphaGraphics Printshops of the Future operation. Managing a franchise chain such

---

Figure 4.1   Pindar's Service Excellence Characteristics

The Pindar Group believe that highly successful excellence organisations share the following characteristics for sustaining customer service:

- They have a strong strategy for service which is clearly developed and clearly communicated.
- They practice visible management and 'walk the job'.
- They have a management who set constant role models for service.
- They 'talk' service routinely and in a language everyone understands.
- They have customer-friendly service systems.
- They temper their high-tech systems with methods that offer a personal flavour.
- They recruit, hire, train and promote for service.
- They market service to their customer, talk about and do it.
- They market service internally to their employees.
- They measure service and make the results available to service people. The most promising way to get the commitment of employees is to put the problem of service quality squarely in the hands of the people who are performing the service. Instead of telling them in microscopic detail what service quality is and how to behave, ask them to define it for themselves. Give people the freedom to develop effective service tactics on their own.

---

as AlphaGrapics is quite different from traditional company structures, because it has to be management by empowerment. The independent owners (the franchisees) have much more clout and leverage than an ordinary customer. Because they are one of a chain, what one store does can have impact on the others, so in a sense the franchisers almost have all their eggs in the one basket. The challenge therefore for Paul O'Sullivan of AlphaGraphics and his team is to listen to customers, whether they are 'captured' or not. Franchisees exist in an environment where they are both employees (one of the family, part of the team) and customers (receiving services to satisfy identified needs). The franchise agreement identifies the rules of play and the duties of either party, but it does not define the types of relationship necessary to allow both parties to live, work and prosper together. This is where a 'partnership culture' comes in. Against that background, the selection of new franchisees for an organisation like AlphaGraphics is very important, since all must subscribe to AlphaGraphics' customer service standards.

One aspect of the franchise operation that allows early success in the customer service stakes is that customers are buying into a system – into a method, a way of doing things. Paul O'Sullivan refers to it as their having 'bought a cake recipe'. He explains:

We provide the equipment, which in recipe terms are the flour, the lard, the currants, the baking powder. We tell them to go and get some eggs, which are the stock, and we teach them how to put it all together. So we provide training, tell them what temperature the oven should be at, how long to bake it for. Sometimes the cake does not come out right and that is where our skill comes in, in that we are the master bakers . . . They must follow the recipe – the systems and procedures – to give us a fallback which will normally enable us to make a good cake.

O'Sullivan also outlines AlphaGraphics' 'service system'. This consists of the physical facilities and procedures available for employees to meet the needs and expectations of the customer. As he explains:

Our store service package must contain not only what the customers need, but what they expect. The more experience customers have without service, the more discerning they become about their own needs and the variety of ways available to meet those needs. In other words, more experienced customers are more demanding. When normal good service is provided, customers accept it without a second thought. They are much more likely to be aware of the lack of service, or service which falls below expectations.

SUSTAINING THE CUSTOMER SERVICE IMAGE

All excellence organisations such as the Pindar Group spend considerable time *listening* to their customers, even their irrational rantings, realising that this is often the key to innovation. At AlphaGraphics' Castle Street store in Edinburgh it is not unusual for the staff to be asked about TV rental or a new sewing machine, sandwiched as they are between Radio Rentals and Singer Sewing Machine Centre. But when its owner, Alex Robertson, was approached one evening by someone who wanted a 'bag of chips', he knew either the chap had to be drunk or AlphaGraphics had a serious image problem! Not so the latter. Indeed, Alex Robertson's commitment to customer service has given an even stronger identity to the store. For example, all staff dealing with customers must, as a condition of employment, wear white shirts, navy skirts/trousers, the AlphaGraphics blue scarf/tie and name badges, which all help to project a professional image. They also get to know all their customers by name, and use their first names where appropriate.

Clearly, Robertson's former achievements in sales and marketing positions with the Mars Company have helped to mould his views on customer relations. He has been running the Castle Street AlphaGraphics store since July 1989, with his wife Dorothy. Despite the recession, the business has seen buoyant growth. During 1993 they expect to open a satellite unit in Edinburgh's West End, adding at least another two in prime locations within a five-year period.

As well as the high emphasis on customer service, the

Robertsons believe in 'sticking to what we are good at and focusing on the core business'. The store opens an hour later each Wednesday morning, so that weekly training meetings can take place. The emphasis is very much on customer service and job involvement, and this has been enhanced through participation on the dedicated courses run from AlphaGraphics' head office. Weekly motivational team briefing meetings take place to promote 'job involvement', explaining forthcoming promotional campaigns and developing selling skills. These meetings can also include specially-prepared discussion packages on subjects like 'dealing with customer complaints'.

'Action planning' is an important element of the Edinburgh store's operation. Each Monday morning, Alex Robertson gets together with the supervisors for customer service and print production, plus the production scheduler, and they plan the work for the week ahead. All staff are given sales training to ensure that opportunities are maximised to sell all the store's services and stimulate 'trading up'. Such involvement and appreciation of the business as a whole are imperative, given the range of activities which the store undertakes. Robertson enthuses on the importance of customer service.

> *It cannot be over-estimated and it is a critical influence in our business development. 'The customer is our boss' is a philosophy that all employees at the Edinburgh store understand and commit to. Every customer must, we insist, leave the store favourably disposed, or better still feeling good, towards our operation.*

To achieve this, specific training is given in the AlphaGraphics' Obsession with Customer Service philosophy (see Appendix 4.1). When I was in the Edinburgh store I heard staff ask a few, brief questions to understand better what their customer wanted in such areas as quality, appearance, delivery, durability, ease of use, flexibility and price. I was impressed. From their knowledge of papers, inks, printing and duplicating methods, bindery alternatives, typesetting and graphic presentations, and a myriad other factors, they decided whether what the customer thought he wanted was consistent with the intended use of the product. Listening was the key skill, enabling the staff to provide advice and guidance to their customers and to find solutions to their problems. Alex Robertson believes that customers buy where they are least abused.

Our goal at AlphaGraphics here in Edinburgh is to exceed the customer's minimum expectations of service. I know that, through out-performing our competition in simple customer relations, we can be assured of a growing volume of business. But the key to success is attitude.

Not just for the Edinburgh store, but across the entire Pindar Group, this covers:

- The attitude and actions of management.
- The attitude of the employees hired.
- The continuous training and re-training of staff.
- The reward of performance.
- The participation of everyone in improving quality and service.

Getting things right has made Alex Robertson's store one of the top AlphaGraphics performers worldwide. His success shows, as he says, that stores with a high level of quality and service 'grow more quickly, are more fun to work in, and offer greater growth potential for employees.' They're certainly more fun. For example, in AlphaGraphics Edinburgh a social secretary has been appointed to organise a range of events for all staff each month, from ten-pin bowling to white water rafting. The importance of this is that it helps to encourage team spirit, which Alex Robertson feels is vital to the success of his business.

CUSTOMER SERVICE – BECOMING A WAY OF LIFE

AlphaGraphics, in common with most other organisations featured in this book, operate a flat management structure. A consistent feature of excellence companies is that the distance between the customer and the 'top' of the organisation is usually in direct correlation to the quality of service given. Ivory-towered or top-heavy management become so distant to the outside customer and to their own internal team that a hidden message is transmitted to that team saying 'Don't bother with customers, as people don't really matter'. The 15 people in the AlphaGraphics Head Office in Scarborough consist of the Managing Director, Paul O'Sullivan, a Finance Director, an Operations Director responsible for all aspects of customer service, and 12 other people who work directly for one of those three. This team of people are all aware of the two-fold purpose of AlphaGraphics' business:

- To transform potential franchisees into franchisees.
- To transform existing franchisees into satisfied franchisees.

As O'Sullivan explains:

These two parts of our business essentially cover growth of the system and the continued well-being of the 'family'. To the first group above we are 'selling the dream' and to the second we are fulfilling it. It is therefore important that everyone within the company understands why we are here, so that they live, eat and sleep quality and service.

In AlphaGraphics' Head Office they achieve this way of life by having monthly team briefing meetings to share information about the whole business. As Paul O'Sullivan says, 'Spending time to ensure that people at the centre – those who work with us, the franchisor – understand the issues of business pays off when they make field visits and spend time with owners or franchisees. It also helps to generate a team spirit because when everyone knows what is expected of them, and of everyone else, then there is peer pressure to perform.' This team-based approach is a constant in excellence organisations, as is a profound and professional knowledge of the business.

However, not all managers adapt so easily to a more 'team-based' style. Often managers equate management position with managing a large number of people in specialised areas. In today's environment, many of the organisations in this book believe that managers should have breadth of responsibility over a number of areas, rather than in-depth tunnel direction through line management. Paul O'Sullivan is in no doubt that:

> we will lose some of our existing staff because they will be unable to adapt to the the team environment which we are increasingly moving towards and which we believe is essential to sustaining customer service. 'Listening instead of telling' is the order of the day, and this is difficult for some to accept and to practise. The service philosophy that companies need is to treat all employees as if they were customers, and all customers as if they were employees. This can be difficult to embrace in every circumstance, and people are quick to point out occasions when it does not work. Sticking with it, therefore, is an act of faith.

Apart from team briefings, Paul O'Sullivan feels it is also important to have a forum.

> This is where all the staff of the franchiser team can highlight areas of concern both within the organisation at the centre, and issues they feel are relevant to franchisees. A monthly customer service meeting allows us to discuss each customer (their franchisees) in turn, and talk through the visits they have received during the course of the previous month and the ways that we are providing support. This could be in marketing, or technical aid with regard to the latest equipment, or training of one of their operators, or helping them recruit a sales team. This approach also allows us to see whether we can then cross-fertilise what worked well in

one area to other areas. It serves to make everyone within the Head Office team, which is fairly small, aware of what is going on throughout the country. It also allows me to report on what is happening within the international arena when I report our UK experience to the master franchisor, AlphaGraphics in Tuscon, Arizona, in the US.'

At the last AlphaGraphics annual conference, the franchisees decided to form themselves into focus groups, or forums, to look at various parts of the business. They have a sales forum, a marketing forum and a technical group which covers their drive for quality accreditation to BSI 5750. Another group is reviewing finance and administration and also covers issues such as personnel and training. There is also a fifth focus group – an operations forum – dealing with productivity issues and skills training for operators throughout their stores. These five sub-groups, which comprise the owners plus one representative from the franchiser, come together twice a month to receive recommendations on what should be done for the future to improve customer service as a way of life throughout AlphaGraphics, for both internal and external customers.

Within a flat management structure and devolved responsibility, empowering people to make decisions can be difficult, and needs constant reinforcement. Excellence companies do not have a 'nanny' type of environment. Staff have to take 'ownership' and make decisions, providing of course that they have been given the necessary skills training. They will get it wrong from time to time, but as O'Sullivan explains:

People learn from their mistakes. Once they accept that it is OK to make a mistake now and again and that they are not being molly-coddled, then people will be more ambitious in the decisions they want to take for themselves. In that way new initiatives will start internally, improving our organisation and administration, and also in the way things are suggested to franchisees out in the field and their employees. They will feel more comfortable with their ability to make things happen.

Adding Value to Customer Service and Satisfaction

In order to find out more about what their customers want, in 1991 the Pindar Group began sending out customer satisfaction appraisals. Peter Wilkinson, Director of Sales Operations, explains,

We asked them if they were very satisfied, satisfied, dissatisfied or had any other comments. I think we were very brave, by the way, and I don't think others always are. I like to use the phrase 'the feel-good factor' – if a customer feels good about us, then he or she will be honest with us. We went through the spectrum of our sales management: were our customers satisfied, did they see their salesmen often enough? We then went on to ask them, for instance, whether they got the right support from Pindar directors. Were they satisfied, and did people respond to them on time, every time?

We had our Law Society customer here today, the legal body of Britain, for whom we produce the Law Society Gazette and their student magazine. They have their own system which Pindar commissioned and trained Law Society personnel to use, allowing us to receive electronic data down a high speed modem which we can output. They're in London, we're in Scarborough. They also use AlphaGraphics. I had no hesitation in introducing him to a customer who was with us for the very first time. I said to our Law Society colleague, 'Would you mind explaining the Pindar experience?', and he said 'Yes, I'd be delighted to'. I could have interrupted, but I didn't!

That type of advocacy gains the Pindar Group commitment in two ways. First, the existing customer feels good in saying he is being served efficiently and becomes a disciple for Pindar Group service and quality. Second, the new potential Pindar customer hears the same story. Adds Wilkinson, 'I honestly think you can bridge the gap between someone being a good customer and being an excellent customer'.

What the Pindar Group effectively do is identify their customers' needs and expectations. They discuss the services they want, and then have a customer disciple who is happy to say, 'I know this company, they will give you customer service'. An essential part of providing superior customer service is, as mentioned earlier, to add value to customers' orders. A customer's order is not simply words on paper. It is a product that has a distinctive mark – a purpose associated with it which is intended to produce results. An excellence organisation will recognise the importance of such an order in terms of what it will do for the customers, and therefore add value to the order. For example, an AlphaGraphics customer creates a CV on their LazerGraphics system, and wants it reproduced on their high-speed duplicator. To add value to the order, their Customer Representative would suggest that the CV be copied on high-quality paper and propose matching envelopes and a blank sheet for cover letters. In this way, the order will have greater perceived value to the customer, because it will produce better results.

It is recognised by the Pindar Group that customers come to them to receive the full benefit of their services. If a customer has a problem, the Group can provide the solution, as they are in the business of solving customers' problems. Their job is to make the customers' task of placing business, of whatsoever size, simple and speedy. It is important to understand why customers choose printers in the first place. Typically, customers put work with the printer with whom they expect to be least dissatisfied! In any event, most customers expect to be disappointed in some way. At AlphaGraphics, and indeed throughout the Pindar Group, they seek to eliminate that negative expectation by providing a superior service to their customers. By serving their customers better at the front counter, for example, and producing orders on time and to a better quality than expected, a positive relationship can be established.

SELLING PERFECTION

With the aim of achieving the ultimate in customer service, Peter Wilkinson ran a series of total staff seminars explaining the company's hopes, aims and intentions. Coupled with the Putting People First awareness training, this initiative brought all types of people together to look at corporate customer service objectives. 'These courses have helped tremendously,' says Peter Wilkinson,

but of course you need to take that further. Together with Marketing, we ran a series of seminars to talk through what we sell to our customers. We sell them perfection. If we don't sell perfection, then anybody can do what we do. Perfection does not come just from the printed product, it comes from the areas such as satisfying the needs of the internal and the external customer, finding out what the customers need, and what their expectations are. There's tremendous synergy between the services we provide and the customers' needs and expectations. The 'feel-good factor' does apply because, if a customer feels good about supplying a superior product to their end user, on time every time, then we of course can score. Our sales costs will reduce because we don't need to look for new customers all the time.

In the USA, AlphaGraphics is called the Cadillac of print stores. In the UK it is the Rolls Royce of print stores. It is a brilliant concept – not just a print shop, but also a business for business. They are not just serving the public, who are of course very important to AlphaGraphics, but also the corporate customer. Peter Wilkinson sums them up:

If I left the Pindar Group, which is highly improbable, I would still recommend to any potential customer that they use AlphaGraphics as a company because they have come a long way and learned a lot of lessons. When you consider the Pindar connection with AlphaGraphics, obviously we have to have a complete faith in them, and their individual franchisees, to service the corporate customer to the same extent and standard that the Pindar Group do. There's a great trust there.'

At this point it is worth remembering that the individual customer perceives service in his or her own terms. The customer alone pays the bill – or doesn't – for whatever reason, or collection of reasons. AlphaGraphics and the Pindar Group know that there is no such thing as a unique complaint. However, as Paul O'Sullivan says,

'Even after a big foul-up, the disgruntled customer can become a top customer, and a better friend, if you call them back and say you're sorry. Astonishingly, that's usually all we need to do to set ourselves apart from the competition.'

In the Pindar Group and AlphaGraphics, complaints are never regarded as irrational – anything the customer says is important by definition. 'Remember the customer perceives service in his own terms, not yours', says Paul O'Sullivan.

We have developed ways of obtaining quick, accurate and varied feedback from our customers and we monitor the feedback closely. We always begin our dealings with customers by making the assumption that 'the customer is always right'. Remember, quality and service are not techniques. They are a commitment by management to its people and products.

SUSTAINING THE COMPETITIVE EDGE

Staff can add value to customer service by doing and saying the proper thing when closing a transaction with the customer. There are two types of situations which are relevant. First, when the customer has placed an order and is about to leave; second, when the customer has collected a completed order. Both situations provide an opportunity to demonstrate superior customer service. In the first situation, it's important to re-emphasise the day or time the job has been promised and that as a company you are committed to meet that deadline. Then, tell the customer that you appreciate his business. This will let the customer know that his order is important, that it has value. This is a consistent factor in excellence companies in this book, who all place much emphasis on the training they give to enable their staff to know the business their customers operate within. In the second situation, it's important to add value to the finished job and to show appreciation to the customer for putting business your way. In AlphaGraphics, for example, they make a complimentary comment about the quality of the finished job, then thank the customer for choosing to come to AlphaGraphics, and ask them to come back again. It is essential that companies leave a favourable lasting impression with customers with whom they do business. Your best customer is your current one.

There is nothing revolutionary about the Obsession with Customer service ethos of the Pindar Group and AlphaGraphics. It applies common sense ideas to help ensure that they have served their customers well. The aim is to provide what Paul O'Sullivan calls a 'memorable business experience'. All over the world people are having to do business in a new economic climate. As we shift from an industrial economy to a service economy, we are shifting from industries which 'produce' to ones which 'perform'. As O'Sullivan says,

> Service has become a powerful economic engine in its own right. In fact, service is really the final product. Where customer service was once viewed as an expense it has now become a strategic tool. It is both a positive force for increasing sales and a method of reducing the cost of sales. It's a way of differentiating our products from those of our competitors.

Andrew Pindar sums up as follows:

> For the Pindar Group and AlphaGraphics, customer service is not a competitive edge, it is **the** competitive edge. People do not just buy things, they also buy expectation. The product is more than a single item it is rather a bundling of items, such as the product itself, the seller, the organisation the seller represents, the service reputation, service personnel, the company he or she represents, and the images of all these in the market place.

This message permeates the Pindar Group and AlphaGraphics, and it is allowing them to not only sustain customer service, but to excel at it.

APPENDIX 4.1

PINDAR GROUP/ALPHAGRAPHICS: SUSTAINING CUSTOMER SERVICE

Part of the AlphaGraphics "Obsession with Customer Service" Awareness Appreciation for Staff.

Prompt Acknowledgement and Quick Service

The first step towards ensuring positive customer contact is to promptly acknowledge the customer's arrival in the store. Customers must be made to feel welcome. You should make eye contact and give them a pleasant smile within 15 seconds of their arrival. Speak to them if you are within normal conversational distance and never shout if you are too far away. Assume control of the interaction by making the first statement.

Move to the point at the counter just across from where they are standing and then greet them 'Hello, my name is Bob. How may I help you?'. Sincerely greet each customer. This will give them an opportunity to begin discussing their order. If they have a problem to discuss, you have already begun to diffuse the situation by having made the first statement. If you are busy with another customer, or cannot move to the counter right away, a non-verbal greeting will suffice. **Be sure you make eye contact with the customer**.

Customers do appreciate a warm welcome. They will understand that you may not be able to serve them that very moment, as long as you give them that 'I'm next' feeling. They will recognise and respect an efficient system in operation, because it guarantees them the same special treatment that everyone else receives.

Try to learn the customer's name as early in the conversation as possible. Simply ask them, 'May I have your name please?'. Often customers will tell you their name just because you have offered them yours. It's very important that you use their name in the conversation. Try to use their name more than once – definitely use it at the close of the interaction. It is an important step toward building a strong relationship with that customer.

Customers value quick service, and they value patient service. This may seem like a contradiction, but it is not. Customers expect you to serve them immediately, to have patience and take as much time as necessary to work out the details of their order, then to produce the order very quickly. This pattern of 'fast, slow, fast' is part of their notion of what superior customer service is all about. Anything less will not be memorable.

Listening to Customers

In AlphaGraphics, we spend more time listening to our customers than any other activity. In fact, listening is the most valuable part of communication activity. It's difficult to understand why a thing we do so frequently can, at times, be done so poorly. Everyone could be a better listener. It is essential to be a good listener on the job in order to provide our customers with superior service. Poor listening not only creates a poor impression, it can also cause mistakes.

How do we become better listeners? It takes practise and time.

- **Prepare to listen.**
  It sounds simple doesn't it? When you approach that customer at the counter or on the phone, get ready to listen. Effective listening takes a lot of energy. So, get ready, get focused on what the customer has to say.
- **Adapt to the customer's delivery.**
  Everyone speaks with a different accent and at a different rate. Be flexible!
- **Overcome distractions.**
  Focus your attention on the customer. Don't allow either the surroundings or your own thoughts break into your concentration.
- **Listen for essential information.**
  The customer may not have their own thoughts organised about what it is they want.

You need to seek out the information which will assist both of you in placing the order. Ask questions.

Find out how the customer intends to use the product.

Listen in order to determine what the customer really needs.

- **Show attentiveness to the customer.**
  Attentiveness is a combination of verbal and non-verbal signals which indicate to the customer that you receive and understand what they are saying. Such behaviour as – sustained eye contact, nodding your head, remaining silent until the customer is finished speaking, and restating what the customer has just said – all clearly indicate to the customer that you are being attentive.

5. Ballygowan Irish Spring Water (Eire)

'A man who is not afraid of the sea will soon be drownded for he will be going out on a day he shouldn't.'

John Millington Synge (1871–1909)

The rain that falls so abundantly on Ireland, and gives the country its legendary greenness, is considered purest in the remote corner of County Limerick in the extreme west. This rain is the source of Ballygowan Irish Spring Water. Launched in 1982, the product has become one of the international marketing hits of the past decade and is the brainchild of one man, the Managing Director and founder, Geoff Read. He first had the idea of bottling an Irish spring water when he was living in London, where tap water is recycled up to ten times. He noticed the increasing presence of imported bottled waters on the supermarket shelves, especially French brands, and realised that here was a chance for Ireland to utilise its wild and natural environment.

So began the quest that was to lead to the creation of Ballygowan, a name that has a distinctly Irish sparkle without sounding too 'paddywhack'. Some 800 years ago a group of Crusaders returning to County Limerick discovered a well of outstanding purity on lands donated to them by a grateful Church. This became known as St David's Well, which was the original source of Ballygowan Spring Water. Today Ballygowan use a number of wells on the western seaboard, which is uniquely protected by the prevailing winds of the Atlantic and free from all pollution dangers. Only here, in the whole of Ireland's 32,000 square miles, do all the conditions come together to produce a water of quality. It is that quality which the company are now bringing to the tables of Europe and the United States.

Today, Ballygowan extract 58 million litres of water per year. This is an average abstraction rate of 2.5 litres for every second of the day, which means that five bottles of Ballygowan are consumed every second of every day. Ballygowan itself owns about 40 acres of land directly above its source, the remainder being owned primarily by Limerick County Council. Interestingly, the Council work very closely with Ballygowan to ensure that no activity takes place within the catchment area that could be detrimental to the source; no herbicides or pesticides are applied to the land. The close working partnership between the company and the local Council endorses the ethos that Ballygowan are in the health quality business.

PRODUCT QUALITY – THE BASIS OF CUSTOMER CONFIDENCE

The frequent rain borne on the fresh unpolluted Atlantic air retains all its purity as it works its way down through the soil and the layers of limestone to the deep subterranean source of Ballygowan. The geological structure of the aquifer is unusual in that it is almost exclusively limestone, while the water itself has a high concentration of calcium, magnesium and bicarbonate and an almost total absence of sodium. It is this combination which results in a hardness that gives the water its distinguishing taste. It's that unique tang which has made this mineral water so popular, even with those who drink the purest spirit, vodka; an 'S & B', meaning Smirnoff and Ballygowan, enjoys designer drink status in some circles. Ballygowan are obsessive about quality; after all, drinking it (without the alcohol!) is making a health statement.

The entire plant and facilities at Newcastle West – the town which has grown up around the spring – have been designed and built to US Food and Drug Administration standards and are the only bottled mineral water company to meet these standards in Ireland. They also meet and exceed the EC natural mineral waters standards, having the finest bottling and in-house laboratory facilities of any bottled water company I have seen in Europe. The operation of the factory is to medical standards, with the emphasis on purity and quality assurance at every step. The filling room is closed, to guard against contamination, and the air supply is sterilised and filtered. In the bottling hall stainless steel underfloor drainage flushes waste away from the factory site, and no product leaves the plant before it has been thoroughly checked, analysed and cleared by quality assurance personnel. Regular visits are made to suppliers to check that the standards Ballygowan require and set are being maintained.

Ballygowan's development has reflected a strategy of growth backed by quality. In many other markets, quality is a relative concept that often means little or nothing outside fairly subjective parameters. In the case of Ballygowan, it is difficult to find fault with the company's claims of quality supremacy. The brand itself has always traded on the distinction of quality, but behind the scenes real effort is made to ensure that nobody can compete with the company on a quality basis.

QUALITY AND BALLYGOWAN

According to Aidan Magennis, Ballygowan's Brands Manager:

> *Our watchwords for success are Quality and Ballygowan. Our quality assurance schemes, exacted by the company at plant level, are impressively comprehensive. Exhaustive tests are carried out every day with every batch of water and, at three month periods, special consignments are sent to the US for extensive chemical analyses. IR£3.2 million was spent in 1991 in improving plant facilities, including up-grading and further quality assurance of the finished product and source. In the water sector, quality is paramount. People will pay for quality only if they are confident that they are getting the best. Ballygowan exudes this confidence. Scientific say-so is not the only benchmark of Ballygowan's quality pinnacle: independent research in Ireland found*

Ballygowan to be the best quality and best value on the market versus the competition.

Surprisingly, the successful production of a top quality spring water is extremely difficult. Without rigorous quality control the water can pick up tastes and odours from the bottle, from the cap, from anything it comes into contact with. Ballygowan is considered, even in the industry itself, as Europe's most advanced water bottling facility. Extending over 50,000 square feet, it represents a significant capital investment and has the capability to produce 8 million cases of Ballygowan products each year. Product excellence and customer confidence have been the keystone of Ballygowan's success, accompanied by an equally remarkable flair in marketing. Today, Ballygowan products are premium goods aimed at the high-quality end of the international market place. And as a result of their outstanding facilities and high-tech production lines, they can offer these premium products at competitive prices.

Quality and innovation have always been inter-linked. For a brand leader or prospective brand leader, survival and prosperity are vitally associated with innovation in the marketplace. The future of bottled water in Europe is in premium brands, of that Ballygowan have no doubt. They now have a 30-strong range of waters and associated soft drinks. As people have moved to healthier, more refreshing products, the company have met demand with quality brands both in aesthetics and taste, successfully anticipated consumer standards, behavioural trends and environmental pressures, and satisfied these in the market, at a profit.

SUSTAINING THE CUSTOMER SERVICE CHAIN

As Ballygowan moves through the 1990s, it is imperative they maintain quality brands and standards. As Magennis says,

As a brand leader in the all-Ireland market, and a dynamic, aspiring market leader in the UK, quality consumer care and attention within the

company play a key role in our overall corporate strategy. Every individual within the company, irrespective of level or function, has an important role to play in the end consumers' perceptions of service and quality. Quality service has been labelled a 'neglected domain' in many countries; however, good pro-active strategies improve our total business, and an understanding by everyone of effective quality marketing, and commitment to its role, leads to overall company success. This, of course, relies upon cohesive consistency in our management philosophy and structure, which leads to effective front-line relations whether company-trade, company-retail, retailer-consumer or company-consumer-direct. Quality is without doubt the overall key to sustaining customer success.

Ballygowan's bond with all their customers – suppliers, distributors and retailers – is a matter of trust. First of all, the company must present themselves properly in order that customers can better understand the Ballygowan business. Ballygowan try to keep their customers informed about the 'water business' generally – who is doing what, what the market is doing and so on. They have developed and published a guide to bottled water, made available to all their customers. They are, therefore, in the education business, as well as selling water. They believe that when their customers know about bottling water, and the logistics of getting it to the consumer in the right quality and the right package, then they will be able to distinguish between a good supplier and a bad supplier.

The people who supply Ballygowan are basically raw material suppliers, such as a glass company. Company reprsentatives make regular visits to suppliers to audit them on an ongoing basis on fulfilment of their stringent quality specifications. Suppliers were in the Ballygowan plant when I was there, being taken through the production process and told about the standards Ballygowan are trying to achieve. As Tom Reid, Ballygowan's Operations Director, says, 'We build up a good relationship with suppliers on this basis, and also with the people we supply to. We bring them into our facilities to allow them to understand our business a little better, and our approach to the business, and hopefully this makes it easier for them to make decisions.' When at the production plant, I saw customers, including Bass and Tesco, being encouraged to meet Ballygowan staff and talk with them. A sign of excellence organisations is that they are open and honest, with nothing to hide and encouraging their customers to see their standards. Says Tom Reid:

We have had customers in from supermarket chains in Japan. We give them hospitality and ensure they can make an accurate judgement about the type of operation we are. It makes it a lot easier in the long term, and you also develop a good relationship with people whereby they trust you and know that you are not going to embarrass them. Also, in the UK now, food safety regulation puts considerable onus on the retailer to ensure that the products which they are selling meet the quality standards that are acceptable. On that basis it is getting easier to encourage people to come to see our business.

At Ballygowan the production plant workers know exactly who is visiting and why, with management keeping them informed as much as possible. They have established a monthly newsletter to facilitate continuous communication and dialogue between all the 70 staff employed in the plant. This ensures that everyone clearly understands what Ballygowan's goals and objectives are. Says Tom Reid, 'We like to reinforce these about every six months, once they start to sag a little bit, so they can have a renewed interest in the customer.'

TOTAL COMMITMENT TO CUSTOMER SERVICE

The ethos of Ballygowan Spring Water is quite simple to Managing Director Geoff Read. 'We believe the customer is king. Obviously, the end-consumer is the final arbiter of our product and they're the person who decides ultimately whether our products will succeed or fail.' Ballygowan's commitment to quality and service is the foundation for their survival. As Read explains:

We have taken a very long-term view of the business and have invested substantial sums of money to enable us to be there in the long term. For many people in the market our raw material is often perceived to be free, coming out of the ground. We would say that's far from the case, because of the necessary environmental controls. We have shown that commitment to quality by investing in real plant, equipment, bricks and mortar, and in people. I think that's the difference between us and many other companies within the market place who would not have made that investment.

The Ballygowan investment in people starts with recruitment. When they originally recruited personnel for the bottling plant, Ballygowan made a point of recruiting operatives who had never worked in a bottling plant before. The reason was that they did not want them to be tainted by prejudices or methodology from other companies. Read says:

We wanted them to come in with a clear mind that Ballygowan was something different. We had a different philosophy, and service and quality were the most important things for us, as opposed to getting bottles of stuff out of the doors as quickly as possible and not caring what the content was. That was a deliberate action which I think enabled us to mould people into the right way of thinking, and to be fairly single-minded in their approach.

Again, in common with service excellence companies, Ballygowan has a flat management structure which is not overly heavy. The company do not like people being put into a specified role and not being able to move outside that role. It's imperative that management and staff understand what the jobs of their colleagues entail, and the difficulties and problems they have. Apart from flexibility, this encourages greater communications between all of them. There are operations meetings on a monthly basis, chaired by Geoff Read, who also chairs the core management team's monthly meeting where they discuss strategy. Any quality and customer service issues are raised at those meetings. Some readers may feel that

Read's role should be more out in the market-place, waving the Ballygowan flag rather than chairing meetings. His response to this is that he believes his job

> *is to ensure that all sections of our management are carrying out their roles as the Board of Directors and our shareholders would wish them to do, and that the company is being run efficiently and to the right standards. I certainly get out there and wave the flag as often as I can, but I do employ management and sales people to do that on my behalf. They are professional people, and I don't need to hold their hands!*

SUSTAINING A SERVICE QUALITY POSITION

Ballygowan is in many ways setting standards and styles for the industry as a whole. For example, they have been involved in the development of the first detailed bottled water standard outside the National Mineral Water Regulations published in Ireland in summer 1992. Some would say it is costly leading the field, spending much time on innovation, which subsequently gets picked up by competitors or others in the industry. Geoff Read sees that as part of their responsibility both to their own company, to the industry generally and to the consumer. 'We see, as a market leader, this ensures that other companies maintain a minimum standard level in the interests of consumer safety.' Ballygowan want and need to protect their industry from cowboys, who ultimately do the market place no good at all and destroy consumer confidence in bottled water.

Ballygowan also want to ensure that no other Irish company tarnishes the name for Irish water that Ballygowan have created through significant investment and marketing. Says Geoff Read:

> *It's really a self-protection mechanism, as much as trying to develop new standards in an industry which is hundreds of years old. We recognise that in the last hundred years, for example, the environment has changed. There is cross-border pollution which did not exist maybe a*

hundred years ago, and there is also greater methodology for testing now. We have been able to set up with all the available knowledge and testing procedures from scratch. Other companies may have found themselves in existence for hundreds of years but have been surrounded by pollution during the course of that time and not adapted in the right way.

Ballygowan remain a small company, but for small companies to prove themselves they have to establish a point of difference. That point of difference, which is important and easier for a small company to adapt to, is the development of a service quality position, which they must be seen to sustain. Read explains:

Companies should consider having independent audits done of their business to establish what they need to do to become a total service quality management company. In Ireland we have audits available to suit the standards authority for ISO 9000 and that's our next goal – that's like the UK's BS 5750. Those independent audits help identify areas within your own company where there may be shortcomings.

Ballygowan also believe a major importance is to understand their customers' requirements totally and to do everything possible on a continuous basis. Companies falter on their excellence route by forgetting this – even good swimmers must respect the sea. Not to do so has resulted in drowning. As Geoff Read says:

You have to talk to your customers. You have got to establish a relationship whereby they will tell you exactly what they need. You must also talk to a number of people within their organisation. For example, if you are talking to a UK multiple store you must also talk to their distribution people to try and make life as easy as possible throughout their chain. Good service quality companies that you deal with are pretty clear on what they actually require and they have their own specifications. But it has to be continuous.

For Ballygowan this means regularly assessing how they have performed against their standards, whether it would be a percentage of distribution getting booked in on time with the right product right down to the rate of sales in their store. Says Read:

> *You must review your performance throughout their system and then review it with your customer to see if it meets their expectation. And I believe this should be done on a one-to-one basis. For example, our distribution people would meet with, say, Tesco's distribution and warehouse people. Generally it is done at a sales and marketing level, where all these statistics are reviewed, and, if there are any problems emerging, then we would address where they are happening, if at all. Then we try and deal with the person on the other side, on the customer side, to ensure a better performance in the future. Effectively we have become a very 'listening' organisation. You have to absolutely understand what your customer wants, listen to what your customer has to say, talk to your customer. At the end of the day it's what they want, not what you want, that's important to sustain customer service.*

Geoff Read believes that his industry will rationalise into big players. They would like to remain independent but it may not be possible in the long term. They are regularly approached by companies who are interested in getting into their market because it has high growth. City analysts believe Ballygowan to be one of the most attractive companies within that market place. To date, however, they have been able to paddle their own canoe. The key requirement for their future is, as Geoff Read says:

> *To always make a point to understand your customers' requirements and establish good dialogue with them, and trust. But it's you, the customer, my customer who is the most important person – you are what makes Ballygowan tick and grow. We must be able to establish a better dialogue with you, the end customer, and we do that through quality packaging and quality advertising, as well as trying to create a confidence among*

everyone that we are going to be a consistently high quality product, delivering all of their expectations in terms of taste and emotion.

There is no doubt that the Ballygowan story is a success. Nature and people have worked together to produce what customers say is one of the best quality products of the 1990s. They are entering new waters, but are well prepared to so do. I wish them a safe and successful crossing.

6. Ryanair (Ireland)

'Welcome, O'life! I go to encounter for the millionth time the reality of experience.'

James Joyce (1882–1941)

Ryanair is the independent Irish airline. In 1985 it commenced air services between Ireland and the UK with its first flight between Waterford and London. May 1986 saw the inaugural flight on their Dublin to London route. The entry of Ryanair on to the Irish market, and in particular into the previously overpriced London–Dublin route, had such significance that air transport in Ireland has never been the same again. Today, the airline employs over 500 people and operates 24 flights daily on their London–Dublin route and around 50 flights daily between Ireland and the UK.

When Ryanair took off in 1985, Ireland took off with it. The number of people flying between Dublin and London quickly doubled and air fares were cut in half. Of more importance to the commuter have been the significant financial savings which the airline are able to offer all levels of traveller. The era of stagnation was over, business travellers began to get value for money; and the rest of Ireland received air service. In fact, Ryanair set a new horizon for Irish enterprise, helped to create a national confidence and, in particular, contributed to a boom in tourism to Ireland.

Ryanair's major UK destination was initially Luton airport, but in 1991 they started services to London's new Stansted airport. The airline's success on the London–Dublin route quickly led to their introduction of a very successful Liverpool–Dublin service, and today they have commuter services on other routes into Ireland such as Cork, Shannon and Knock.

Since the commencement of operations from Stansted, Ryanair have entered into a marketing alliance with Air UK. This has resulted in a comprehensive schedule for passengers travelling between Ireland and Europe to destinations such as Paris, Brussels, Amsterdam, Dusseldorf, Frankfurt, Munich, Nice and Florence. A similar partnership also exists with American Airlines and this allows interlinking from Ireland to Chicago, via Stansted. Since Ryanair's inauguration in 1986 the London-Dublin route has become one of the busiest in Europe, with the business traffic representing 80 per cent of total revenue. The airline now offers the business traveller a reliable and frequent schedule, and what many regard as superior on-board service.

In keeping with all airlines, Ryanair can only secure their commercial future by carefully expanding their customer base. This requires a pragmatic approach to customer service and will take time. However, unlike larger airlines, Ryanair can never afford to become complacent. Says Mary Hurney, Sales Manager for Ryanair in Ireland:

For us, good customer services is a necessity, not a luxury. We have put the customer first, always. Our policy has always been to create new services for air travellers – in other words, to lead from the front. At the same time we realise that we have to listen, and react with extreme care, to what our customers tell us about the sort of service they want.

Ryanair has effectively been in the process of re-educating the air traveller. For example, they no longer have to pay high prices to cross the Irish Sea, nor do passengers have to fly into London's Heathrow airport. Passengers now have an alternative. With this in mind, Mary Hurney says, 'Maintaining a high standard of customer service is an integral part of this process. After all, our best salespeople are our customers.'

AGREEING YOUR CORE BUSINESS FOR SERVICE EXCELLENCE

To Conor Hayes, Chief Executive of Ryanair, the core of their customer service excellence is not to 'hype' but rather to offer a consistent and caring service at a reasonable cost. The airline do not claim to be something that they are not. If a customer or passenger has a need to fly first class or on Concorde, then he or she is travelling with the wrong airline if they fly Ryanair. What Ryanair do is provide a relatively basic service, aiming to do it as well and as consistently as possible.

Conor Hayes joined the airline in 1992, from a non–airline background. His personal approach differs from that of many who have grown up in the ranks of the airline world. He believes all businesses are businesses first, something he feels that a lot of airlines have forgotten:

> *There is an institutionalised approach to airlines and in a lot of cases the business aspect has been forgotten. By the 'business aspect' I mean that people are in business to make a profit. I don't see anything wrong with that. Equally, you will not reap a profit if you do not satisfy the needs of consumers. You may not always be able to satisfy all of your customers' aspirations, but what you are trying to do is to satisfy them to a sensible level, and the more acceptable the level the more people you are going to attract. All businesses live or die on what the customer ultimately thinks of them.*

In reality, Ryanair has gone through much trauma as a business. In common with many of the world's airlines, they lost a great deal of money up to 1990 before returning to profit in both 1991 and 1992. As a result they have had to cut costs and refocus on exactly what service they are trying to provide. For example, they decided to discontinue providing a business class service on their Shannon and Cork routes. As Hayes says: 'We were not doing it properly anyway, and if you are not doing it properly then don't bother doing it. It's going to be a failure from a business point of view, but also, as a company, you are going to end up with disgruntled passengers.'

What Ryanair are now doing is increasing their market share, particularly on the London–Dublin route, which is one of the top three busiest air corridors in Europe. A central goal, therefore, has been to establish a degree of credibility in that corridor. Ryanair also wanted to utilise the fact that they fly into Stansted airport, which has its own customer service commitment, guaranteeing the provision of quality facilities.

As Hayes explains, the method Ryanair chose to achieve their market share and service objectives was, first of all, to increase the frequency of flights:

We increased the frequency of flights by about 60-70 per cent. The idea was, essentially, to provide a morning shuttle and an evening shuttle, so that if a customer arrived and could not get a flight, they could get the next flight within an hour. That made the service more attractive to a wider number of people, and in particular to the regular business travellers. Leisure travellers on the other hand tend to be less time sensitive.

In 1992 Ryanair offered another product service for their customers, through greatly expanding their charter activity – a different, but essential, part of their business. They increased the number of charter passengers in 1992 alone by about 150 per cent. Hayes says that there were essentially two motivations:

Obviously we were trying to provide a service and, in that instance, the customer is really the tour operator. What we are saying is that we can provide this service, at this price and with these ancillaries. This is where our reputation for reliability is so essential. If you say you are going to do this at a certain time, then you have to do it at that exact time.

In effect, Ryanair are propounding the customer service pledge: 'Do things right, first time, on time, every time.'

Ryanair also recognise that they are operating older generation aircraft and that they must replace their existing fleet with newer aircraft. Hayes feels that:

If you want to offer a better customer service, you must have a better plane, and to afford that you have to have more customers in the first place. If you want to have more customers, you must give them something they want, and at a price they want it. Value for money and offering a decent reliable service is not a high frills or very exciting concept. Nevertheless, you are offering something that people need, at a price they can afford, reliably, efficiently and safely.

SUSTAINING CUSTOMER SERVICE THROUGH SPARKLE AND STYLE

Ryanair is a small fish in a big pond. They have competitors who are bigger operators on their main route. In their case, the main competitors are British Midland and Aer Lingus, the latter being state-owned and part of the Irish national debt. It has been necessary, therefore, for Ryanair to establish a strong and distinct identity. The best route to this has been through their own staff, who are treated as vital internal customers. Says Hayes, 'Their attitude, image and general vibrancy are what we have that I don't see in our competitors; our staff sparkle.' Conor Hayes claims no credit for that, describing the staff as:

A very good bunch of people, very committed and motivated. Like all companies, we have a few who are not, but the majority of people are very motivated, very committed, very interested in what they are doing. Probably because we are a young airline, they have not been corrupted by the institutionalisation that takes place in some of the bigger, more established, airlines.

The attitude that 'this is the way that we have been doing it for 45 years, so this is the way we are going to do it for the next 45' simply does not exist in Ryanair, as far as Hayes is concerned:

We are highly autonomous, so we get a lot of younger people who have been faced with challenges at a very young age and who have come up with their own solutions. Sometimes the solutions are good, sometimes they are not so good, but at least there is a willingness to try it out that way. We also have a lot of people who have come through the ranks – people who have started off as baggage handlers and are now pilots, people who were initially in-flight hostesses who now work in marketing and sales. There has been an opportunity, and ability, to move through the company and to develop at a relatively fast pace. We are a newish company, and in the past we have had our share of financial difficulties, but there has been a certain degree of buzz about the place, for trying new things and doing new things. It's that buzz which gets through to the customer and sustains service.

From the brief Ryanair customer sample I have taken for this book it is clear that this vibrancy, buzz and sparkle delight most of the customers. All the staff I talked to, from baggage handler to stewardess, pilots to check-in staff, were persons uniquely focused towards the company objectives. It was as if they all had a mission. As Conor Hayes says:

Being with Ryanair is interesting for our staff. If you make it interesting for your people, they in turn will be more interested in their work and that will definitely come across to the passengers. Our passengers in turn are going to be more comfortable and they will like us better. If they like us better then they are going to fly with us again. If they fly with us again, obviously your market share will go up and we will make more money. If we make more money, we can update or upgrade our aircraft fleet, and we can expand. Everyone understands that that is the mission and that there is something in it for everybody; our customers and our staff.

To sustain customer service Ryanair place great emphasis on communicating with as many customers as possible. As well as a continuous programme of market research, they undertake regular customer surveys to monitor and maintain service. One example of this type of survey is their 'Post-Flight Monitoring System', which involves telephoning the customer after a flight to ask how they feel about the service Ryanair provided. This provides an instant feedback which can be acted upon immediately.

There are many other Ryanair initiatives, all of which concentrate on both identifying customer needs and satisfying them.

- Uniformed pilots and in-flight staff visiting corporate clients and large travel agencies, talking to them about the service Ryanair provide and finding out how the airline can assist them.
- Presentations of the service the company provides are given direct to major companies on their own premises.
- Telephone surveys of travel agents are undertaken to solicit ways of improving the service Ryanair can provide.
- A 'hotline' has been introduced to facilitate queries from agencies.
- Ticket desks are located next to check-in desks to allow customers who have to collect their ticket at the time of departure to do so with minimum effort.
- Ryanair has introduced specially-designated group check-in desks to prevent congestion at other check-in areas.
- Reservation opening hours have been extended to include weekends.
- Customers in business class are issued with a newspaper at check-in and are provided with refreshments on board, prior to take off.

Ryanair have also introduced computer software which processes all forms of customer contact and correspondence. The system, called 'Computer Quality Assurance Network', records all forms of customer contact, telephone calls, correspondence, comment cards, etc.

A Total Involvement Strategy for Customer Service

Ryanair are committed to the concept of what they call the 'total involvement' of all staff. From the start, all Ryanair employees are given a clear picture of how they fit into the company. They are shown how their individual work contributes to the success of their department, and how their department's work impacts on other departments, and ultimately impacts on the customer. This is done through a variety of measures, ranging from initial staff induction courses through to in-house communications and training programmes.

Ryanair's company structure directly assists customers in two ways. First, the management structure is flat. There is a thin layer of middle-management, and this enables the rapid flow of information between front-line staff and senior management. Second, the flatter company structure encourages inter-departmental communication, allowing each department to play its full part in improving the overall service to customers.

Customer Service – Ryanair's Major Route

The Ryanair route to customer service has not been one of razzmatazz. Conor Hayes feels it has been more a question of setting objectives and trying to communicate them:

> The method I chose was through my own managers. I am not the kind of person to stand up in front of a room full of 2,000 people and try to persuade them of anything. I do not have that kind of personality, it's difficult for me and it just doesn't suit me. There are a lot of people here who are willing to champion the service message, and hear that message.

Most of the ideas concerning improved customer service are coming up through the ranks in Ryanair, they are coming from operators and in-flight teams who have made observations through being in daily contact with the passengers. It is all part of the 'willingness' culture – staff feeling comfortable about presenting ideas upwards. Maybe an idea or suggestion will work, maybe it won't, but staff are committed to making the whole Ryanair experience more attractive, more entertaining, and more comfortable for their customers.

For Ryanair, customer service is a route. Conor Hayes would be the first to admit that not all the things they have done have been correct. Nor is he happy that Ryanair have gone far enough. It will be some time before he and his fellow directors can evaluate whether all the things that they are trying to achieve are actually achievable, or indeed are the right things to be achieved. As he says, customer service:

> *Is a significant effort. We would not try to maintain that we have a perfect service, or that there are not a lot of improvements to be made. However, the objective is to provide a good reliable service at a reasonable price. If you want to reach that objective, you have got to make a certain commitment to resources. And then you go back and you try and achieve that objective at the lowest possible cost.*

An example of this is Ryanair's decision to have a back-up facility of a plane in Stansted and in Dublin to minimise delays for passengers to 40 minutes.

The Ryanair story illustrates that you will not achieve the objective of total customer service if you do not have a lot of very committed people. It doesn't really matter what the directors think, the staff have to *want* to do it. Conor Hayes sums it up when he says:

> *You can pay people big money, you can provide all sorts of inducements, but at the end of the day if people don't want to give wholehearted customer service, and they don't actually enjoy doing it, you're not going to get the results you want. In the short term you will, but not over a consistent period. Of course, ultimately, it is the job of management to create a climate within which everyone will want to come on board, and in a lot of small companies you will often have that by default. Probably*

one of the big dangers when you grow, as we have, is that you lose it; all the more reason to reinforce the personal touch message. Probably the big challenge for us is to maintain customer service favour and flavour, but at the same time to grow the business. We can then become a much more financially viable and healthy operation. We can never achieve the latter, however, without accepting that former challenge.

The reality of the experience of excellence companies could not agree more, nor could their customers. I personally wish Ryanair well with their challenge.

7. CR Smith (Scotland)

'The race that long in darkness pin'd have seen a glorious light.'

Scottish Metrical Psalms 1650

CR Smith is based in Dunfermline in Fife, Scotland, and was first established in 1915. Acquired by its present management in 1976, it is today considered one of Scotland's foremost window and door replacement companies. Although many people know that it sponsors both Glasgow Rangers and Celtic Football Clubs, many more in business are aware of CR Smith for its progressive advances in customer service. The company manufactures, sells and installs replacement windows and doors to private householders. Most people would refer to this as 'the double glazing business', which has long suffered from a reputation of poor workmanship, low standards and poor customer service. CR Smith believe the customer deserves better from the industry and have produced standards that are second to none for their particular type of business, including a Code of Customer Service Practice (see Appendix 7.1).

Independent market research has shown that the company have a very high rate of customer satisfaction, which Managing Director Gerard Eadie says is 'possibly the highest in the industry'.

> Our products must be right; right quality, right delivery and what customers want. Our products must be tried, tested and constantly improved, based on customer response and anticipation of their

requirements. It is customer service which makes the difference. We listen to what customers are looking for and do everything we can to provide it. Every single person in CR Smith must focus on satisfying customers, turn up on time, keep promises, respond to queries and requests – in fact, treat customers the way you like to be treated yourself. We totally recognise the way we treat customers is as important as the products we provide.

MAKING CUSTOMER SERVICE A WAY OF LIFE

There are problems within the replacement window business which make the sustaining of customer service a tough challenge for CR Smith. As Gerard Eadie explains,

There are natural cultural differences in labour forces. For example, in the hotel industry subservience is natural. When a customer says 'jump', you ask 'how high?'. The hotel industry is established and nearly always meets the customer face-to-face. Contrast this with an industry such as our own, where the communication with the customer is on the telephone, which makes it easier to be impolite and awkward with the customer, and therefore harder to gain consistent levels of quality service from the workforce.

This has required their joiners to acquire an image which is conducive to customer service, not only because they have to work in private homes, but also because their customers are buying expensive products. Says Eadie:

They cannot have the image of the typical joiner who is macho, works on a building site, is two steps removed from the customer and is motivated by bonus. Also, our joiners' technical ability is only part of their job. What is vital in our business is how he handles the customer. The natural culture of our labour force is different and we have to work hard to change their way of thinking. We train them in customer care as well as how to fit windows. We have to show an interest in our joiners and make them feel they belong to the company.

Joiners are expected to demonstrate the professionalism CR Smith portray in their marketing advertisements. For example, they must:

- Appear in a clean blue and white van.
- Wear clean overalls.
- Treat customers' property with respect.
- Never panic customers.
- Sort out customers' problems with discretion.
- Communicate with customers and explain how products work.
- Protect a customer's property with sufficient dust sheets.
- Clean up properly afterwards.

Says Eadie: 'We believe joiners are a transient breed. To overcome this, and make them more loyal to CR Smith, we involve their families by offering good rates of pay, pension funds and private health care. All our joiners are employed by the company and not sub-contracted.' Salesmen, surveyors and administrative employees must also embrace the CR Smith customer service philosophy. Salesmen demonstrate professionalism in everything they do, the way they speak, dress, drive, and so on. They are constantly reminded to keep in touch with customers before, during and after installation and must explain and clarify every point. Surveyors must be knowledgeable and pay attention to detail, ensuring that the customer understands exactly what they are getting. They are helped to do this by training and also through customer documents, such as the Surveyor's Checklist, which clarifies all points on contract and requires the customer's acceptance and signature as well as recording any amendments to the contract. Such clarifications serve to avoid confusion later on in the job contract, which is sadly too often the case of the industry within which CR Smith operate.

To CR Smith, the attitude of administrative staff is also vitally important. Although office staff do not normally meet customers face-to-face, they have a responsibility to meet their internal customers' expectations. The company, therefore, put great emphasis on telephone communications, using the most up-to-date equipment, and training their staff to a high professional level. They provide an excellent working environment, bistro facilities and the services of a company doctor. Gerard Eadie believes the working environment is only part of making customer service a way of life. He maintains:

> *Everyone must have a positive attitude. The attitude and behaviour of the workforce comes from those at the top. Management have to accept that things are not perfect, be prepared to do something about it, and then pass it down the line. Of course, you must have measurement and traceability to make things work, and you also need facts and figures. But you must have the attitude right. There must be no hiding place for anybody, and that's why traceability is so important. Every single person has to be accountable so you can trace to every level.*

CUSTOMER SERVICE ACCOUNTABILITY AND ACTION

Accountability for customer service is backed up by CR Smith's approach to performance measures, of which there are a great many. All performance results are published – everyone knows how they are doing, by comparison. One of the major reasons for this is explained by Eadie:

> *The handling of a CR Smith complaint can be different from one, say, in the hotel industry. For example, it is easy not to charge for a room or a meal because of the low order value, whereas our average order value is £3,000. Very often, quantifying the remedy actually becomes the problem to solve, rather than rectifying the window. We require a different level of skill in performance measures and problem solving techniques to achieve customer satisfaction. There is only one way to do things – the right way – nothing else is acceptable. Also, success, and*

being associated with success and achievement, is one of the best motivators. Through effective feedback, all staff can share in the 'pat on the back', but also know where we have gone wrong and can sustain, and improve, our customer service.

In other words, CR Smith are 'closing the gap' between meeting the needs and expectations of their customers and the standards of service that must be rigorously applied and reinforced in order to meet a total quality of service delivery. An 'evaluation team' meets fortnightly to analyse the results of all the various performance and customer service standard measures and research conducted by CR Smith on a regular basis. They implement corrective action, evaluate all customer recommendations and action customer service policies.

GUARANTEED COMMITMENT TO CUSTOMER SERVICE

Over four years ago the company decided to produce a customer guarantee that would be stronger than anything else offered by any other double glazing company. They consulted the Office of Fair Trading, who told them what they would look for in ideal trading standards, and took further advice from trading standards officers and from consumer bodies, as well as from customers and potential customers, to see what they wanted. All this feedback produced input to the CR Smith Code of Customer Service Practice (see Appendix 7.1). According to Gerard Eadie,

It demanded plain English, no-nonsense contracts. It demanded tight customer guarantees and spelt out procedures for the handling of complaints. It demanded, most unusually, that we set up an entirely independent panel of experts, an Ombudspanel, who, if all else failed, would adjudicate cases of conflict. As a company, we were required to agree to its findings, and do exactly what the panel recommended. Our system for handling complaints was already sound. Nevertheless, meeting the Code's conditions meant a total revision of our contracts and procedures. It meant retraining our employees, and it meant accepting the word of an outside body if we could not settle complaints within our own procedures. In short, it meant setting standards so high that only the best would be good enough to meet them.

The selected panel consisted of three people who had spent their lives fighting for the rights of the customer. One was a retired trading standards officer, another the author of a book for the Consumers Association on *How to Complain*, and the third a board member of the British Standards Institute. In essence, a panel of 'enemies' of the company would now arbitrate! CR Smith agreed that, in cases where it could not sort out a problem direct with the customer, the panel would independently investigate and CR Smith would do exactly what was recommended. The panel meets three or four times a year and say they can 'smell a troublesome customer a mile off'.

In a number of cases the customer has been found to be wrong, but in these cases the customer is always told that he or she can take legal action if the verdict is not acceptable. Of course, there were problems at the beginning. For a start, the company did not like being told it was wrong, and was particularly miffed when the panel told it to pay substantial compensation in a couple of cases. Gerard Eadie recalls the first time that he and another director, Ian Campbell, went to a local hotel to meet the panel.

We were in a good frame of mind. We were feeling good, thinking 'We will go down and meet the panel and have dinner with them'. Within ten minutes I had to restrain myself from saying 'To Hell with you lot, I'm away'. The reason for that was we got what we did not expect. The panel went through the first two or three job complaints and basically we got a lecture. After 20 years of telling people, often in no uncertain terms, where they have gone wrong, it was hard to accept such lectures and reprimands of the type received from the panel on that occasion – especially when they were right! But it was a necessary discipline to focus my mind on the detail required to drive customer service levels to a standard that gives us a competitive advantage.

CR Smith has always argued its case strongly. It has even threatened to disband the panel – but has never ignored it and regards it as having proved to be a major success. Customers know they can get a fair and objective hearing, whilst CR Smith has discovered that it is only by keeping its standards of customer service very high that it can avoid the panel's criticisms. What is exciting is that the staff are now determined not to lose a panel case, and that has led to a higher awareness of customer expectation and commitment.

According to Gerard Eadie, the panel has also brought some unexpected benefits. 'As we try never to lose a case, so its existence keeps us all on our toes. Also, we use the case studies for training exercises and this makes all our people feel that the panel is there to help, not act in judgement.' This is a first-class example of turning mistakes into opportunities – a constant experience in excellence organisations. As Eadie emphasises,

Now that we have done this, and gone down the road of the Ombudspanel, and our Code is in operation, it is the strongest customer guarantee in the business. It is far stronger than the protection offered by the Glass and Glazing Federation, an organisation which we believe exists to help the member company and not the customer.

CR Smith is an impressive company. Research conducted for this book, with both happy and dissatisfied customers, illustrates a major point: customers get instant action. Even more important is that those customers who felt the product or service could have been improved on would still recommend CR Smith as a firm to do business with. This advocacy is the reward for total commitment to customer service throughout the organisation. However, as Eadie reminds us;

Laying down the Code of Customer Service Practice is one thing, but it is worthless unless you have an Employee Code of Practice which proclaims the commitment from the employee to the customer. This must start from the Managing Director and everyone must believe that strong customer commitment policies lead to greater profits. The link is direct:

our customer commitment programmes help us win business. When there is little to choose between price and product, it is customer service that wins the contract.

How right he is.

APPENDIX 7.1

CR SMITH CODE OF CUSTOMER SERVICE PRACTICE

The Climate of Concern

We acknowledge that the replacement window industry (the double glazing business, as most refer to it) has been the focus of consumer concern. The selling practices and misleading claims for the properties of the products themselves, the terms on which business is done, the way that work is carried out and paid for and the guarantees offered have all been criticised, most notably by the Office of Fair Trading.

CR Smith believes the customer deserves better.

The Business of the Company

CR Smith manufacturers, sells and installs replacement windows and doors to private householders and tenants. The company is not a member of the Glass and Glazing Federation (GGF). CR Smith prefers, instead, to offer its customers a standard of service and reassurance which exceeds that available through the GGF Code.

The company, based in Dunfermline, was first established in 1915 and was incorporated as a limited company in 1972.

The present management acquired the company in 1976 and it is in the period since that CR Smith has prospered to its current position in the double glazing market.

Selling and Marketing Practice
Coming to the home:

- Our sales and installation representatives arrive only by appointment at a time agreed by the householder. Therefore, there is no cold calling or unsolicited telephone canvassing.
- All sales personnel carry cards identifying them as representing CR Smith.

- The name, address and telephone number of our sales personnel are left with the householder as is the telephone number of our headquarters.
- All sales personnel are employed by CR Smith and work under the strict supervision of an Area Sales Manager.

Purpose of the Code

This code sets out for the benefit of the staff, agents and customers of CR Smith the policies and practices of the company. We accept that it is the duty of our company to trade fairly and believe that to do so is also to trade profitably. The code defines what we mean by this and how we intend to put the idea into practice. This code has benefited from consultation with Trading Standards and Advisory Authorities. We are happy to acknowledge that help but would underline that the responsibility of formulating the code and discharging the obligations set out in it is ours alone.

The Provision of the Code

The code covers the areas of:

- Selling and marketing practice
- Consumer contracts and other documentation
- Manufacturing procedures
- Installation: timing and quality of work
- After sales service: guarantee and complaints

The Survey

- The customer will be notified of their survey date within seven working days of having signed the contract. this will be by telephone. Notice is normally at least twenty four hours and this can be confirmed in writing if necessary.
- Whereas the measurements made by the salesman were for pricing purposes, an installation surveyor will visit the customer

on the agreed date to take further measurements for manufacture.

(Readers please note, only part of the above is given in this appendix)

8. British Rail – InterCity

'Even if the Doctor does not give you a year, even if he hesitates about a month, make one brave push and see what can be accomplished in a week.'

Robert Louis Stevenson (1850–1894)

British Rail (BR) is a holding company, whose businesses include Regional Railways, whose name almost speaks for itself, and Network South-East, a commuter-driven operation which looks after people who live in the south-east of England (some would say to their misfortune). Then there is InterCity, generally running between the major urban centres of the UK, typical examples being the Edinburgh–London and London–Birmingham connections.

InterCity, in effect, operate Britain's high-speed rail network, with 750 trains per day providing a frequent service beween major towns and cities. At the end of the 1980s it became the world's first national rail network to operate at a profit. Of the 80 million passenger journeys made every year in the UK, 30 per cent are for business purposes. InterCity is certainly big business, with assets of around £2 billion and an annual turnover of £1 billion. They are proud not only to be Europe's only profitable express rail network but also to offer more trains travelling at over 100mph than any other European country.

Britain's railways have a 150-year-old history, and a future which promises dramatic change. Over the coming two or three years there

Figure 8.1 InterCity: Vision, Strategy and Values statement

InterCity Vision	InterCity Strategy	InterCity Values	Core Behaviours
The best, most civilised way to travel at speed from centre to centre	To focus on quality as seen by our customers and deliver a consistent, safe and relaxing service	We will value our people, using their creativity to innovate and bring about continual improvement	Respect
			Empathy
			Enjoyment
			Visibility
	To improve efficiency and reduce unit costs	We will empower individuals and teams with responsibility and accountability	Courtesy
			Personal discipline
	To grow profitably in an open, competitive environment		Teamwork
	To provide an environment where our people can achieve their potential and so enhance our competitive advantage	We will behave with clarity, trust and openness, encouraging participation and giving support when needed	

are going to be major disruptions arising from the Government's policy of privatisation, including the creation of a separate authority to own the track, possibly the selling-off of stations to different people, and certainly competitive provision of train services. There are questions about the European system of railways and equal access to it, relating in part to the Channel Tunnel rail link. These and many other issues, many of them not new, have to be addressed between now and 1995. Many people in InterCity, as well as many customers, find this all timely and challenging.

The first important point about InterCity is that they are in more direct competition with coach, car and airlines than other BR operations. Second, whereas other parts of the BR network are state-aided, InterCity get no Government subsidy. Their success depends on their ability to convince their customers that they are worth buying a ticket from. The InterCity operation is still within its first decade of existence, having started off as a BR marketing concept, subsequently achieving rapid growth. But almost from inception,

InterCity have had to stand or fall by their own efforts and level of profitability.

InterCity are very prone to the effects of recession. The number of people travelling on trains during the last year was far fewer than in 1991; revenue has declined while costs have remained constant, even increased. In light of these factors, they were very fortunate to make a profit in 1992, albeit a small one of approximately £2 million, compared with £50–60 million in 1991. If costs continue to go up, and if the number of people travelling does not increase, InterCity are in for another very modest year. For this reason alone, they have no alternative but to try to attract more customers by giving special attention to customer service improvements.

Given the creativity and innovation in telecommunications – such as teleconferencing – it could be that businessmen need not travel as much as previously, or even that InterCity are in effect in competition with the telecommunications industry. However, no matter how good the audio–visual and electronic magic on offer, at the end of the day people still want to have conversation face-to-face. Over the telephone, it is often less fluent and fluid, and therefore less constructive. InterCity believe that there is always going to be a need for individuals to meet and 'see the whites of each other's eyes'. Moreover, there is considerable scope for InterCity to work in partnership with British Telecom (BT) and Mercury in applications of telecommunications for rail passengers. For example, InterCity already have telephones on their trains and pagers for their Senior Conductors.

Chris Green, the Managing Director of InterCity, admits 'We are in tough competition for your business with air, coach, car and telecommunications, but I believe that ultimately it is our customer service that will shape our future.' To this end, InterCity have adopted their Vision, Strategy and Values statement (see Figure 8.1), which represents a major first step towards creating a central focus for long-term success. The statement highlights the need to provide improved levels of customer service by taking a 'quality' approach: this, InterCity believe, will contribute to a better understanding of, and reduction in, basic costs. The result will be a better-run business which is more capable of reaching its targets for customer service and for profits.

GIVE THE CUSTOMERS WHAT THEY WANT

One of the things a customer-aware organisation must be wary of is the accidental substitution of good communication for good action. Good customer communication is important, but good action is actually what is needed. In this respect, British Rail is often seen by its customers – internal and external – as an example of poor practice. Many people find it very frustrating as rail travellers to read on huge trackside posters that British Rail met its quality objectives 87 per cent of the time last month, when the train you are waiting for has not appeared and the announcement which might have explained why is inaudible.

British Rail has been asking its customers what kind of service they want for some years now – and customers have not been short on ideas. They want the simple things to be right: clean trains and stations; trains running on time and frequently enough to ensure the fare-paying passenger actually does sit on the seat he has paid for; and information that is directly relevant to the journey, delivered in such a way he can make use of it. Chris Green agrees wholeheartedly that you have got to give the customer the basic service first, before you worry too much about the 'added value'. 'I, like you, want InterCity to be seen as the best, most civilised way to travel at speed from centre to centre. This vision will be achieved if we provide a quality product – one that fulfils the service promise on a consistent basis to all our customers.'

Green believes that InterCity's strategy for the future must be to build on its strengths. 'We have managed to expand turnover by over 1 per cent in the worst recession for 60 years. Now we must plan for the big opportunities, when the economy recovers, with a mixture of product improvement and creative marketing.' Top of InterCity's product improvement list is the £750 million total route modernisation on the main UK west-coast line, involving new trains, depots and signalling. Equally important is the development of frequency as well as speed. In fairness to InterCity, who would have thought a few years ago that Swindon would have a 15-minute peak service to London, or Edinburgh a half-hourly service for much of the day?

Recently appointed Managing Director of InterCity after six years working elsewhere, Chris Green used his first three months as an opportunity to experience InterCity with fresh eyes. He says, 'This was an ideal time to see the product from the customer's point of view, to identify needs and opportunities and to overturn the compromises of the past.' He made as many trips as was humanly possible, travelling both first class and standard, and stayed away overnight at least once a week to join a morning business train into London. The object was to get views and experiences, to which end he encouraged staff to talk to him.

The biggest change I have noticed in my six years away from InterCity is the willingness of the cabin crew – the Senior Conductors and Chief Stewards – to 'own' and manage their trains. It is not easy to be the fall-guy for 500 passengers when things go wrong down the line, but I have been both impressed and proud at the willingness of train crews to take this on.

Figure 8.2 InterCity Customer Service Action List

- Making the train run on time. The timetable is a promise to be delivered and if schedules are unrealistic they must be adjusted.
- Keeping the buffet cars stocked and operational, insisting that trains must not run out of basic commodities or lose sales through failed equipment.
- Keeping toilets clean and hygienic throughout the whole journey – not just at the start.
- Completing the provision of radio telephones for Senior Conductors on all InterCity trains to accelerate information when things go wrong.

Green's travels and conversations suggested that his first task was to give the train teams real support in providing top-class customer service. He has fed his early impressions into a customer service workshop comprising a cross-section of InterCity and he has been 'delighted' by the response. 'There was immediate ownership of the problems and a near-crusading zeal to find solutions. We are a complex industry and it will take time to get things right, but the will and means are already identified.' His action list for customer service is shown in Figure 8.2.

GETTING THE PRODUCT RIGHT

As Chris Green states, 'The recession has savaged many of InterCity's competitors, but InterCity is riding the storm better than most.' Arguing that InterCity should strive to survive the recession and 'in style', he continues:

> We must not make stupid cost reductions which hit our income, and we must do everything we can to protect our customers from the recession. It means finding genuine productivity in everything we do, including our Headquarters costs, our procurement policies and our overheads. The long term is very much up to myself and the InterCity Headquarters team to get agreement for the big product improvement investment funds that we will need as soon as the recession is over.

Green is emphatic about total commitment to safety never being compromised. 'We have one simple motto in InterCity: "If it is not safe, don't do it!" Safety is an absolute number one priority . . . If for some reason the money dried up, we would rather stop parts of the railway than do anything unsafe or reckless.'

Another aspect of the commitment to customer service through product improvment is undertaken at the retail outlet level. InterCity and BR's European Passenger Services Division are investing over £12 million in a joint distribution system (JDS) to retail their products at stations throughout Great Britain. The JDS is integrating BR's fares, timetable and reservations databases, to help the retail clerk give a quicker response to customers' needs. The Channel Tunnel will have particular needs regarding security and check-in procedures; as a result, airline-style ticketing has been chosen, since this will allow the customer's reservations and connecting services to be shown on a single travel ticket.

Customer service initiatives at the retail point of sale are important to InterCity. As Roy Woods, their Retail Systems Manager points out:

There are further benefits to the new retailing system, such as the opportunity to hold a record of our most frequent and valued customers in order that their travel preferences can be taken into account automatically, considerably cutting transaction times. The JDS also allows the customer to make a provisional booking and to convert that into a firm order, with the tickets posted or collected at a convenient station, allowing customers to avoid stations at peak times.

In early 1993 the JDS will be on stream in more than 40 main stations, and a further 400 stations were due to be equipped later in 1993 and in 1994.

Another recent contribution to customer service is in their telephone sales. They have set up a one-number Freephone credit card booking service, which enables customers to purchase tickets in advance without having to make a separate visit to the station. This initiative is in line with plans to rationalise the list of telephone numbers published. Faced with a confusing range of numbers, a customer seeking to make a booking or an enquiry may not always be certain whether his destination is in the South Midlands, East or West Midlands, and so does not know which number to ring. Concentration is now being focused on ease of access and convenience, together with on-going objectives of maintaining response time targets and training staff to be courteous and helpful. Of course there can still be improvements, but I have noticed faster response times to telephone call enquiries in the sample conducted for this book of 60 UK stations.

Chris Green and his team are open about what they face in seeking to deliver optimum customer service.

When we publish a timetable, advertisement or pamphlet we are publishing a commitment to the customer. It's quite simple – if it's not deliverable, don't publish it! We should make 100 per cent certain that the customer is going to get it. I worry when drivers tell of schedules that are almost impossible to deliver punctually. We still have trains that are cancelled far too regularly, catering that is not up to the published promise either through equipment failures or trains being transposed at the last minute. We have to re-think our product, decide how we are going to deliver it, and if we can't deliver the promise we should not pretend we can.

WINNING HEARTS AND MINDS

Graham Smith was brought in from British Airways (BA) as the Head of Customer Service and Retail for InterCity. He is by no means unique, in that at least three members of the InterCity Directors' group have outside experience of private organisations. InterCity are anxious both to retain traditional railway management skills and to marry them to the skills which some people have brought in from the outside.

According to Graham Smith, sustaining and improving customer service starts as an idea, which does not take root and grow unless it is in strong soil and good compost. The board of directors is that compost.

If the rest of us who work in InterCity feel that the idea for improving customer services is rooted in good soil then the roots are going to grow. Ultimately the strength of the plant is the people on the ground delivering the product. They are the real root of the plant that makes it grow and survive. Therefore, if it has a healthy start in life, it has a reasonably good chance of continuing its growth. It's the boardroom that provides that essential compost, and good soil, and without that the plant just will not grow.

The excellence companies covered in this book and its predecessor all illustrate the truth of the maxim 'If you don't start in the boardroom, you don't start'. Some managers disagree, believing that an organisation should start with the market research to discover what the customers want, and then provide that service. To me, and to many executives featured in this book, this is back to front. At the heart of a company, which is traditionally the boardroom, there has to be a desire to change and improve the service to customers. When the will is there to change, then you can commission the research. As Graham Smith puts it:

> It is rather like Wimbledon. The players have to go out there believing they can win. They are then surrounded by all the coaches in the world, the physiotherapists and psychiatrists who help them, but the will to win is the beginning. You can then engage all the necessary assets that translate the will into a plan of action. I think that market research is very valuable and important, but it has to start somewhere – someone has to generate the idea.

To win hearts and minds InterCity need the commitment of their board, at the very least to sanction resources for the training they have to undertake on customer service. They have identified that in the next few years their staff must be trained so that existing vocational skills are supplemented by attitudinal, customer-aware and behavioural skills. Senior dedicated project teams have been given very specific changes to bring about in areas such as punctuality and station appearance. So InterCity are trying to generate changes in their services at the same time as attitudinal changes in their staff. 'At some stage,' says Graham Smith, 'the two meet, so that we can say to our customers, with our hand on our heart, not only that we are doing our best to make their journey more enjoyable and punctual, but also that the people driving the trains and serving the meals will be better at their craft.'

The reason why commerical organisations place so much stress nowadays on the importance of customer service is because it has become a way of life among the public. We all expect it. The days when British customers suffered in silence are over. It is therefore easier today to transfer the message to the boardroom, and to the managers and individuals at the sharp end. As Smith says:

In the last two or three years there has been quite an awareness building up that if we do not get our act together somebody will come and pinch our act. There are already enough competitors out there – coach, car, plane – and we know that we have competition. We also know that the only way we will retain our customer loyalty is if we are rewarding them in terms of the service we give.

SERVICE IS A LONG JOURNEY

InterCity have upwards of 30,000 people scheduled to go through their customer service training programme. The chief priority has been their main customer contact staff, who can do so much to win the loyalty of customers. These seminars began in late autumn 1992 and were targeted on staff at certain key locations, such as some of the main London termini and the larger provincial locations, for example Bristol. 'Obviously the focus has been on those most often directly in touch or contact with the customer', says Graham Smith, who adds, however: 'The interesting thing is that one way or another all our staff have an impact on the satisfaction and experience of the customer. The train driver may very seldom see a customer but how he drives his train, and his attitude towards punctuality, impact on the total customer service.'

InterCity need, therefore, to start from an awareness that every one of the 30,000-plus employees has some degree of impact on how the customer perceives the service. Everyone who works for InterCity should have some awareness of their impact on the customer. However, the practicalities of the logistics, time, cost, and management of such training have to be recognised. Accordingly, InterCity prioritise, focusing on employees who have the most instant effect on customers, especially on-board staff, those who sell tickets and people who answer the telephone. At InterCity these 'frontliners', numbering somewhere between 5,000 and 8,000, are the first people they are trying to influence in terms of their behaviour towards customers.

InterCity believe that it is essential that their seminars cross-fertilise and that, for example, the booking clerk should sit next to the train conductor or steward. One of the strong lessons Smith has drawn from his BA experience is that you must mix people together. There the pilot sat down with the baggage loader and ticket checker, sharing for the day their common and contrasting experiences. He explains, 'If you did not do that you would lose out on a lot of the common cultural feelings you want to get over, and also on the 'societas' or sense of belonging that comes from meeting different people in the same organisation.'

As the start of something new, InterCity are not certain where all this customer service training is going to take them. They think it is the right approach, and are borrowing from other people's experiences. They know that some of their staff will be cynical, some will be over the top with enthusiasm and some will be middle of the road. But they also believe that at the end of the day the large majority of staff will want the initiative to succeed.

LISTENING TO YOUR CUSTOMERS

One option for organisations like InterCity is to invite customers into staff training seminars. This gives the customer the opportunity to reflect on the organisation, and to indicate what it is like from the customer's point of view. To get real customers in a controlled environment such as a training session is a form of instant market research which can be extremely instructive.

With or without the inclusion of volunteer customers, what these events should be trying to say, says Graham Smith, is that 'excellence comes down to consistency and predictability of service'. He explains:

> If I know that a train is going to be clean, that I am going to be comfortable and welcomed and am going to get off at the other end feeling good, if you achieve that consistently, that is what I would regard as

approximating to sustaining service excellence. You are then getting value for money, being appreciated for your custom, and are arriving on time for appointments etc.

Smith admits that if the train arrives late the impact of excellence on board is destroyed. He knows that if the train is late, and passengers have not been told why, InterCity are double-damned. He recognises of course that, often for reasons outside InterCity's control (although sometimes within), they do not always get people to their destination on time. 'It is therefore doubly important that we explain to our customers why, and that when you get to the other end there are good facilities to speed you on your journey.'

InterCity now have their Passenger Charter and have to live with its compensation aspects, which have been criticised by many people. To many more, however, such as Smith, it is

bolder and more specific than anything I have read relating to the transport industry, in terms of making promises, and we now deliver the promises. If we don't deliver the service, we repay in terms of vouchers . . . I think our customers will forgive us if, when things go wrong, we try to put them right. What they will not forgive us for is when things go wrong and we give up on them. Then they would say 'Never again will I travel InterCity'. So the first objective is to get it right, and get it right first time, which is when you reach the pinnacle of excellence.

Several BR stations now invite customers to come along on a particular day or evening on a 'partnership' basis. This is all about listening. There is not always a structured agenda, but there is a chance for customers to meet a lot of the people who work at their station and to give an opinion on what they want done better.

Occasionally, says Graham Smith, we do get compliments, but we would like to see the ration increase. I have a vision of this customer forum approach being more widely used, not just to come along and meet us but to influence how we use future products. Help us design change! What we are doing is good and healthy, but you have to keep evolving its scope and purpose. I do think that the next important focus is to use customers in face-to-face situations to help us design what they would like to see from InterCity.

BRITISH RAIL'S VISION FOR INTERCITY

Mike Carroll is Quality Manager for InterCity. He identifies 'a total quality process' as the way forward in sustaining customer services success. He says that this total quality process is changing InterCity's whole management style, cutlure and behaviour.

It is one of many strategic initiatives which are now being progressed within InterCity in an overall approach to managing the future organisation and achieving customer service excellence. The strategy is about understanding and satisfying the agreed requirement of our customers, both outside and inside InterCity. Simply put, it is about giving our customers what they want, when they want it, every time. It also requires that we become good customers ourselves, stating our requirements clearly to internal and external suppliers. It is central to InterCity's future success, and is helping to create an organisation which is flexible and able to respond to changing needs.

The quest for customer service quality within InterCity is based on six key principles. These are:

- Identifying customers' requirements.
- Getting it right first time.
- Tackling variation in performance.
- Involving all employees.
- Identifying the costs.
- Working towards continuous improvement.

An InterCity Customer Service Strategy is now being developed to determine the future direction and priorities for satisfying customers' needs. The strategy is based on a promise to provide InterCity customers with a quality service which is characterised by:

- Personal service throughout each journey.
- Consistency of care throughout each journey.
- Complete 'end-to-end' service.
- Departing and arriving on time (delivering the timetable promise).
- Consistent and reliable information.
- Security and reassurance.
- Quality of service that focuses on continuous improvement.

'Introducing this strategy,' says Mike Carroll, 'is a major step in helping to ensure that InterCity is a customer-focused, correctly-resourced organisation with well-trained staff – and continues to be sustained in the future. Quality and service is taking root in British Rail and it is changing the way we work. Eventually it will change the quality of service we provide and transform the way our customers perceive us. As a result we will have a more efficient and effective railway.'

For a company of the size, complexity and age of BR – InterCity to adopt quality as an aim implies a great deal indeed. Says Mike Carroll: 'Quality implies nothing more or less than doing the job properly.' He lists the following demands upon his staff if they are to meet the quality requirement:

- Put the customer first in everything we do.
- Know what the customer requires.
- Know whether we can meet those requirements.
- Know precisely how to meet those requirements, fully and regularly.
- Understand how to achieve continuous improvement in our performance.

Carroll adds:

In order to achieve the position where every job done is a quality job, InterCity and British Rail obviously have to change. We all share a view of what we want InterCity to stand for in the eyes of our customers. We want InterCity to be the best, most civilised way to travel at speed from centre to centre.

The basic message InterCity need to keep reinforcing is that commitment to quality of service is their most important business priority. InterCity is determined to be recognised by everyone as a quality service organisation meeting agreed customer specification first time, every time, but they must ensure that each individual is responsible for the quality of his or her work and that all have a role to play in making InterCity a quality service organisation. Such statements are the key to the way InterCity will run their business, now and in the future. They make it clear that 'quality' is one of the most important words in the InterCity vocabulary (see Figure 8.1). But this means change in the way management behaves:

- Managers need to act as team-leaders and role-models.
- Managers need to understand the importance of trust and empowerment.
- Managers must switch from a hierarchical approach to work to a team-based approach which identifies, secures and develops skills and competencies throughout the workforce.

As Chris Green states:

We are clear on our priorities and our processes – now we have to harness them and make customers really welcome from the moment they make contact with InterCity. So we have a challenging task ahead. I feel, as does my management team, excited about the future prospects for InterCity as a whole. Unlike Robert Louis Stevenson's patient we are hale and healthy but, just as he is encouraged to be, we too are determined on rapid and lasting improvements.

9. Hotels

Doyle Hotel Group (Dublin)
Gean House (Alloa)
George Hotel (Edinburgh)
Hyatt Carlton Tower (London)
One Devonshire Gardens (Glasgow)

'The Welcome – Come in the evening or come in the morning, come when you're looked for, or come without warning.'

Thomas Davis (1814–1845)

Service today has become a vital element in the battle for the hearts, minds, money and support of the customer. Throughout this book total customer service is referred to in its widest sense, to reflect an organisation's 'mission and value' statement, internally and externally. Also crucial are the organisation's philosophy, people, policies, processes, procedures and personality – all of which are geared to meet customers' product needs and expectations of service. The central message is, of course, that the customer is the final arbiter – service must always be measured from the customers' point of view. Customer service, throughout this book, is perceived on three levels:

- The actual product or service delivered
- The way it is presented and served to the customer
- The after sales service and support

A major theme of all these studies is that all these things must be provided with *consistent* excellence. Sadly, this is where far too many organisations fail, in that they do not have sufficient dedication to providing sustained service for their customers – getting it right first time, on time, *every* time.

Service excellence is a balance between purpose, people and process.

- **Purpose** – This is the 'mission and philosophy' statement, the values and the ingrained vision of the organisation. It is these beliefs, emanating from the boardroom, which drive service behaviour through the organisation.
- **Process** – This means adapting systems throughout the organisation to suit the needs of the customer. It also means the provision of support for all the people who work the system and are the service deliverers.
- **People** – The staff, who need to understand the value of the customers and the general public they serve. To do this, they need to understand what business they are in and their role within that business. They must be energised and empowered to make decisions and improve the system to better satisfy their customers.

Total customer service may be executive-driven, but much depends on the attitudes and behaviour of all the people in the organisation. Being a customer- and service-centred culture is a profound philosophy and commits all concerned to change. Effectively, it becomes an indigenous way of life. It means constantly supporting the front line of the organisation, the 'coal face', and it also necessitates communication with customers – both internally and externally. It also means being *seen*. In customer excellence organisations, managers are seldom in their offices. Rather, they are visible, walking the job and effectively coaching and counselling the players 'on the field' as well as 'in the dressing room'. For all the managers I meet in service excellence organisations, sustaining customer service is a process of continual improvement; turning mistakes into opportunities, and regularly reinforcing the rhetoric that 'it is the customer who, ultimately, pays the wages'. Nowhere is this better witnessed than in the hotel industry, and in particular the hotels selected for this book.

The hotels I have chosen are, indeed, successful. But, as Irving Berlin said, 'the toughest thing about success is that you've got to keep on being a success'. My Highland granny once told me of six essential qualities that are the key to success:

- sincerity
- personal integrity
- humility
- courtesy
- wisdom
- charity

Upon reflection I see that these qualities could also be considered essential in customer-centred organisations. Certainly they abound through the hotels reviewed in this chapter. Of course, hotels are all about prime locations, luxurious interiors, comfortable and spacious rooms, good food, ambience and value for money. But the most important feature for the hotels mentioned here is the consistency of the calibre and commitment of *all* their staff. I have met many people who say that success is simply a matter of luck. This is true, if you ask any failure. As I have said before, success is a journey, not a destination. The organisations throughout this book have to continually strive to not only sustain customer service but also to improve it.

A great deal of research goes into selecting the companies and organisations for a book of this nature. They have to meet some three dozen criteria to justify whether they come anywhere near the mark in terms of customer service. This method of judging covers principles and standards encompassing the *purpose, process* and *people* elements I have mentioned. To achieve excellence in these three major areas of organisational activity is, of course, more difficult in a larger concern than a small one. This is certainly true of hotels, particularly when they are spread over a number of locations aiming to achieve consistent standards. The three major hotel groups covered in this chapter have consistently fielded high ratings against the excellence criteria. But all would admit, in the words of Michael Gray, the General Manager for the Hyatt Carlton Tower in London, that they must, 'try harder because we have not arrived yet. We feel that we can always do better – we are never complacent – we are only as good as the service experienced by the last customer.'

To my mind, one way of judging a good hotel, of whatever size, is how long you remember the experience of staying there after your departure. Two hotels which colleagues, and myself, still talk about months after a visit are both in Scotland. I mention both the Gean House and One Devonshire Gardens, albeit briefly, in this section because they not only met the customer standards crtieria mentioned above but exceeded it at a dramatic, memorable level.

'WE ARE HERE WHEN YOU NEED US'

The Gean House is listed among Egon Ronay's top ten Scottish Hotels. It was the 1992 winner of the Scottish Field and Caithness Glass 'Interiors Of The Year Award' and it has the 'four crown' deluxe accolade of the Scottish Tourist Board. Our research showed not one complaint among current customers, with comments about the service ranging from excellent to extravagant. The Gean (Scottish for 'wild cherry') House is run by John Taylor and Anthony Mifsud, whose motto appears to be, quite simply: 'We are here when you need us.' They delight their customers by excelling at the basics.

Like the Gean House, One Devonshire Gardens has established a reputation for outstanding customer service. It is also a small, luxury, award winning hotel built for those who expect, and appreciate, fine standards – what some of us might call the old-fashioned values of personal service. The hotel operates at the opposite end of the market from the three large hotels discussed later in this study. It has fewer guests at any one time, but they are demanding customers who want the one-to-one relationship expected of a smaller establishment. Ken McCulloch, the proprietor of One Devonshire Gardens, explains:

> *Part of the reason we get business in the first place is that we are appealing to people who really don't want to be staying in a hotel as such, so we work to that customer base, in that they are coming to a hotel which is a kind of 'non hotel'. Only having 27 bedrooms we are in a position to keep a good customer record and history of what they like, and what they don't like.*

Both the Gean House and One Devonshire Gardens are part of the trend towards small-town house or country mansion hotels offering a different type of business from the larger hotels. This means that they have to put a lot of emphasis on the quality of people that they hire. Both hotels realise that before they can service the outside customer properly they have got to look after the inside customers – their staff. Ken McCulloch says:

> *When you are in the quality business, you are in a stronger position to attract that type of person. Therefore, like sticks with like. It is much easier then for them to have a one-to-one relationship with the clients that we attract. The more quality that we build on internally, the more we will be successful externally. Success is the sum of many small things correctly done, it is not one thing that is any more important than any other. The more we dictate our standards, and discuss them with our personnel, the more they take them on board, and the more they are able to transmit them to our guests.*

The hotel industry is notorious for not paying its staff well. However, many managers would say that you cannot give good customer service without getting the financial rewards for staff right first. Our research shows, however, that semi-financial rewards are at least as important as take-home pay. Such rewards include a recognition by the management and one's peers that you are doing a good job. As John Taylor at the Gean House puts it:

It is not just the money you pay to a staff for doing their job, but the money you spend on them, and the care you take in making them feel successful, important and, in fact, loved – not just by the management but by our guests. It is not enough that they are just working at the Gean House; rather, the important thing is that they get satisfaction at all levels from doing their job. We have a high quality product and if our staff are not proud of it they are certainly never going to come across as sincere, which is the way customer service has to be. Everyone, quite simply, has got to believe in the maxim 'we are here when you need us'.

For me, the basis of customer service excellence was probably summed up by Ken McCulloch at One Devonshire Gardens when he said:

With all of our guests we never say 'no'. Whenever the customer comes to our reception area or speaks to any member of our staff, the brain is automatically clicked into 'yes'. Before we even know what the customer – our guest – wants, we are saying 'yes'. That is the way it has to be in this business.

THE DOYLE HOTEL GROUP

'To be sure sir, that's no problem'

Founded by the late P V Doyle, the Doyle Hotel Group is Ireland's largest privately-owned hotel group. It has seven hotels in Dublin, one in London and two in the United States. They have been in operation for more than 25 years and their Dublin hotels account for more than 40 per cent of the capital's hotel bedrooms. The present managing director of the Group is P V Doyle's son David, who took over the reins on the sudden death of his father in 1986. According to David Doyle:

The success of the hotel group can be attributed to not only offering products which meet the highest international standards, in prime locations at value for money prices, but also because all staff, at every level, are committed towards the prime objective of delivering the very best in customer service.

How, then, do Doyle Group achieve this? It is a member of 'The Leading Hotels of the World', a prestigious network which includes two of their hotels, the Westbury, a five star international hotel in the heart of Dublin city, and the Berkeley Court, in Dublin's embassy district. Both these hotels have not only met our researchers' standards of excellence consistently, but have constantly exceeded them, over two years of study.

Recently, Neil Garnett, Manager of Corporate Communications for Texaco UK said of the Berkeley Court that he had never before witnessed such high quality customer service at every level within the one hotel. He continued: 'The reception area was one of the most welcoming I have ever come across. I immediately felt comfortable, although I had never stayed at that hotel before'. What Neil Garnett has highlighted is an essential feature of high-excellence hotels – their care in promoting the 'sense of arrival'. All of the hotels in this chapter not only displayed this care but, as important, and too often forgotten, the 'sense of departure'. Many hotels concentrate on the guest on arrival; too few appreciate the importance of leaving the guest with a good impression as they leave – hopefully one that will make them *want* to return.

'YOUR BUSINESS IS OUR PLEASURE'

The Doyle Hotel Group are committed to ensuring that the highest possible standards are maintained. The growth and development of the Group has depended on ensuring customers' needs are met with the greatest possible ease and efficiency. At the Doyle Group you will find our staff courteous, attentive and discreet. Your business is our pleasure at the Doyle Hotel Group.

(Doyle Group Mission Statement)

The Berkeley Court and Westbury hotels each have approximately 200 bedrooms, all with en-suite bathrooms. Both hotels also have a wide variety of suites including, at the Berkeley Court, the penthouse, which offers total privacy in some 7,500 sq.ft. Surprisingly for their size, both of these hotels retain a 'guest house' status, offering the customer a home-from-home atmosphere. Each guest's arrival, stay and departure are treated with the utmost care and personal service, the aim being to consolidate the already high level of customer loyalty.

When you ask Doyle Group staff about their management they consistently say that managers 'listen to staff in the same way as we listen to customers' and that 'they're always there, and approachable'. I am confident that this is why Doyle hotels gain a huge amount of repeat business and retain staff, in an industry otherwise known for its high labour turnover. David Doyle is 'known' by everyone around Dublin – taxi drivers, kitchen porters, guests and VIPs alike. He visits each hotel every day and appears at all important functions in them. In an industry which is so service-orientated David Doyle knows that a keen eye is required to ensure that all areas within his hotels are run as smoothly and efficiently as possible. To this end, he is always 'visible'. In fact, colleagues have even seen David working in one of the bars himself, to keep in touch with his guests.

The Berkeley Court and Westbury hotels have played host to a large number of world leaders, celebrities and VIPs. What attracts such guests to stay and to return is, to my mind, not only the excellent facilities but also the discretion with which they are treated. As a seasoned and well-travelled hotel guest the one thing I value – perhaps even more than service – is my privacy. To me, discretion and courteous attention to my privacy represent added value. Indiscretion in a hotel is indefensible. 'As a jewel of gold in a swine's snout, so is a fair woman which is without discretion.' The same is true of a hotel. It is the policy of the Doyle Group not to cash in on publicity opportunities by releasing the fact that a celebrity is in residence, or by disclosing any weird and wonderful things he/she ordered while staying! Well-known personalities are not harassed for autographs and the like. The privacy of all their guests is of paramount importance, the aim being always to respect that each guest must have the freedom to enjoy their stay the way *they* would like.

SUSTAINING SERVICE THROUGH STAFF DEVELOPMENT, INVOLVEMENT AND RECOGNITION

It is often difficult to follow in a father's footsteps. David Doyle was, he will admit, much more comfortable being in the background, rather than in a one-to-one, visible leadership role dealing with staff and guests. At first he tried to step back, as he is shy and modest, and to form a more structured hierarchy in the Group. However, he soon realised the very reason why Doyle Hotels were such a success was because his father had been so accessible to both staff and customers alike. Fortunately, David Doyle has all his father's ability at setting the sort of management style required to ensure that the best customer service is sustained.

Members of his staff confirm that David Doyle has developed a distinctive style of management which encourages employees to make an input into decisions which affect themselves and the customer. He actively encourages staff to experience the role of the customer, to heighten their sensitivity to the customers' needs. This is a feature in many excellence organisations, and encourages staff to know the competition. Travelling abroad as part of his own market research has made David Doyle very aware of what it's like to be a customer. This has been a tremendous asset, enabling the Doyle Group to make new strides in providing quality customer service, and also in appreciating the needs of seasoned business travellers.

Because of their excellence reputation the Doyle Hotel Group are recognised to be one of the best hotel groups to train with and work for. As such, they attract some of the best talent in the hotel industry. Responsibility for training in the Group is placed with the general manager of each hotel. Their overall policy is the diligent development in staff of initiative and attention to detail when dealing with customers. The philosophy of getting to know the customer, meeting and greeting, recognising potential problems and solving them to the benefit of the customer are paramount in all training programmes. Although all employees adhere to the policy of the Group, they are not stereotypes, but rather are encouraged to develop their own personalities.

There is a strong and insistent emphasis on weekly meetings between heads of departments and the general manager to discuss progress, problems and ideas. The general manager depends on his heads of department to motivate their staff and ensure the very best of customer service is provided. Every general manager knows all the staff in each department and they therefore benefit from a good working relationship where senior management is accessible and approachable. Problems can be discussed, solutions put forward and, if accepted, put in place. As with other excellence organisations featured in this book, the key elements of such meetings are: that they are held regularly; that they involve managers from the boardroom down; and that quality of service is top of the agenda.

For example, David Doyle is a great believer in staff putting forward ideas in their own area, becoming more actively involved in their department and in recognising what the customer wants. A recent example of this came in the drive to revitalise the two restaurants in the Doyle Group's Burlington Hotel in Dublin (Ireland's largest, with some 500 luxury bedrooms). A team for each restaurant was drawn up consisting of the food and beverage manager, the chef and the head waiter. A short-list of successful restaurants in Dublin was also drawn up and each team dined in each restaurant. This not only acted as an excellent method of motivating staff towards new trends; it also assisted them in understanding customer needs, by being customers themselves. It also made them aware of what competing restaurants were offering customers. After each visit these teams met and decided the pros and cons of what they had experienced and what would be appropriate to introduce for Doyle Hotel Group customers.

Each month an employee who demonstrates outstanding commitment to customer service is rewarded for his/her efforts. This 'employee of the month' is selected by the general managers of

---

Figure 9.1 Criteria for Selection of the Doyle Hotels 'Employee of the Month'

- Service to customer
- Attention to customer queries
- Efficiency and courtesy in solving customer queries/problems
- Disposition and attitude to one's position
- Standard of work
- Ability to work with others
- Punctuality
- Hygiene, uniform and appearance

---

the seven Dublin-based hotels in consultation with their heads of department, according to the criteria shown in Figure 9.1.

Each recipient is awarded with a plaque, and the employee's photograph is displayed behind reception. At the end of the year each general manager selects an overall winner for his or her hotel. Each winner goes forward to the grand final and an overall winner is crowned 'Doyle Hotel Group Employee of the Year'. The winner is selected by a panel of three judges consisting of not only the Doyle Hotel Group Personnel Manager, but outsiders, for example, the Chief Executive of the Irish Hotels Federation and a representative from the Irish Tourist Board. This reinforcement of the importance of sustaining customer service, accompanied by the media coverage, acts not only as a motivator to other members of staff, but endorses the 'recognition' message highlighted earlier in this chapter. If staff value themselves, and one another, then they will value their work and their customers.

It is no coincidence that my opening quotation should come from *The Welcome* by Thomas Davis who, in the 1830s, was one of the Trinity College Dublin generation defining new destinies for Ireland. Today, within ten minutes' walk from Trinity College, stand two of the 'Leading Hotels of the World', sustaining standards of service well ahead of their competitors. 'That's not enough', says David Doyle 'It's hard getting to the top, it's even harder to make sure we stay there.'

The Doyle hotels are not only surrounded by tradition, they have become one. Perhaps the final word should be left to a member of staff who, on receiving a seemingly impossible request from one of my colleagues at a ridiculous time of night, said with the usual Doyle smile: 'To be sure sir, that's no problem.' P V Doyle would have been proud.

THE GEORGE HOTEL (EDINBURGH)

Service With No Excuse

Listed amongst Edinburgh's premier hotels, the George has 195 rooms, including some dating back to the hotel's opening in 1881. Complacency can breed contempt every bit as much as familiarity and the George, as with so many hotels, fell into the trap of saying: 'We're successful, why change?' A misguided arrogance allowed it to coast – and when you're coasting you're going down hill. I personally recall staying at the hotel a few years ago and being disappointed at the lowering of its service standards. They were not poor, but for a hotel which enjoys one of the finest reputations in Europe service levels were neither consistent nor sustained. Today it is different, and research feedback over the last year has illustrated a returning to customer service excellence worthy of this grand establishment.

Now part of Inter-Continental Hotels, the George displays a commitment to customer service which comes right from the top. As with many excellence organisations, they have inverted the traditional pyramid to allow its broad base to be the front line, interacting with the customer. But the boardroom and management are steering the change in culture, from being a reactive organisation to being a proactive one in taking care of customer needs. Today the George is committed to a new organisational culture, empowering people and departments interacting with the customer to make decisions. Every part of their corporate strategy is geared to winning the hearts and minds of all their customers, both internal and external.

A vital component in customer service is the communication factor, meaning that a 'vision statement' should go out to all staff, and be followed up with actions to implement that vision. Campbell Black, the George's General Manager, uses the phrase 'plan your action and action your plans' in connection with the commitment of his board and management to opening communication channels and putting plans into place. He says:

Vision statements for most people should be very clear and easy. Vision statements of too many companies relate too much to levels of profit and their position on the marketplace. At the George we want to get back to basics. Our basic vision statement is quite simply 'Service With No Excuse'.

Creating the environment and the culture of customer service must start at the top. However, in making it start at the top the George believes in the need to ensure they are getting it right when they employ people. Campbell Black views the Human Resource Department of the hotel as being the cornerstone of the organisation:

To get the culture that we want, their brief is to employ the right people. The ethos here, of course, is that through employing the right people we have a solid base to build upon. As we start to bring in more and more people, they then become part of the structure. If the foundation is strong and the structure is strong, the results will then follow. It is essential, in this area of human resources, that training and development are not just talked about, but actioned time and time again.

The George Hotel's human resources function covers a multitude of opportunities for employees. Campbell Black has found that one of the most effective ways of measuring the change in culture is through the use of an 'Employee Opinion Survey', which is completed by all staff. As he says:

It is an exhaustive questionnaire, offering confidentiality of response from the employees on how the hotel is doing overall. In our busines, 85 per cent of staff have an interaction with the customer on a daily basis. It is as important to discover what the employee thinks of the hotel as what the customer says. The survey is certainly not designed to be a 'bitch' session, but it is designed to build the self esteem of the employee and to provide feedback with action to management.

At the George they consider it essential that management undertakes *action* in response to the comments made in the Employee Opinion Survey. In this way employees feel they have a much more active say in addressing the issues of running a hotel. Nevertheless, Campbell Black points out that this does not, in effect, mean that the front line is the entire business:

They are a component of running the business. At the George we operate on a global, regional and individual hotel unit base for all our various training programmes. On the global scale of training we 'think global, action local'. Through this approach we try to consistently deliver the philosophies of the company in the local environment, so that when a guest goes to an Inter-Continental hotel anywhere in the world there are always certain standards that will be consistent. This is vital to reassure the customer. Regional actions add flavour to the consistency from country to country. The real feel of a hotel from city to city is, therefore, unique – training activities on the local level cap things off, hopefully, to provide a unique experience to the global traveller.

CUSTOMER SERVICE RECOGNITION

To ensure that the climate and culture are right, the George consider it essential that a well structured and progressive training programme is implemented for both existing and new employees. That first day on the job must be a very special one, says Campbell Black:

The new employee's first impression must be one that is positive. Too many times their first day is cluttered with confusion, paperwork, ill-fitting uniforms and misunderstandings, and the employee often ends up feeling abandoned. At the George we produce an Induction Programme that includes grooming and hygiene, a full tour of the hotel, and introduction to the general manager and the executive committee of the hotel. The programme also includes an introduction to Edinburgh for those employees coming from out of the city, or abroad.

One thing they also do at the George, which is first class, is to offer employees an overnight stay, with their spouse if they have one, so they can experience being a 'guest' in the place of their employment.

Constant emphasis on training geared to the 'vision statement' of customer service is a constant throughout this book. Over the last couple of years the George have had to introduce a new culture and to gain commitment for it. Training is a major part of that effort, but it takes more than that. 'Commitment can really only be gained if our people see the leaders of our hotel lead by example,' says Campbell Black. 'It is essential we have "management by walking around". You must be visible, watching, talking and listening – being totally immersed at the front line of the business.' In effect, by doing this, management are both recognising and reinforcing the service mission to their staff.

Another form of recognition the George believes in, is that those employees showing high standards of customer service should be rewarded. As in the Doyle Hotel Group, the George have an 'employee of the month award' and a departmental 'Star Award'. The principle behind this is explained by Campbell Black:

Just like any customer receiving recognition from an employee in the service business, it is equally important for employees to receive recognition from customers, internal and external. Our 'employee of the month' is customer-led – that is to say, it involves votes from guests of the hotel, as well as votes from the hotel management. It rewards those individuals who are recognised as helping outside of their area of responsibility.

Campbell Black recognises that there is always a need for staff to have some way of seeing how far they have progressed, where they are at now, and whether they are going in the right direction.

There are various forms of measurement that can be utilised both from a customer's point of view and from the staff's point of view. Follow-up to our Employee Opinion Survey is one way to measure the way that our staff perceive what we are doing. Another measurement tool is turnover statistics of staff. What departments are turning over most? Why are they turning over? Interviews of those staff should be able to identify what the problems are, and exit interviews are always carried out on any member of staff who leaves our employment. The interview is held by the personnel department and not by the department that the person worked in. The reason for this is that if a person is leaving because they don't like their supervisor, they are unlikely to tell the supervisor that.

In this way, at the George they can recognise why, at the very least, they have not delighted their internal customer and can do something about it.

DELIGHTING THE CUSTOMER

Delighting a customer should always result in the loyalty of that customer being retained for your business. For the George, delighting a customer does not mean pandering or grovelling to guests. As Campbell Black says 'It just means doing the basics – a welcoming smile, a confident, warm sounding voice, an offer of help!'

Further delight can result if just that little bit extra is done to cater to a customer's needs or wants. The key to this is *anticipation* of what would delight. For example, the George keeps many different records of the guests who stay there. These vary, explains Campbell Black:

. . . from their dates of birth to their wants such as having firm pillows or down pillows, still spring water or gaseous water. Once we know what the needs of the customer are, we should be able to deliver 100 per cent of

the time. Information can be gathered from a variety of sources. To get your birthday, all I need on my reservation card is the month and day of birth. The year is irrelevant! Certainly, in a chain-operated hotel company, when that customer needs a reservation in another part of the world, we should be able to communicate the particular wants and needs of the customer to the other hotel. Just by doing that, we are able to delight the customer in an alternative location, no matter if it be in Hong Kong, Los Angeles, Stuttgart or even here, in Edinburgh.

More important, however, is that over a period of time the floor housekeepers, maids and Guest Relations Manager should get to know the regular guests more and more, and specifically ask them what their needs are. Today's sophisticated business traveller is well versed in giving various pieces of information when they enrol in travel clubs such as the Six Continents Club, British Airways Executive Club, and so on. All that we do is process that information into our in-house computer systems and the rest of it is very easy. Also, recognition of a returning guest is vitally important. In today's age of computerisation and technology, it is very easy for us to determine how many times a guest has come back to us, so that we can be ready for that next visit. There really is no excuse for getting that service wrong.

IMPROVEMENT STRIVING FOR SERVICE EXCELLENCE

The hotel business is judged by its customers in terms of quality of service and value for money. The George is steered not only by its 'vision statement' but also by its 'Ten Commandments of Quality', and 'Ten Quality Benchmarks' (see Figures 9.2 and 9.3). According to Campbell Black:

Each one of these two items relates to a service delivery. If we are going to have quality service, we need both the benchmarks and the commandments to be put into place within the George Hotel. They must be a constant reminder and the goal, for not just the individual, but the organisation. That really is the way we are going to sustain customer service.

Certainly customer service is being sustained at the George. In common with other hotels covered in this chapter the hotel always finds a way to delight its customer and make them *want* to return. One of my researchers, who had always previously stayed at another local hotel, recalls having a dinner party in the George's superb *Le Chamberlin* restaurant. Asking for a haggis, he requested a piper to toast the dish! A ten-minute wait (with a drink on the House to compensate for the delay) produced both haggis and bagpipes. The entire restaurant applauded. 'What service', said an American lady. 'What style' said my researcher!

Figure 9.2 The George Hotel, Edinburgh

TEN COMMANDMENTS OF QUALITY

1. There is no such thing as acceptable quality. It can always get better.
2. From the corner office to the shop floor, quality is everybody's business.
3. Keep your ears open. Some of the best ideas will come from the most unexpected sources.
4. Develop a detailed implementation plan. Talking about quality isn't enough.
5. Help hotel departments work together. The territorial imperative is your biggest obstacle.
6. Analyse jobs to identify their elements and set quality standards for each step.
7. Take control of your process. You must know why something goes wrong.
8. Be patient. Don't expect gains to show up next quarter.
9. Make extraordinary efforts in usual situations. Customers will remember those best.
10. Think beyond cutting costs. The benefits of improving quality should reach every part of the organisation.

Figure 9.3 The George Hotel, Edinburgh

TEN QUALITY BENCHMARKS

1. Quality is a hotel-wide process.
2. Quality is what the customer says it is.
3. Quality and cost are a sum, not a difference.
4. Quality requires both individual and teamwork.
5. Quality is a way of managing.
6. Quality and innovation are mutually dependent.
7. Quality is an ethic.
8. Quality requires continuous improvement.
9. Quality is the most cost effective, least capital intensive route to productivity.
10. Quality is implemented within a total system connected with customers and suppliers.

HYATT CARLTON TOWER (LONDON)

'Let us never forget that it is not the guests who need us but we who need our guests . . .'

Research in the early 1990s resulted in London's Hyatt Carlton Tower being selected for an in-depth study in my first book in this series. Since that book was published in early 1992, research has indicated that this hotel is sustaining its high customer service standards. Also in 1992, their chef Bernard Gaume was voted 'chef of the year' by *The Hotel and Caterer*, a tremendous tribute from his own industry.

Michael Gray is the General Manager of the 225 room Hyatt Carlton Tower, which is located on London's Knightsbridge. He says there is ever more effort being given to sustaining customer service, with the executive continually aware that competitive edge can be lost more from internal inefficiency than from outside competition. Their service 'mission statement' (Figure 9.4) remains the prime focus of their energies. They admit that not only is change a constant, but the more you change, the more you *have* to change and the more you *can* change.

For the Hyatt Carlton Tower, customer service does make a difference to their bottom line, day after day. They know that the only difference between competing hotels in the 1990s will be quality of customer service. They know that success requires that quality of

---

Figure 9.4   Hyatt Carlton Tower – Mission Statement

Objective

By 1995 Hyatt Carlton Tower will, by consistency in its operation, be established as one of the top three hotels in London and one of the top ten hotels in Europe.

Our marketing objectives will position the hotel to achieve a performance that exceeds our natural market share, maximises room yield and creates a significant improvement in our market awareness.

Product

A planned cycle of refurbishment and upgrading of guest rooms, public areas and food and beverage outlets will continue to ensure that, only within the limitations of the physical structure and of available funding, we will offer a product that reflects the luxury status of the hotel. The 'consumable' food and beverage and rooms products will be imaginative and reflective of all current trends and market demands.

Customer

The success and acceptability of the physical product will be dependent on our guests experiencing caring, efficient, personal and friendly service that will be achieved through a 'back to basics' and 'attention to detail' service philosophy, and achieved by a total commitment to progressive and on-going training.

Employees

We will continue to maximise employee productivity and contain payroll expenditure through the training and development of a flexible and adaptable work force, whilst maintaining the service levels guests expect at the Hyatt Carlton Tower.

We will maintain our image as a caring, progressive and sought-after employer with the implementation of competitive and rewarding remuneration packages, a fair and consistent management offering career opportunities, and on-going involvement with education institutions.

---

service receives constant attention, if it is to be sustained, and that all staff must think about it every day.

For customer service to work, all excellence organisations understand that you must commit in the boardroom. For the Hyatt Carlton Tower, this involves a daily executive committee briefing which goes through every guest arriving that day. They will discuss such topics as:

- Number of previous visits to the hotel
- Special requirements based on previous guest history, including which room number was assigned
- Time of arrival
- Previous special gifts
- Room Service alerted to welcome the guest and ascertain any special requests
- If first visit to the Hyatt Carlton Tower, who will follow up during visit including potential future sales

All service-related departments receive a copy of the guest arrival list and each division has its own daily briefing to pass on the relevant information. All members of the Exeuctive Committee, whatever their primary role, contribute ideas towards customer service – it is not just those more directly involved with guest service such as Director of Rooms or Food and Beverage.

'WE'RE ALL IN THIS TOGETHER'

What is important to the Hyatt Carlton Tower is the constant interaction, not only between staff and suppliers but also across departments. This communication on a regular team briefing basis is of maximum value when things go wrong or service fails. Team briefings help staff come to terms with mistakes and turn them into opportunities. As Michael Gray emphasises: 'We are in the service business and people are our business – people are human and therefore *do* make mistakes.' But as a recent regular Hyatt guest said to me 'When things do go wrong . . . Hyatt is the best at putting them right.'

The assertion that 'the customer is always right' is put into practice at the Hyatt Carlton Tower. Every written guest comment, good and bad, receives a written reply, and copies are distributed to the department head concerned. Where a particular staff member is mentioned, a copy also goes to them. All guest complaints are investigated and the guest informed, where appropriate, of the reasons for whatever problem has arisen. There are *never* excuses. The majority of complainants are rewarded with some sort of compensation and the majority return to the hotel. Handling the complaint gives the hotel another opportunity to communicate with the guest and find out what their expectations are. This is then recorded in the 'guest history' in order that the needs can be met on the next visit.

To improve service further, Hyatt Carlton Tower have formed partnerships with customers, which they call 'Customer Encounter Groups'. These involve both guests and employees, not just management, and encourage the guests to tell Hyatt Carlton Tower honestly how they are performing, especially in the area of guest service. An example of this is the lunches that are held on a regular basis by the banqueting department, for both existing and potential customers.

Ultimately, it is the customer who spreads the word and sustains the service mesage. Often staff have not only delighted their customer but exceeded the 'call of duty' and taken the appropriate action to meet the customer's individual needs at the time.

The Hyatt Carlton Tower stays ahead by insisting on allocating resources to their customer–centred mission. In the hotel industry the most important aspect is ensuring that financial resources are constantly available to maintain a high standard of service.

In the hotel industry it is not only a case of delighting the customer but also, whenever possible, anticipating their needs and exceeding their expectations. That is what every hotel featured in this chapter has excelled at. They make the customer never forget the experience of being in their hotel and ensure that they become an advocate for them. The referral network is the best marketing tool any organisation can have, after their staff. In the hotel industry it is critical.

10. Hastings and Rother NHS Trust

'There is no higher religion than human service. To work for the common good is the greatest creed.'

Albert Schweitzer (1875–1965)

National Health Service (NHS) hospitals within the Hastings and Rother area of south–east England deliver care locally to around 170,000 people, known as their 'customer base', and employ more than 3,000 staff. Such an organisation needs clear leadership and accountable management if it is to perform effectively and give sustained quality of service. Management priorities are twofold:

- To focus on responsibility to the local community for maintaining and improving the standard of local healthcare delivery.
- To provide leadership for staff, and to guide and motivate their work with patients.

Hastings and Rother NHS Trust provides care and treatment in hospitals, clinics and old-people's homes. The Trust's primary aims and healthcare principles are shown in Figure 10.1.

Geoff Haynes arrived at an early point in the Trust's development, as Chief Executive. His major concern as Chief Executive has been to create an organisation, of more than 3,000 staff, that is able to deliver a quality, cost-effective service. In the

Figure 10.1 Aims of the Hastings and Rother NHS Trust

Statement of Purpose

The primary aims are:

1. To offer an integrated and comprehensive range of hospital and community services, responsive to local needs and aspirations.
2. To provide a high-quality service at all times, combining clinical excellence with patient satisfaction, recognising the contribution of all staff to the quality of patient care.
3. To minimise patient dependency on hospital-based services through an increasing focus on community care and health promotion.

Healthcare Principles, Purposes and Values

Our aim is to provide healthcare to people living in and around Hastings and Rother. Our guiding principles will be:

1. To offer an integrated and comprehensive range of hospital and community services, responsive to local needs and aspirations.
2. To provide a high quality service at all times, combining clinical excellence with patient satisfaction.
3. To value our staff, implementing policies that attract, retain, develop and motivate each individual employee.
4. To develop a culture which thrives on dependence, rewards individual achievement and encourages innovation in all its activities.

nature of the latest NHS review and reforms, only that type of service is going to survive. Hastings and Rother have a Clinical Directorate structure. One of Geoff Haynes's tasks has been to empower the Directorates to look at its organisation and structure to establish what they do in terms of service and quality provision. His aims are to gain acceptance for a 'quality menu' (incorporating a 'productivity/activity agenda'), to put in place appropriate systems and to secure staff commitment to them.

DEVELOPING A SERVICE MENU

The single biggest problem, in terms of getting that menu and menu agenda in place, is employees' perceptions of what they are able to do within their own roles. Becoming a Trust has provided more freedom, including the flexibility to do some interesting and exciting new things. But, as Geoff Haynes admits:

The thing which will stop us achieving our aims is if people operate in what might be described as 'traditional mode' – thinking that all they have got to do is bang the table and money will appear from somewhere. Instead, they must look at what they are doing, think laterally about the service they are giving, and produce new, innovative ways of doing things that deliver better quality and better activity, for the same base-line cost.

A major part of achieving a quality service menu must be to change people's attitudes. But how can that start? How does an organisation like the NHS move from 'traditional mode', which may also be a very cynical mode, to where they need to go? Geoff Haynes suspects that this quandary is true of every Health Authority in the UK.

There will always be people who are very cynical about what's going on, for all sorts of reasons, and in a sense we've got to try and understand that. But first we have got to create an organisation that has a vision, that knows what it wants. I am not saying Hastings and Rother do not; I am just saying that this is a pre-requisite, and that all things have got to be measured against it. We've got to create an organisation that actually knows where it's going and can see how to get there with the resources we have got. We've got to have a value statement for the organisation, to set down very precisely the type of environment we want – for example, where information is exchanged freely, where people are able to get on in their jobs, where they can make suggestions and have them acted on.

Most important, therefore, has been the work Hastings and

Rother have done with key managers within the organisation, to help them to understand the above. Haynes believes that this approach succeeds, and that potentially obstructive people get marginalised in the process. 'We have to have a positive incentive for people to be innovative and forward-looking, and a positive disincentive for people to be traditional and backward-looking. Gradually we are creating an organisation which understands that.'

MANAGING SERVICE DILEMMAS

The paradox facing a manager such as Geoff Haynes is that he wants his organisation to have freedom, flexibility and scope for innovation, but knows that there have to be parameters, otherwise chaos will reign. There has got to be a boundary, he says.

> *The Executive must say that it prefers you not to step outside those parameters, because it thinks that would be unhealthy for the organisation. If you do, there are a number of measures that can be used to disadvantage you. In other words, stay within the boundary and managers can have the flexibility and the freedom to do what they think is right, and can determine their own destiny within their broad objectives.*

For many observers, part of the 'NHS attitude problem' lies with the consultants, who are often the Clinical Directors of a Trust. At Hastings and Rother a definite decision was taken to manage the organisation via the Clinical Directors. The problem is that the consultant body has not been trained to take a broad management overview and continues to be oriented towards individual patient care. Yet consultants are intelligent people, manifestly capable of adopting a wider perspective and of looking corporately at the way things function. They are not always altogether happy with such an idea, but they usually realise that the alternative is, ultimately, that decisions will be imposed on them. At the same time, a sensible approach by the executive authority is to say 'We appreciate the dilemma and our role is to help you. We will support and put people alongside you, give you access to training and experience, so that you can become true managers.'

Experience in Hastings and Rother NHS Trust shows that, where consultants feel a conflict between patient care and management requirements, support at board level is crucial. As Geoff Haynes points out: 'Part of the success process here at Hastings and Rother is to say to them "Look, we do actually understand the dilemma that gives you, so what we want to do is get alongside you and perhaps share some of the responsibility".' Service excellence management is, therefore, very much about enabling and empowering, as opposed to controlling. But in my view it must be genuine management if you want to deliver quality service. In a public sector organisation such as the NHS this means, among other things, making individuals see that 'things are not as they used to be' and that priorities have to be established in light of finite resources. For Geoff Haynes the basic issue is that of

> *empowering people to look at their own situation and to create an organisation that allows them to do it. The quicker I can dispel ideas that I've got a secret back pocket to solve people's problems, the better, because I don't have. I do not think that leaves me as a weak Chief Executive; rather, it leaves me as someone who can enable solutions to come from other places. My biggest challenge has been to explain that as an issue, and free up the space for innovation. That is what ultimately makes the service deliverers deliver.*

OWNERSHIP OF QUALITY AND SERVICE

Hastings and Rother NHS Trust firmly believe that ownership of quality and service must be with those people who have the greatest contact with the customer. Haynes has been very encouraged by the way this approach has enabled issues to be progressed by staff. For example, at a meeting which began very negatively, a colleague said to him 'Do you mean that if we wanted to get rid of two staff nurses, and employ a much better, higher-graded nurse, we could do that?' He responded 'Of course you could do that. You cannot sack people, because we do not do that sort of thing . . . But next time a couple of nurses leave take someone on temporarily to fill the gap, and then recruit the person you really want, and fund it that way.' In other words, 'Take the initiative, come back with some objectives and then we'll talk it through'. As a result, the logic of the required new approach began to click into place in his mind. He is anticipating a long haul, because 'a lot of them can be very cynical', but he believes that the important message is that the organisation must trust its own system.

If we put in place a service system that requires doctors to manage, we must not go round it and say 'Well, that problem is too difficult for our system, so we will find another system'. It is essential that we use our own system, even if this is incredibly painful at times. Once everyone begins to see that we actually do mean that, and that there is no hidden agenda to build up some huge bureaucracy in the headquarters, hopefully everyone will want to come on board.

The Trust made a conscious decision not to produce a strategy document for quality and service at senior management level without first seeking the views of all their staff. This was in line with the Trust's belief that ownership of quality and service must be vested in those people who have greatest contact with their major customer, the patient. The first step in developing their customer strategy included the presentation of a Quality Roadshow to all Directorates. About 75 per cent of the contents reflected customer-focused quality initiatives developed by staff in the workplace. Other aspects included presentations by the Consumer Relations Officer, the Senior Nurse Quality Assurance and the Director of Quality. This facilitated questions and answers, and provided a forum in which quality and service ideas could be shared. Feedback from the Roadshow was presented to the Board, the Quality and Consumer Committee and the Complaints Panel, and is now assisting the formulation of plans for improvements in customer service from 1993 onwards.

SUSTAINING CUSTOMER SERVICE

Hastings and Rother want their Clinical directorate structure to be totally representative of its constituent clinicians. In other words, they want the clinicians to have regular meetings and discussions on corporate objectives. That is not happening in all cases at the moment, but there is no reason why it should not. At the other end of the spectrum, the Board favour some system of monitoring outcomes and quality at the point of exit. Are their systems actually delivering the service they think they are? Do GPs get letters about their patients within the prescribed fortnight? Do patients wait longer than half an hour in Outpatients?

Communications, especially between the Board and staff, is something which interests Geoff Haynes, who says, 'An enfranchised, informed employee is a powerful and very valuable asset for us to get to where we want to be in sustaining both internal and external customer service. A disenfranchised and uninformed workforce is really a recipe for suicide.' Media aids likely to help in communications with internal customers include video and phone-in help-lines. Also useful will be the planned introduction of regular 'away times' enabling groups of managers to think through conceptual and strategic issues. The Trust publish a very good internal newsletter, but it could still be refined, enhanced and built on, particularly in its coverage of quality and service issues. The most important communication method of all will be the 'management by walkabout', ensuring that all managers get out and about talking and listening to people. Geoff Haynes admits that at present 'We are all very bad at this'; however, the fact the weakness has been recognised, and is being acted upon, is a credit to Hastings and Rother.

COMPLAINTS AND QUALITY ASSURANCE

'The hallmark of a service which cares for its consumers is an open complaints system which provides courteous, critical and thorough investigation of grievances.'

(Health Service Commissioner, Annual Report 1989/90).

One of the major areas for sustaining customer service is through complaints handling. Hastings and Rother NHS Trust acknowledge the importance of complaints to quality assurance, both as a means of reviewing the standard of services provided and as an opportuntiy to improve communications and delivery of customer service. They do it very well. In fact, they see complaints handling as such a vital part of customer satisfaction that their procedure and the thinking behind it are worth covering in some detail. Dolly Daniel, the Trust's Consumer Relations Officer (CRO) says

We all have a responsibility for complaints whatever our position in the organisation. Complaints give us a wealth of information about the quality of our service, and the way we respond indicates to the consumer what kind of organisation we are. Our prime aim is the courteous, critical and thorough investigation of all complaints, and to encourage comments and suggestions on how we can improve our services. But responding to complaints requires a team effort. It is also essential that an investigation is carried out close to the point of service, and for this reason the Business Manager or Nurse Manager in each Clinical Directorate is the designated manager with whom the CRO can liaise. The role of the manager is to co-ordinate multi-disciplinary comments and to provide a courteous, sympathetic response based on an analysis of the original complaint.

Many of the complaints Hastings and Rother receive relate to issues which could have been resolved at the time of the incident if complainants had known who to go to. That is why the introduction of posters and leaflets into hospitals and clinics is an important feature of an 'open' complaints system. The Trust circulate a customer satisfaction survey leaflet (under the title *Help Us to Help You*), which publicises 'how to complain'. Dolly Daniel explains:

Business Managers and Nurse Managers are asked to ensure the effective distribution and introduction of publicity material such as the survey

throughout the hospitals and clinics in this district, and to lead staff in a positive 'problem-solving' approach to complaints. Minor complaints are frequently dealt with at ward or department level and may require no further action. Such incidents must be noted in writing, however, in case of more serious developments at a later date. We ask our Business and Senior Nurse Manager to review the use of a ward complaints book or a departmental complaints book and to establish a mechanism known to all ward and department staff where all complaints can be listed and reviewed by the appropriate manager at quarterly intervals.

If a member of staff is implicated in a complaint, that member of staff has the right to be informed of the nature of the complaint and naturally has the right to consult his or her professional organisation or trade union. More serious complaints (whether written or verbal), which cannot be resolved at ward or department level, are directed to either the Business Manager, Nurse Manager or the CRO; the complaint must be acknowledged within two working days, and notified to the CRO for registration. Two days is a first-class turn-around time and is an illustration of the importance attached to customer complaint management within Hastings and Rother. On receipt of a complaint the Business Manager or Nurse Manager informs all relevant staff (at ward or departmental level) of the nature of the complaint received: (i) to enable staff to give their comments, and (ii) to ensure that staff are given the opportunity to review practices and amend where indicated. Staff are always informed of the outcome of a complaint, together with any action management may need to take on issues such as staff training, organisation of service or district policy.

Within Hastings and Rother the aim of the investigating officer is to look into a complaint as thoroughly, impartially and expeditiously as possible. They appreciate that delays can lead to an increased sense of frustration, even anger, and will inevitably make a complaint more difficult to resolve. Complaints must therefore be investigated and responded to within 28 working days. 'I find', says Dolly Daniel, 'that it is valuable to meet the complainant, as matters can often be more easily resolved face-to-face than by impersonal correspondence. The complainant can be invited to the Trust's offices or, in some cases, a home visit to the complainant may happen. Where a complainant is invited to attend a meeting on Trust premises I can book hospital transport for them, or re-imburse their public transport cost, or pay their mileage.' If, after a thorough investigation, the complainant is still dissatisfied, the options of referral to the Health Authority Commissioner or to the Regional Health Authority for an independent review are carefully explained. The monitoring of complaints is taken very seriously. It is done by quarterly returns of complaints, which are then submitted to a Complaints Panel. This Panel reviews the handling of all complaints in the district, and will approve a quarterly report on complaints by the CRO for submission to the Trust. This report, together with information given to visiting groups on specific complaints, ensures that the Trust and the commissioning authority retain an overview of all complaints in the district.

TURNING MISTAKES INTO OPPORTUNITIES FOR SERVICE IMPROVEMENT

An important aspect of complaints and other feedback is how they are used to improve patient care. As Dolly Daniel says:

> *Where a complaint highlights a shortcoming in the service, the investigating officer must advise the CRO of this, together with a note of what action is being taken. Once a complaint has been investigated there may be a number of issues which particular staff groups need to address. The Business Manager or Nurse Manager, in liaison with the CRO, then ensures that feedback on complaints is given to the appropriate staff. This is considered vital. Staff need support and encouragement from managers to deal sympathetically and courteously with comments and complaints. Where Business Managers or Nurse Managers identify training needs of particular staff groups in respect of complaints they contact the training officer or the CRO for assistance. Hastings and Rother are now exploring the possibility of a multi-disciplinary staff*

training programme on a district-wide basis which would encompass complaints and consumer relations.

Complaints provide an important measure of customer satisfaction, although they can demoralise staff if they appear to be the sole yardstick of outcomes. At Hastings and Rother small-focus patient satisfaction surveys have been drawn up in conjunction with staff in selected areas, for example, Accident & Emergency and Outpatients. The results are fed back to staff to enable them to draw up action plans for improving services. It is worth noting that 'action plans' abound. They really do follow through on the axiom that without an action plan you might as well plan for nothing to happen. As indicated earlier, Hastings and Rother NHS Trust have launched consumer satisfaction publicity, inviting consumers to make comments, suggestions and advising them how to complain. Drafts of this literature were sent to staff for comments, and the overwhelmingly positive response gave Hastings and Rother confidence to launch the publicity in line with the opening of their new Conquest hospital. Originally they favoured a high-profile press launch, but finally decided to distribute the literature to Business and Nurse Managers over a period of several months, asking them to introduce the publicity via team briefings. These explain to all staff how Hastings and Rother are using literature as a tool to improve communication with service users.

Dolly Daniel says that early indicators from their complaints monitoring 'give us cause for cautious optimism that our communications with the public are slowly but perceptibly improving'. Along with a number of other service industries, the Trust have recently experienced an approximate doubling of the number of complaints year on year. However, since they have begun to heighten staff awareness, the handling of complaints and queries has won back dissatisfied customers. This can take time, effort and energy, but what would be the cost to Hastings and Rother NHS Trust of not turning complaints into credits, and mistakes into opportunities?

THE SERVICE WAY FORWARD

At Hastings and Rother NHS Trust the culture is changing, and much of it is a question of self-esteem. Once you start to go down the customer service road you end up with your product champions, people who want to be there, doing their bit for the quality and service menu. Hastings and Rother have moved appreciably down that road. They are starting to cross professional boundaries, and people are confident about challenging past practices and services; So there is a challenging time ahead as the Trust seeks to build an organisation that has the necessary flexibility, with managers unconstrained by yesterday's principles. Flair has to be encouraged, because new ways of doing things are, in a sense, the answer to stagnation. The NHS must learn to be an effective, managed organisation. Much of industry had a headstart and enjoyed a longer learning period than time permits for the NHS. The latter are having to do a crash course in commercial management to understand the system on which their survival depends. Now they have actually got to deliver service and quality over and above traditional capacities. 'If we don't', says Geoff Haynes, 'we'll go out of business.'

The trend at Hastings and Rother has definitely been towards a more focused approach. People appear less threatened by consumerism and in some areas are actively seeking ways in which to improve their customer services. As Dilly Millward, Director of Nursing and Quality, emphasises:

For us, improving and sustaining customer service must always be a constant. Quality of service is built into absolutely every single thing each of us do. Of course, this means there is a massive onus on us for training in this awareness, and organisations have got to bear that in mind. However, unless quality is integral in the culture and everyday life of the organisation, there's not much hope of your ever achieving genuine customer service excellence, let alone sustaining it.

11. The Clydesdale Bank

'The perpetual obstacle to human advancement is custom.'

John Stuart Mill (1806–1873)

The Clydesdale Bank has some 350 branches, including departments and supply divisions, mainly in Scotland. The Clydesdale is probably no different from any other bank in that it took time to realise that service is a particularly important aspect of its business. Traditionally, if one asked members of staff what they provided, they would sum it up as 'the opportunity for customers to save, and borrow, and for customers to involve themselves in the money transmission system'. In many respects it has taken years for the banking industry generally to recognise they are in the service business as well, and some still do not see it!

Accordingly, the Clydesdale now recognise that there is an opportunity to take the high ground by ensuring that the Bank provides a quality of service that meets their customers' expectations and rapidly changing needs. According to Douglas Corner, General Manager of the Banking Division of the Clydesdale, there are several reasons for the change.

> I would never wish to be disparaging about the consumer, but I think the UK has tended to be fairly long in patience and lacking in demand. That was true in the past, but because of (i) increased competition and (ii) increased awareness as a result of consumer and lobby group activities, it

is no longer the case. People now tend to be more aware of the fact that there is actual choice.

One of the goals which the Clydesdale Bank has set itself is to provide customer service of the highest quality on the way to becoming the pre-eminent Scottish bank. In order to succeed they know they have to recognise, and respond to, the individual needs of all their customers. This basic philosophy is enshrined in the Guiding Principles which form part of their Customer Charters. Like other organisations covered in this book, the Clydesdale agrees its codes of customer service in the boardroom and then seeks commitment to them throughout the organisation.

The first of the Bank's business objectives are the development and maintenance of customer relationships 'based on high quality service' (see Figure 11.1).

The basic philosophy is translated into the detailed commitments of their Customer Charters and Codes of Practice for both business and personal customers. Reviewed at least once every year, these texts are designed to promote good banking practice and set out the standards to be observed by the Clydesdale in dealings with customers. Among other things, the Bank undertake to:

- Act fairly and reasonably in all their customer dealings.
- Help the customer to understand how their accounts operate and give a good understanding of banking services.
- Maintain confidence in the security and integrity of banking and card payment systems.

IMPROVING SERVICE PERFORMANCE

With regard to customer service, the Clydesdale recognise that they should not unilaterally determine what the customer wants. Therefore, the Bank carry out research to establish service quality benchmarks, which are continually monitored. What can happen in such research is that the organisation discovers customers want something which the existing structure is not able to supply. This can be a major minefield. However, the whole purpose of market research is to find out what the customer really does want. An organisation must recognise that it can be constrained, but it may, like the Clydesdale, realise that the potential benefits of quality customer service outweigh the costs. The starting point, after the boardroom 'mission' commitment has been made to customer service, is to find out what customers are experiencing.

Surveys are of course one approach in this journey of discovery, but feedback from staff actually dealing with customers is also vital. It is impossible to develop service standards against which performance can be measured without tracking the feedback of customers and those who serve them. Clydesdale Bank have got this right – they have put much energy into disseminating the right message from the top of the organisation and also into improving customer service. A variety of research approaches have been used, for example:

- Qualitative stage: to identify the service attributes which can influence the customers' overall views and impressions, and to understand how the service can be improved.
- Quantitative stage: to quantify the importance of these attributes

---

Figure 11.1   Clydesdale Bank's Mission and Objectives

Our Mission: To provide core banking and selected financial services professionally, efficiently and competitively to achieve a pre-eminent position in chosen markets.

Objectives: Develop and maintain mutually beneficial customer relationships based on high quality service. Quality earnings generated in core markets. A diverse high-quality business base. Strong capitalisation. Create shareholder wealth. Disciplined growth strategy. Market leader in efficiency and productivity. Management style and practices that contribute to the well-being and development of a fully responsible and accountable workforce. High standard of corporate and business ethics.

---

and evaluate the priorities customers place on service improvements.

- Performance measurement surveys: to measure service quality on a continuing basis.

Performance measurement can be conducted in many ways, such as using 'mystery shopper' techniques, as well as questionnaires, telephone sampling, market surveys and so on. One of the feedbacks from the Clydesdale Bank's research was dissatisfaction with their complaints procedure. Says Douglas Corner:

Our complaints procedure at the moment, while it is quite structured, is actually centralised. Now, I do not think that meets customers' needs, because people in the centre are answering customers' complaints. I think complaints should be answered by the people who made the mistakes in the first instance.

The Clydesdale Bank work on the basis that the customer does not want to complain and that, therefore, a 'get it right first time' attitude can eradicate many complaints. However, having said that, the Bank recognise that there will always be complaints of one nature or another, e.g. from people who have had loan applications turned down, and including many where the customer wants access to the manager.

The Clydesdale experience suggests that most customer complaints would not have escalated if they been dealt with in a common sense way at the outset. In other words, it is essential to prevent any polarisation at the early stage of the complaints process. Says Corner:

Complaints can tell you a lot about the organisation and your performance. That's where it starts. Every branch in essence should be its own little quality of service unit, because they have got to be aware of their own performance. They must record and monitor that performance and they are required to ensure that they are meeting the standards the Bank requires.

In a number of excellence companies it is policy that all complaints should be seen at a very high level, so that the directors know what is going on. Douglas Corner is sympathetic to that view, but does not believe

> . . . *that the people at the top should actually be dealing with the complaints. I think they should be aware of the complaints that are being dealt with by the organisation and we will maintain – in fact we do maintain, although it is not as robust as I would like – complaint data. We have a database of customer complaints in order that we can analyse the type of complaints that come into the organisation. This enables us to know, at a high level, what the customer is complaining about, and how these break down. We know whether it is service or whether it's a turn-down for loans or for whatever reason. We also, obviously, receive a number of complaints ourselves at the centre, and in many instances I will follow through that complaint myself, in the same way that the Chief Executive does from time to time.*

CUSTOMERS ARE REALLY EVERYTHING (CARE)

To sustain service performance the Clydesdale Bank have instigated what they call the CARE initiative, standing for 'customers are really everything'. They have put everyone from top to bottom, including the Chief Executive, through a two-day course of customer care training led by external experts. In fact, it is under the auspices of such intensive staff training sessions that much of the research mentioned earlier on service improvement is obtained. Questionnaires are used to obtain the feelings and views of those staff who are in direct contact with internal and external customers. Such questionnaires discover not only what staff feel about their own company's customer-centred image but also their own strengths and weaknesses in contributing to the CARE style of service. The feedback is also vital for the directors, for without having their fingers on the attitude pulse of the organisation they could find they are 'asking dead staff to perform live service'.

The Clydesdale bank have established within their marketing department a Service Quality Unit, which is responsible not only for establishing service quality benchmarks but also for monitoring the Bank's performance against these benchmarks over a period of time. The Clydesdale's Service Objectives are closely allied to the corporate Mission and Objectives statement and Customer Charters mentioned earlier. They are inculcated during the initial CARE training course and regularly thereafter at departmental team briefings held throughout the Bank. During these team meetings, the CARE initiative and its service quality aspects are given particular attention. Staff also carry out their own internal measurement process, marking the performance of their managers and answering such questions as: Do they feel they are providing a high quality service? If they think they are slipping in any way, what can they do to improve the situation?

Although the Service Objectives are internal, the Clydesdale are aware that there is an external perspective to customer service. They may think they are providing good quality, but if the customer thinks the Royal Bank of Scotland provides better service, the Clydesdale appreciate that they are not providing good quality at all. That is why there is maximum effort on reminding staff they are customers of one another as well as having outside customers. As Corner explains:

> We have to be into the internal as well as the external customer. I know that the perspective some of our people took originally was that we only had one set of customers, i.e. the people who we serve out of the network. There is now a realisation that support units service the network, and that if we do not provide good quality service internally to the sales end, how can we possibly expect the sales end to provide quality service to our customers? That was why everybody participated in the two-day programme, and why we are now establishing service-level agreements. They are levels of service which we agree between the support staff, the operations units and ourselves. For example, they will guarantee to have automated teller machines (ATMs) working for a

given number of hours per day; in other words, they agree that ATMs will be operating at 99.5 per cent efficiency, or thereabouts.

'THE CONTINUING DRIVE TO PRE-EMINENT SERVICE'

In 1992 the Clydesdale Bank restructured their organisation to one that more reflected their new service image. They used to have an operation unit embracing all the services provided to the network, such as information technology, cashiers department and legal services. Today they have 'inverted the triangle', in that all of these support organisations now back up the front-line staff who serve the customer. The Clydesdale Bank admit that there are people in their organisation who have found it difficult to come to terms with the new customer service ethos, especially some who joined the Bank some years ago. Such custom and habit can be an obstacle to progress. As Douglas Corner says,

If we were asked, 20 or even ten years ago, what banking would look like now, I do not think we would be predicting what we have now got. Having said that, it is quite remarkable, when the situation is explained clearly to individuals, how ready they are to buy into it. One of the most important things of all, in getting over, or getting through, a cultural change, or change process, is communication. I believe we've communicated reasonably well. Obviously the two-day CARE course itself was a form of communication, because we touched every single soul and everyone knew that every one else was being touched by it. However, it's a constant, through other media, whether this be circulars, videos, or staff newspapers such as Carecall, our quarterly newsletter dedicated to CARE issues and problems. It's through communication, which is disseminated through the regional management departmental system, down through the branch meetings, and so on. I think people have a reasonable picture of the sort of organisation we actually work in now, and the objectives of our organisation, and what constitutes the important customer service aspects of that organisation.

A consistency in excellence companies is a degree of autocracy, which is the board saying 'there is no alternative' and 'this is the way we are going'. The Clydesdale are no exception, especially when habit and custom have to be overcome. Douglas Corner agrees.

In any event, when you have 330 outlets, as we have, you have to give guidance as to what you should be doing, otherwise you are going to get a potential of 330 branches plus all the departments, and all the 7,000 staff, doing their own thing. The one thing that we are open to is the idiosyncrasy of the individual. It is a very difficult thing actually to maintain consistency across a network, and I like to think that the Clydesdale Bank proposition and service in Piccadilly London are the same as in Ayr Scotland.

The Bank accept that there is a cost to quality, but know that there is a benefit too. They also know that a customer care programme and service quality cannot be sustained unless they constitute a fundamental aspect of plans for the future. As Corner says:

You identify service quality as being something you would wish to strive for in the organisation and that has to come from the top. Everyone, and everything, is involved in this mission which, quite simply, is to provide core banking and selected financial services professionally, efficiently and competitively to achieve a pre-eminent position in chosen markets. Our principle market is obviously Scotland, and our aim is to achieve that pre-eminent position in banking in Scotland. I believe that fundamental to that objective is our ability to deliver, and sustain, high-quality service to our customer base and to obtain that recognition within the market as a whole. We, in fact, do have the quality high ground.

I could not agree more!

12 . T.G.I. Friday's

'When I make a feast, I would my guests should praise it, not the cooks.'

Sir John Harington (1561–1612)

London's Covent Garden has the highest grossing 'Thank God It's Friday's' ('Friday's') restaurant in the world. Holding that record for the last two years, it has some 240 seats and around 125 staff, and is run by a team of seven managers. Probably around 5,000 'guests' come through the doors each week, and the restaurant has a turnover in excess of £120,000 a week. It is a hugely successful operation for the UK Drinks, Food and Leisure chain, Whitbread, who are their parent company.

Friday's is a very high-volume operation *per capita* and must be operated on a triple A (high-volume) site. At Friday's they buy the best materials and products for their menus, and work, very effectively, at giving the guests the best customer service. They have to take a lot of money to pay for that. Friday's is really about having lots of people and bringing them all together for a party-type experience, as opposed to just a meal experience. Their reputation for achieving this adds to the customer volume.

Whitbread brought Friday's to the UK in 1985 after visiting the United States, to find the restaurant operation best-suited for transfer to Britain. They settled upon Friday's, which had been running for 27 years in a market where restaurants go out of business every week. It is a hugely successful operation and today is regarded as the market leader in its sector.

The first UK opening was in Birmingham in 1985, and proved to be more successful than anybody had anticipated. After Birmingham, Covent Garden was the next site to open, in 1986, and sales went on a straight line upwards. Then Friday's opened a further restaurant in Fareham, effectively giving them three different types of restaurant: one on the outskirts of Birmingham, another in the centre of London and the third in Southampton at an off-city-centre 'drive-to' site. All three quickly became very successful, enabling Whitbread to expand the operation to the rest of the UK and to commit themselves to building Friday's as a UK brand. They now have 11 restaurants, and the latest opened in London's Haymarket in October 1992, with 170 full-time staff.

SELECTING STAFF FOR CUSTOMER SERVICE

At Friday's they call their staff recruitment sessions 'auditions', because they look at job applicants' personality rather than their skills, biographical background, attainments and so on.

Alison Finnigan is Human Resources Manager at Friday's, responsible for the strategic direction of staff. This entails recruiting the right kind of people, ensuring the most appropriate training tools, looking at methods of measuring employees' performance and the investment of the Friday's recruitment training programme. Alison Finnigan says that Friday's employs people who have intelligence, a service attitude and charismatic personality, who love to interact with people and who can cope with any situation. She adds:

They must also have common sense and be able to solve problems, and of course have fun! If they have those type of elements in their personality we know our training systems are such that we can train them to do anything. So we have auditions to attract this type of outgoing individual, who is going to be right for our interaction with guests. We look at their personality when they come along to see us and then they go through an interview system. It's not that we just want wild and wacky people – that's not what we are about. We are about guest focus, fun, and charismatic people who can provide absolutely superior guest service.

At Friday's, they do not screen out in terms of age. Anyone can come along to these auditions, although the majority of candidates are in the 20–34 age group.

Basically, what happens is that potential candidates come to the audition theatre and see a few videos about the organisation. Around eight different screen tests are then held for them. These tests are all run by Friday's employees and are designed to put people in alternative situations and observe how they manage. There are activities, such as a guest role play situation, where a candidate will be put in the position of being one of Friday's 'dub–dubs' (waiter/waitress) and be required to handle a given situation. There are screen tests for selling techniques, and to discover if someone has flair as a potential bartender. There is also a freestyle section where recruits can do whatever they want. At the audition for the London Haymarket operation a twenty-year-old candidate portrayed his personality by reciting from *Henry V* and juggling at the same time! The candidates have a score card and this is marked by each of the employees on every screen test.

It's good to see Friday's using their own employees as part of the audition procedure. Employees are selected from restaurant staff who have been with the organisation anywhere between 18 months and four years. Some of them are probably trainers, having been taught how to train new employees in their restaurants. According to Alison Finnigan:

We give our employees quite a lot of responsibility and we do use them in the hiring process. We also do this with our managers, allowing them to have an input into the hiring of other managers. You can get much more information out of an employee interacting with a candidate – probably better than a manager interacting with that candidate – mainly because the latter will let down their guard and show the employee who they really are underneath.

In the summer of 1992 Friday's were looking for 170 staff for their Haymarket operation. On one day, nearly 400 people passed through their audition programme, and in total more than 1,000 people were seen. That is just the beginning of the process, because once auditions have started, word gets round and people keep ringing in. In reality, therefore, Friday's usually process up to 3,000 people while auditioning for a particular restaurant.

Out of that 3,000, Friday's would probably conduct some 600 first interviews, and then use 'profiling'. This focuses on skill areas which the organisation believe contribute to guest satisfaction – such as teamwork, service attitude, ability to work within a structure and emotional consistency.

Those people who get through the initial interview process and profiling will then have a final interview. At this stage some 250–300 candidates will be interviewed, from whom the final 170 will be selected.

CUSTOMER SERVICE STYLE – COST OR INVESTMENT?

Despite this emphasis on recruitment selection, Friday's still have movement within their employee group, in an industry notorious for its high levels of labour turnover. Alison Finnigan explains:

Friday's recruit people between 22 and 34, and part of the reason they come to work for us is that they are fun, outgoing, and adventurous types of individual. What they will typically do, therefore, is come and work for Friday's for maybe a year or two, and then travel the world for, say, a year. They will then come back to us. For instance, one girl has been training dolphins in Florida and has just recently returned to us. Others are actors or singers in their spare time; others may go hiking on the Himalayas or scuba-diving in Australia. This is all part of their make-up, what they are and what we want. Whenever guests come into the restaurant they are not conversing with staff who are just waiters and waitresses who don't have anything to talk about. They are talking to really charismatic, interesting people who have done things with their lives, and who have interesting things to talk about.

Friday's live with all the cost factors associated with such a demanding and sophisticated selection process. Alison Finnigan explains that the high cost is regarded as an investment:

We want to look at our people almost as you would look at a profit and loss account. Friday's pay people on a commission basis, and we have the technology and systems to measure the sales that various individuals generate. So we can look at someone and say: 'OK, you have cost us this much to hire, to train, to develop, and it's taken this long to reach your optimum sales level. But across the time you have been with us, you have generated this much profit for us.' It is all about looking at people in those terms.

What we also do is measure our top performers. Through profiling, and measuring what's important, we want to replicate those top performers. Through our systems we can see the difference in sales generation on a shift between a top performer and an average one.

Friday's are one of the few companies in the UK today who do continuous profiling of their front-line people in order to sustain customer service. They measure factors related to service orientation, working in a team and so on. First they profile a number of their top performers and form a 'norm group' of those individuals. They will then test new people against that profile. The company say the typical staff reaction to this profiling is exciting. As Alison Finnigan puts it:

They are extremely impressed with the fact that we take this much trouble, and indeed cost, when selecting waiters and waitresses. At the end of the day they are our front-line people, interacting with our guests. There could not be anyone more important than that in our organisation.

The remuneration system is commission based, which means that staff can directly influence what they earn. Each restaurant has elaborate technology, including electronic point of sales (EPOS) systems and screens, allowing staff to view every second of shift activity. This tells them who has sold the most, what the sales target is, what they have to do to achieve it. Staff therefore know, on a moment by moment basis, exactly how much they are earning.

But could this type of incentive scheme not result in customers going into the restaurant for a meal, and being badgered to eat food they do not really want? Alison Finnigan explains why this does not happen:

> *What we want to do is guide guests through our menu. That's part of why we need excellent sales people. We have a very broad menu and if you are a new customer, it would take you about half an hour to read through it. Therefore, the waiter/waitress is there to assess and help the guest in terms of the 'experience' they want to have during their visit – what type of food they like – and they can then recommend dishes from the menu. If the guest is sold too much food they are going to leave feeling very uncomfortable and unhappy. Therefore, part of the employee's role may be to suggest a customer should **not** have a particular menu item.*

SUSTAINING GUEST LOYALTY

At Friday's they know that their repeat customer business is as high as 80 per cent because they do a lot of guest and market research. For example, during 1992 they surveyed 15,000 of their customers in ten restaurants. For the surveys, they use external companies, whose researchers come to their restaurants and talk to customers, as well as surveying exit guests. They ask questions such as 'If you were not here eating at Friday's where would you be having your meal?' to discover what customers themselves think of as Friday's competitors. Another question is: 'What is the most important aspect about your experience at Friday's?' Invariably, guests explain that the most important dimension for them is the interaction they have with the staff.

The company can relate this feedback directly to their investment in recruitment and training mentioned earlier. Says Alison Finnigan:

As it is the most important consideration to our guests so we have to invest in it. Guests tell us they do not really notice if the hinges on the toilet doors are brass or not – therefore this may not be an area on which we need to focus. Our researchers will always ask customers about the menu, the pricing and the drinks we offer. What we want to know is where we should be focusing our energy.

This approach is akin to value engineering. At Friday's they spend large sums on their restaurants, building everything to the highest quality. Their guests may not notice that the bars are made out of seven different types of wood, but they may well want Friday's to spend more of their energy on having interesting and enthusiastic employees or more vegetarian items on the menu, etc. It is vital that the company receives this feedback on a regular basis.

Friday's also sustain service through committed managers who grow through the organisation. Their policy is based on providing people with constant challenges, which are considered an essential component in what keeps people interested and motivated at work. There are around 14 different positions in their restaurant structure, giving their staff the possibility of different career opportunities. Later, staff can progress into management positions, around 30 per cent of which are filled by people from line-level employee grades.

The company consider that internal communication is vital to sustain guest service. The various Friday's restaurants have an average 130 employees each who are working on shifts. It is essential to communicate thoroughly, and to ensure that everybody gets to know all that they should know. It's not just about communicating to employees. It is about letting line-level employees communicate upwards to executives as well – a two-way relationship. To facilitate this, Friday's have what is called a 'shift meeting'. This occurs daily before every morning and evening shift and allows the managers to prepare staff. It is a team briefing, and it is as a team that they counsel and then combat whatever problems the restaurant may be experiencing.

Alison Finnigan is quick to acknowledge the valuable role of such open lines of communication:

Feedback is of prime importance within Friday's. One of the things that makes us so successful is that we always want to have feedback. We want to know when things aren't quite right so we can improve. On every shift that we run with our front-of-house employees, a different person takes turn at being shift leader. That person is responsible for setting up the shift, ensuring everything is clean, and doing anything else that needs to be done, such as setting up the salads and desserts. They organise the rest of their team and, at the end of the shift, produce a report and have an end-of-shift debrief. That employee will rate and recognise other employees who have done a good job on the shift. There is, therefore, a lot of peer pressure going into this feedback mechanism. Everyone gets to give feedback on everyone else.

If a person has done a good job, and they are praised at that meeting, their performance is rewarded. There are a lot of recognition systems in the system which are ultimately linked to how staff have served their guests. For example, Friday's have 'star' programmes – a gold, silver and bronze star that can be awarded to people. As Alison Finnigan explains:

We have things like 'wow' pins, idea pins, MVPs (most valued player) awards. If someone, for instance, did a particularly good job on a shift everyone in the team would recognise that, and that person could be rewarded with something like an MVP pin. To our staff it is really like getting a medal. It is a very strong reinforcer. When any other employee meets someone who has a pin, for whatever reason, they know they have really achieved a lot in terms of either their teamwork, or their obsession with guest satisfaction and service.

One of the benefits of this type of system in a service excellence company is that mediocre performers will not stay. Because Friday's pay on a commission basis, it becomes a self-regulating system. The people who work hard, and who are excellent at what they do, can earn a lot of money. Mediocre staff will not be so good at what they do and, consequently, will not earn enough money in terms of their commission. There simply is no room for mediocrity. Add to this the constant performance appraisal at Friday's where, in addition to the shift-by-shift appraisal already described, employees are reviewed every three months. On this occasion they have a full sit-down review, with their manager, of their work performance.

Friday's are investing a lot of money in people and are looking for maximum benefit from it. The company is committed to ensuring that its employees receive the very best service and support from the organisation. That is the Friday's mission. Employees should be able to look at it as *their* company, and believe they have received great service from Friday's in the same way as their guests look at the staff and, hopefully, decide that they have received good customer service from them.

As to what makes Friday's successful regarding total quality customer service, Alison Finnigan suggests that it is something that happens through 'total guest obsession' at every single level.

Everybody talks about sustaining customer service, from the managing director to the dishwasher. With each decision that is taken, at whatever level, the first question we ask ourselves is: 'How is it going to affect the guest?' With any initiatives or systems that we create, the first question we ask is: 'Is this going to take our staff away from the guests?'

Friday's know customer service is not about running a customer service programme once every three months. It has to be something that exists in the culture all the time. Alison Finnigan aptly reminds us: 'It's the very reason for our existence in Friday's. All the technical knowledge we give people is to help them provide great guest service.'

13. Bradford & Bingley Building Society

'Let us train our minds to desire what the situation demands.'

Seneca (4 BC–AD 65)

Bradford & Bingley Building Society (B&B) has approximately 3,800 staff, of whom some 2,000 are based in its 260 branches across England, Scotland and Wales. The Society has around two million customers, and its head office is near Bingley, West Yorkshire. Up until 1986, as with all the other societies, B&B was a traditional building society. After 1986 there was a change under the Building Societies Act, which gave societies wider powers, for example by allowing them to be more like estate agents or to give investment advice on products which were not traditional deposits. From 1987 societies could also give advice on unit trusts, life assurance, pensions, PEPs and so on.

The way in which B&B differs from most of the other societies is that it is not tied to one single supplier of financial services and can therefore give independent advice on a range of products from different suppliers. According to Mark Gerdes, Head of Central Marketing, B&B chose to go as an 'independent' for two main reasons. 'One is our corporate mission statement, which quite simply says "B&B must do the best thing for the customer". If you like, there is therefore an aspect of moral high ground to our being an "independent".' The second reason was that B&B was taking a longer-term view of the market place. As Gerdes explains:

In five or ten years time, if we are advising a customer on an investment portfolio or a life protection scheme or on their pension arrangements, we think from a commercial point of view we might be better able to place a greater amount of business by advising our customers on the best products in the market across all those individual sectors. We felt that if we were tied with one individual life assurance company they may have very good life assurance contracts but their personal pensions might not be so good and their investments might be only average. Or, alternatively, if we proceeded with a different supplier they might have average life assurance contracts, very good pensions but poor investments.

Having decided to be an independent financial adviser, B&B set out to identify what the costs would be; many of them proved quite substantial compared with those of other building societies who had opted for being 'tied'. This was mainly because the supplier to whom the Society became tied would usually supply the financial resources in terms of organising training, arranging compliance systems and so on. B&B, on the other hand, had a substantial investment in terms of having to meet those costs themselves. It was a major up-front investment, but then they were taking a 10/20-year view of the marketplace.

Independence has meant that B&B has had to reorganise to sell a broader spectrum of products. It has also involved a comprehensive training programme. The Financial Services Act generated a lot of new rules and regulations, plus a range of complicated compliance-related procedures. Therefore, many changes were necessary in the way B&B geared its staff to giving information to customers. This, in itself, led to its customer service focus. When B&B took the decision about independence, there was already an ethos statement in the corporate plan that said it 'Wanted to be in a position to give its customers the best products on the market'. Says Gerdes:

We did not specifically say at that time, or in that mission statement, that we wanted to give a 'quality service', but that ethos was encapsulated within the corporate plan. Having stated that, B&B clung very firmly to

*the mast of independence, and we set out on a programme to bring
quality products to the customers on the high street.*

B&B's corporate philosophy – Codes of Conduct – today
stresses the customer and service. The Society also has a Customer
Charter which spells out to all customers how B&B will never lose
sight of 'our primary aim, which is to provide you with fast, efficient
and friendly service'. The Charter booklet sets out, in an easily-
digested format, B&B procedures and responsibilities in managing
customers' accounts, investment plans, insurance and pension
policies and also gives details on 'how to complain' should a
customer be dissatisfied with the standards of service provided. The
Customer Charter is seen as a pledge and commitment by B&B to
sustaining service.

DISCOVERING WHAT CUSTOMERS ARE EXPERIENCING AND GIVING THEM WHAT THEY WANT

Today B&B sees itself as having three main business areas. One is
deposit-based savings, the traditional business of building societies.
Second, its lending division deals with mortgages and unsecured
loans. The third core business is financial planning, which
encompasses life assurance, personal pensions, private health
contracts, unit trusts, PEPs, investment bonds, or related saving
schemes on all the types of regulated products that are available to
B&B in the marketplace.

The society has got to have the right products to offer to its
customers; to do this, it has to ascertain what the potential
marketplace wants, as well as what existing B&B customers would
like. As Mark Gerdes explains:

*To achieve this, we have several bits of research that are pretty much
continuous. Some of it is consumer research to identify what customers
need now. For example, in terms of their being catered for in life
assurance, are they under-insured? In pensions, who are in company*

schemes? Who is not in a company scheme? What are the rates of people coming on to the private pensions market, and what pensions would they like? What gaps are there for them? Also, in terms of investment, we look in particular at the 45-plus market, where people are gaining an increasing amount of personal savings and income to invest. We are really trying to determine what products can be the best for their capital up until their retirement, and an income after retirement. We also use some traditional research techniques, such as bringing together a group of individuals and having an in-depth structured interview with them, about what their financial situation is and what their needs are.

B&B has an extensive national television advertising campaign designed to put the message across about the society's independence. It stresses that with nine out of ten building societies you do not get a choice if you go to them for investments or pensions, but with B&B you do. Apart from this medium, B&B has three distinct arms in its network which seek to persuade potential customers to use its services. First is its 260 high street branches around the country. Second, it has also developed, as a result of research, a direct sales force of 65 financial planning consultants who can conduct home visits or see people in their offices, according to preference. The third method is aimed at especially busy professional people. For this group, customer service is provided by a telephone–based financial service unit in London, where a team takes incoming calls and conducts a full telephone 'fact-find' with the customer, followed up by a full written recommendation.

Of the financial planning advice that B&B offers, roughly 78 per cent is branch-based, some 20 per cent via the direct sales arm, and the remaining 2 per cent is done on the telephone. B&B also has customer-orientated marketing teams reviewing what customers want, and identifying their longer-term needs, by research:

- into customers themselves to calculate what they need; and
- having identified those customer needs, trying to identify the best products that are suitable.

As an intermediary, armed with the above information, the society can select those companies it feels offer the best advice and product for individual customers. B&B has a rigorous selection procedure, which it applies in customer interviews when a dedicated research team will consider what the best individual products are for that customer's specific circumstances. Says Mark Gerdes:

Certainly, in terms of the financial planning business, B&B is totally customer-orientated in we act as an 'independent' intermediary. The whole rationale behind that is we do a detailed fact-find to consider and calculate on an individual basis exactly what the customer's circumstances are. We have to look at what the customer's life-long objectives are, for example, in terms of when do they want to retire? Do they want to grow their investments from nothing or, if they have existing investments, do they want to protect those and receive a future income? Also their personal objectives in terms of protecting income in case of accident, disability or death, for themselves and their dependants. So, having taken the customers into a fact-find, worked out what they've got at the moment, and having then discovered where they want to get to, we construct, on an individual basis for each customer, a portfolio of advice that says 'We believe that, given your circumstances and where you want to get to, we would recommend these mechanisms, and financial products to enable you to get to where you want to go'. That's really the business we are in. Giving the most personal quality advice that's suitable for the customer, given where they're starting from and where they want to get to.

B&B then selects individual products which it believes to be the best advice for those individual customers, and the selected products they select are based on all of the background research being constantly undertaken by the society. To give an illustration of that, Mark Gerdes explains a survey B&B conducted at the end of last year.

We said, given the customer could walk into any of the top ten building society branches in the UK, assuming they needed some life assurance and they are a male, aged 40 next birthday, and they wanted £50,000 worth of cover on a level term assurance policy, how much would that actually cost them? Given that most societies are 'tied' and B&B is not, we found that the product we would recommend for the customer was some 20 per cent cheaper, on average, than the rest of the competition or those we consider as our direct competitors.

SUSTAINING LONG-TERM CUSTOMER SERVICE

B&B recognise that it must keep in constant touch with its customers because of ever-changing needs. Needs are never constant, they may change every six months, so B&B hold a review with the customer through a timescale that is set according to customer needs. That can vary from a review on a six-monthly basis to a review on a three-yearly basis. B&B subsequently updates its customer recommendations from the discussions. As Mark Gerdes says, 'We have a fairly regular review programme with those customers that we think need it, or those customers who want it. That's really intended to maintain and sustain the level of service with those customers.'

It is a difficult balance however, because the person selling the products, the advisor, must judge whether keeping in touch is supportive or whether the customer perceives B&B as being interfering and a nuisance. Mark Gerdes agrees:

It is a difficult one to judge. A lot of that judgement is left to the discretion of the advisor, but in conjunction with what the customer wants. If you take, for example, personal pensions, what we are trying to do is to maintain contact with each one of our personal pensions customers on an annual basis.

This represents very personal customer service for the million or so people who walk into B&B branches each month. It demands staff who have been trained to the highest possible standards of excellence and expertise. Evidence of the success of this training came in 1988 when B&B became the first building society to win a Department of Employment National Training Award, and this success has since been repeated.

As with all the excellence organisations featured in this book, sustaining customer service demands a major commitment to training from the directors. At B&B Roger Bonfield took over as Head of Training in 1992, and his department has 22 people servicing the training needs of 3,800 employees. It has divided into five sections under five training managers. One looks after Head Office and three look after product knowledge, sales and computer-based training respectively. Another is spending much time in arrears training, and also in an area B&B admit it needs to improve, namely telephone techniques. The Society has done some 'mystery shopping' exercises and believes that its staff do not always recognise that the telephone is a source of business. As Roger Bonfield explains:

> Because branch staff are so busy they can regard the telephone as an interruption, and therefore treat a caller as an interruption rather than as a potential sale or as a customer needing quality service. We are very good at the counter, as we spend a lot of time training staff in that area of work, but our staff don't always give a quality service on the telephone. Giving quality service can obviously generate future business, and that is why we are putting an emphasis on telephone training.

Skilled telephone techniques are seen as relevant to B&B's approach to counselling customers in difficulties. Says Bonfield:

> As a Society, B&B would not have thought of arrears training 18 months ago. As an example, we have still got a card-based system which we have been operating for some 30 years. We have never needed to improve the technology until recently. Therefore, for the past year, we've actually done a whole tranche of training focused specifically on arrears.

Currently B&B has approximately 335,000 main accounts, of

which 9 per cent are, apparently, in arrears. On the branch side of its business B&B has undertaken three specific activities relating to arrears work. It ran a face-to-face workshop for one person in each branch to familiarise that staff member with talking to customers in arrears in a people-focused way. Essentially, B&B was encouraging the trainee to talk to customers as human beings in trying to solve their arrears problem, and this required an empathy role. There is a lot of pride involved when customers get into arrears; they do not always come to the Society immediately and say 'I have got a problem'. B&B's overall policy is to encourage customers to come to them as soon as they have a problem, because it's then easier to solve.

As Roger Bonfield says:

We will make some arrangements to help customers if they have got a temporary problem – for example, the husband may have been put on short time as his company are between orders. If they come to us at that time and say 'I am going to have a problem for 3-4 months, please give me help', we can do so by taking a reduced subscription for a few months, maybe two-thirds of the normal repayments, or lower if we have to. If we can do that, if we can encourage people to come to us, the problem will often solve itself more quickly, because ultimately we are much more likely to keep people in their homes if we can solve the problem after one or two months rather than after six months.

A second specific activity relates to training in the Government Mortgage Rescue Unit Scheme. B&B's training for this customer approach was packaged in a very short time span. It ensured that all staff were aware of the scheme, and also covered customer arrears and staff attitudes. As a third intiative, B&B launched a full interactive video dealing with arrears and covering aspects such as interviewing a customer, what to say, how to negotiate arrangements, etc. Roger Bonfield admits that training on handling arrears problems can be dispiriting.

It's depressing for both the individual customer and for the member of staff. What we have therefore produced is a very creative approach to it, and there is actually a lot of fun in the interactive video. It's a package about dealing with people. It emphasises the point with this type of customer that you must have empathy, rather than sympathy, and you must make customers own their problem and try to solve it.

TRAINING MINDS FOR SERVICE DEMANDS

As part of its recent training initiatives B&B has made a series of three videos on sustaining quality in customer service. Its 14–minute video on quality assurance is accompanied by a pack for the manager and his staff who study it together, with the manager subsequently leading a departmental discussion. Six weeks later a further video is distributed to reinforce the quality message, focusing for example on the need to ensure that B&B is taking on the right kind of customers. This training medium allows the Branch Manager to sit down with his or her team to discuss its implications, applications and difficulties for every member of staff's job role.

An approach such as this is often used in excellence organisations, bringing real–life customer service training to those at the sharp end, but in a participative manner involving the line manager as well as the service deliverer. However, Bonfield adds:

It is very important to understand that this was not specifically a training exercise. It was about attitude changing and it was the training department who acted as the vehicle for delivering. It was not a specific training activity but it obviously had training spin-offs. The important point is that this was an opportunity to bring major customer service quality issues down to the level of the service deliverers. It is all about working with the business to deliver what the business wants. It is one of those happy coincidences where giving good service to the customer is good for our business. For example, we are not going to lend to people who are not going to be able to afford to pay. You are not doing anybody a service if you are going to give them a loan they cannot afford.

Another lively feature of B&B's training efforts for sustaining quality and customer service is its production of audio cassettes for all their branch and Head Office staff. Again, this is produced by the Training Department staff, who act as the facilitators for it. The content varies: it might be about customer service on retail investments, or a new computer development, or unsecured lending or what other departments are doing. The tape has a mixture of questions and answers, interviews, and so on. 'Anyone in the company can have these tapes,' says Bonfield. 'They are sent on a regular basis and there are about five a year. It's really a news magazine on tape called *Sound Advice*.'

B&B produces these tapes because it believes staff are more likely to listen to them away from the office, when in their car or doing the ironing. As Roger Bonfield says:

When we send out a circular about a change of procedure we have discovered that a lot of staff do not necessarily read it. However, if we send a cassette, the individual who is responsible for that change of procedure will talk to staff directly on the cassette, and explain why we need to make the change. We have discovered that staff are more likely to listen to that than read about it. Also, they hear the voice of the person who is actually responsible for introducing and steering the change. In this way we can build a relationship between, say, a branch in Cornwall 300 miles away from us in Bingley, where the originator of the procedural change may be based.

B&B produces 2,400 copies of these tapes each time, at a very high cost. Training, especially to achieve 'corporacy', has been historically expensive. In keeping with other organisations, B&B is reviewing its training cost basis. However, Bonfield insists:

High quality training gives us a competitive edge. Being independent means that we have to have a higher premium on training than someone who is 'tied'. We have gone through a lot of heart-searching on things like our Sound Advice cassettes to decide whether the cost of the cassette – somewhere around £9,000 each time – is actually worth it. We've decided that on balance it is. It would definitely be cheaper on paper, but the side benefits of knowing our staff listen to it, as our research has shown, wins the day. I know it sounds phoney, but you can build up a relationship between branches more easily on a tape than you can on paper and we have decided that is valuable and we are going to carry on.

There is one other aspect of training for customer service that appeals to me at B&B. This concerns the induction process, which B&B has revamped during 1992. Previously, anyone who came to work for the Society used to be immediately sent on a two-day course at Bingley. It did not matter at which branch they were based, they had to go to Bingley. Now things are different, as Roger Bonfield explains.

We were not convinced that it was actually giving us what we wanted, so we have introduced an induction interactive video plus a workbook. This has two advantages. The individual can do the induction at home or in their own branch at their own pace. Not only does the individual get the book, but again the manager becomes part of the process and gets one as well. The manager then has to work the individual through the induction process and exercises in the book. That gives the line managers much more direct ownership with the new recruit because they are responsible for making sure the exercises are done, and he or she can progress the staff in a much more controlled way and have mechanisms to do that.

B&B has, therefore, established a direct line-level responsibility for the quality of service training and subsequent in-job development. This input is geared essentially to ensuring that there is sustained customer service, it being appreciated that good customer service does not happen automatically. As Roger Bonfield says, 'B&B's training commitment is all about the ethos of satisfying customer needs. We are certainly focusing on the customer first.'

14. Board Products (Eastern) Limited

'Seeing is deceiving – it's eating that's believing.'

James Thurber (1894–1961)

Board Products (Eastern) Limited are an £11 million turnover company, employing 120 people and located in Sandy, Bedfordshire. Until January 1992 they were part of Trinity International Holdings and are now a fully autonomous company within Danisco, the Danish Sugar Corporation. The company was set up to underpin a group of paper mills and was therefore purely in business to consume paper. According to Eric Nutter, their Managing Director, it didn't really matter how many mistakes were made, the more paper the company consumed the better the group and papermills liked it. Quality and customer service were irrelevant: the sole aim was to consume paper. They confess to having been a cheap and cheerful 'brown box company'.

Today they are at least as good as, if not better than, any of the competition in high-quality post-print flexography, which is water-based printing. Post-print means that they make the board first and print it second. The company has the ability to design and manufacture a full range of corrugated packaging and is today considered a high-quality producer of corrugated cases.

In the late 1980s the company was in decline and steps were taken to change it from being a paper consumer into a profit centre and a cash generator. Eric Nutter was brought in to achieve this objective.

He found a labour force who felt they were doing a reasonable job. 'Nobody ever thought they came to work to do a bad job,' he says, 'but equally nobody ever showed them that there could be a better job done by doing things properly, right first time, and thinking about customers.'

Board Products began a journey of cultural change. The first thing they did was to invest heavily in information technology to achieve 'corporacy' across departments. Originally each department was a little company in its own right: Board Products Sales, Board Products Production, Board Products Despatch – all doing their own thing. The resultant communication gap between the departments was bridged by technology investment, which brought everybody together by making the information system uniform within the company. They also invested in manufacturing technology to ensure that the production equipment was the best available in the industry at that time. However, the most important investment was to embark on an attitude change programme to improve customer service. This was named 'Quest for Quality'.

In launching Quest for Quality Board Products decided, first of all, to conduct a survey of their labour force to ascertain management and staff attitudes to the company. They also surveyed all their customers on their perception of Board Products. Not surprisingly, there were vast differences between the employees' perception of their company, the management perception and the customers' perception. Says Eric Nutter, 'As far as our customers were concerned we were a nice company to deal with, but we weren't particularly professional. As far as our employees were concerned, all we were interested in was running as fast as we could – quality and service were irrelevant. As far as management were concerned, they thought they were doing quite a good job trying to get things together.' As a consequence of these surveys Board Products decided that the only way to survive was to embark on a customer service approach and the Quest for Quality programme started in late 1989.

What Board Products mean by Quest for Quality is, says Eric Nutter, 'a way of life'. It is a management style that first of all 'gets decision-taking down to the levels where it should rightly be taken, as those are the people with all the information.' Most of the time Eric Nutter does not believe he has enough information to take decisions. Often it's filtered out before it gets to him and, as he says,

I take a major decision on the minimum amount of accurate information, whereas someone perhaps in our Despatch Department, who has all the information, can make the right decision for the customer. Therefore, we encourage decision-taking down the organisation, and employ people to take those decisions. They have the authority and responsibility to do that.

The Quest for Quality initiative was a major cultural change for Board Products, and a considerable investment, involving a great deal of management time, effort and training. Its success was built on two major pillars. First, the company invested a lot of money in training; second, they invested a lot of time and effort in communications, so that staff, and customers, knew what Board Products were trying to do. It was vital to keep everyone informed of where the company was going and what the senior management were trying to achieve.

THE ROLE OF THE FACILITATOR AS AN ENABLER

In common with many of the organisations covered in this book, Board Products started by training facilitators, eight in number. Facilitators are the people who can make things happen, and are an essential ingredient for change to succeed. (See Appendix 14.1 for details of their role.) Board Products selected people for the role of facilitator whom they believed would take the message through the company. These were people who were flexible in their approach to work, who would be receptive to the training, as well as enthusiastic and erudite in taking the Quest for Quality ethos down the organisation. They came from different departments and were seen by those around them to be people who were potentially active rather than static, and capable communicators. They were asked by their heads of department if they wanted the role, which was entirely voluntary. Some said 'no' because they did not think they could take on the type of training necessary for being a change agent.

Facilitators are trained in a broad spectrum of subjects, such as effective presentations, running meetings and time management. At Board Products the course lasts for four days and is run in a participative style, with the delegates taking part rather than just sitting and listening. (Some of the aims and approaches of that training programme area given in Appendix 14.2.) Facilitators have to 'sell' the message, which is not always easy. One reason is the abundance of recalcitrants harbouring in many company ports, Eric Nutter agrees:

> I would be overstating if I said everybody in Board Products has come on board with our Quest for Quality and Service initiative. We've got the sales, finance, planning and the bulk of the work force on board but there are always going to be the cynics who don't want to take part in this sort of thing. They come to work, do their job and go home. I can accept that, even though I shall try to bring them on board and make some of their latent talents usable within our company.

Company experience in this book shows that cynics become fewer when they live through success. This has certainly proved to be true for Board Products, which have now had some 80 different quality and service improvement initiatives, of which 78 have been successful. Says Eric Nutter,

> An unsuccessful project was one of the very first that we carried out, but the second project we carried out was the most successful, on customer service, and we improved our delivery reliability on that particular project from something just under 70 per cent to somewhere between 98 and 99.5 per cent, depending on what type of work mix we were having on a particular week. That project was run by the operations manager and he was facilitated by a planning assistant.

The most unsuccessful project was run by a works manager, and was facilitated by a sales assistant. The main difference in the management style at Board Products today compared with pre-Quest for Quality days is that the company are now operating in a climate of counselling and coaching, delegating and training. They ensure that if people are going to take things on they have all the facilities to do the job they have been asked to do by management. Senior management are very much there to 'help' rather than to 'tell'. This participative approach is a constant within excellence organisations.

Today at Board Products their Quest for Quality initiatives are stronger than ever, and sustaining the ethos is still very much the role of the facilitator. It's worth adding that Board Products use facilitators at all meetings, selected from among enthusiastic volunteer staff. It's the facilitators who are change agents, who make the meeting work and encourage the workforce to get involved in the customer service programme. As Eric Nutter explains:

> *Because we have wanted more initiatives on total quality, from improving customer service to energy management, from waste reduction through to productivity improvements, these are the things that we have been able to get off the ground through using facilitators with groups of people who know what has to be done and know how to do it.*

SUSTAINING CUSTOMER SERVICE

Customers who purchase corrugated cases usually have a number of key criteria against which they would buy from a particular supplier. These might include delivery reliability, consistent quality, help in an emergency, delivery time, presentation and design facilities. Board Products regularly talk to their customers in a fairly informal way about the company's performance versus the key criteria. In that way the company are better able to develop business, because customers know Board Products (Eastern) Limited are interested in them. As Eric Nutter says:

> *We can go back to that customer and say 'This is what you told us, this is*

what we have done in order to try and improve the situation for you as our customer'. In other words, 'We have tried to get your customer requirements built into our system, so how are we performing now?'.

Great Yarmouth Cardboard Box is Board Products' largest customer. 'They take about 12 per cent of our output', says Eric Nutter, 'and are a very important customer, who rely on us delivering good quality, on time and presented properly, because they have obviously made a promise to their own customer on our promise.' In 1988 Board Products lost the Great Yarmouth Cardboard Box business, but subsequently got it back again. The company believe that they won the customer back again because of their Quest for Quality and customer service programme.

Quality and service are what we got wrong, says Eric Nutter, in all the things they were buying from us. They were buying products, but they were also buying service. We were not delivering it on time nor were we presenting it right. So we spent a lot of time with them, trying to confirm their customer requirements, and then explaining to our work force what we had to do, and obviously then improve it.

Today, Board Products (Eastern) operate in the way their customers want them to operate. They have, for example, a regular business meeting with Great Yarmouth Cardboard Box, about service, quality and any customer complaints. Whatever the agenda is, says Nutter,

We will have the information ready to discuss all these issues so that we can try and get them right. I will take with me to that meeting the people inside my company who can put those matters right. In the old days it might have been me, the sales director or works manager, but today it's more likely to be one of the despatch controllers, probably one of the production supervisors, or one of the girls in the sales office. That would be quite normal in our company now.

INFORMATION TECHNOLOGY AND CUSTOMER SERVICE

Having access to total customer information is part of the major information technology investment mentioned earlier. When Eric Nutter joined Board Products, virtually all they had was a sales order processing system and invoicing and accounting system. The company now have an integrated computerised system which operates from the moment the customer places an enquiry with them to the time they pay into the bank for that corrugated case. Everything known about the customer, including service requirements as well as product and works specifications, is loaded onto the computer. This never used to be the situation. Previously, if a customer complained, the complaint would never get back through the system to ensure that it didn't happen again. Now, if Board Products do something wrong, and the customer complains, the company can ensure that their computer data will prevent any repetition.

TURNING MISTAKES INTO SERVICE OPPORTUNITIES

In Board Products, customers get an immediate response to a complaint. If it results in a credit note, that note is raised immediately. Says Eric Nutter:

> *If you were to complain that we had delivered five cases short in an order for 1,000, we would accept that as a complaint. I would make sure on the day of that complaint that a refund was credited to your account on that day. There is no hold up in terms of the financial systems. What we then do is find out what happened in our system as to why we thought we'd delivered 1,000 and you only received 995. It is important that you as a customer receive a credit note as soon as possible.*

Board Products turned over £11.3 million in 1992/3, in which year they had a target provision for customer complaints of 46,000, i.e. less than 0.4 per cent of turnover. Interestingly, because every department takes its own decisions in this area, future targets are more ambitious than the board would set. Nutter finds that:

They all set themselves targets which are more ambitious than I would set for them. They have the facilities to take decisions, and they have the authoirty and the responsibility that goes along with it. I would never change a decision that has been taken at lower levels, we might counsel them and coach them into making a better one on a different occasion, but we will not change it.

Eric Nutter's hope for Board Products is a continuing total quality service programme sustained with more initiatives rising from the shop floor and offices than down through the organisation from people like himself.

When that happens I know that I will have got the message across. Seeing the results of those initiatives will be our customers, because we will be delivering even higher quality and better levels of service because those who are going to be providing that quality and service are the same ones that are involved in the projects.

At the end of the day that is the fundamental foundation for sustaining customer service.

APPENDIX 14.1

THE ROLE OF THE FACILITATOR

What is a Facilitator?
When we look at training courses which we have been on, and compare the good ones with the bad ones, we often find that the courses which have had the most impact are those where we have had an opportunity to participate and to make immediate use of the things which we have been learning. The less worthwhile courses, invariably, turn out to be the ones where we have just had to sit and listen without taking part.

A good trainer is one who will, through instruction and practice, bring course participants to the desired level of understanding in an interesting and memorable way.

A facilitator is someone who helps participants learn by additionally helping them to understand the ways which their new knowledge can be used, and by coaching them in its practical application.

To facilitate is *not* to tell and instruct, but to help and to coach.

The role of the facilitator:
To enable others to take part in the 'Quality and Service' process, by equipping them with the necessary tools, techniques and skills, and by helping them to identify ways in which they can apply these, in order to make improvements in their own activities or to work together with others to make improvements.

It is probably worth looking, then, at what the facilitator's role is *not*:

The facilitator is not just a trainer – there is far more to it than just standing up, talking for an hour about Quality and Service then sitting down again.

The facilitator does not take responsibility for everyone's improvement plans – it is the job of each individual to contribute to improvement through Quality and Service, not just the facilitator's.

The facilitator does not provide the answers to everyone's problems – People must take ownership of their own problems, the facilitator's job is to help them find ways of tackling them.

The facilitator does not do quality and service management for everyone else!

The Facilitator's capabilities:

To fulfil their role the facilitator will need to acquire certain knowledge, skills and attributes.

Knowledge

They will need to understand all about Quality and Service and to understand the Quality and Service training material. They will need to be able to produce examples to support their understanding and will have planned the training modules themselves to reinforce that understanding.

Skills

They will have developed their presentation and facilitation skills in order they will be able to stimulate discussion within training groups and to encourage participants to initiate their own improvement plans.

Attributes

They will be enthusiastic and committed to the success of Quality and Service management and will be in a position to help people outside their training sessions, not just during them. They should also be able to demonstrate Quality and Service in all the things they do, not just in what they say.

APPENDIX 14.2

The Facilitator Training Programme
Aims

The facilitator training programme is designed to enable you to fulfil your role as a facilitator. In doing that, it will need, first, to ensure you fully understand the material in which you will be required to train people. It will then familiarise you with the facilitating skills and techniques which you will need to deliver that material. Finally, you will have the opportunity to practice your facilitating skills and, through the help you receive from your trainer and from your colleagues, to gain the confidence necessary to take on your new role.

Approach

You will acquire the necessary skills and understanding through introductory awareness, practice and application. You and your facilitator colleagues will work together, helping each other through this learning process.

It is important that, in order to help each other, we all follow some basic ground rules. Learning can sometimes be an uncomfortable experience and it is essential that you, as a facilitator, are as open, honest and supportive as possible. This will be equally important once you begin training others as it is now while you are on the receiving end.

The facilitator training programme will give you the maximum opportunity to put into practice the things which you are learning, and to develop your training techniques in front of your colleagues. To get maximum benefit from these practical sessions you will be asked to provide a critique of the performance of your colleagues and vice versa.

A good critique is a valuable aid to helping you to improve your skills and to gain a better understanding of the training process. A critique, badly handled, can be a very destructive thing so it is important that the attached guidelines on critiquing and on giving and receiving feedback are carefully observed.

Outputs

The facilitator training course will help you to develop the skills and understanding which you will need to run the Quest for Quality and Service training sessions. By the end of the course you will also have played a major part in assembling the final training formats which you will use in those sessions.

To deliver these successfully you will need to do more than just read course notes to the participants; you will need to be able to discuss them in terms which they understand, using examples with which they are familiar, and in a style which is natural to you.

Your trainer will help you to select and adapt exercises and examples which you may decide to use when you deliver your training sessions. The final decisions, however, will be yours. To be able to deliver the training with conviction you must be able to OWN the material which you are presenting.

Course Critique

At the end of this course you will be in a position to look back over the training which you have received and, through the eyes of a trained trainer, suggest ways in which you might improve this course.

Your feedback gives us the opportunity to practise what we teach and to look for ways of continuously improving our service to our customers!

15. Olivetti UK Limited

'Perfection is the child of time.'

Bishop Joseph Hall (1574–1656)

Olivetti UK have made such strides in customer service in the last five years that it is worth briefly recording their progress here. A major player in the information technology field, the company operate in a highly competitive market place. They believe that sustaining customer service throughout their large organisation will provide a competitive edge.

They are a company of some 1,400 people dealing with around 50 corporate accounts. About 1,000 staff are employed in the 'Customer Support Group' (CSG). This represents quite a high ratio of staff to customers. According to Paolo Tosi, Managing Director of Olivetti UK: 'In terms of customer care, we have a strong partnership with the people we are working with, with very good supportive resources.' The company not only stress the importance of their high staff ratio for servicing their customer accounts but also insist that a strength of their 'partnership' approach is the frequent refocusing on, and revisiting of, their customers.

QUALITY POLICY

'Our policy is to provide a consistent quality of products and services which meet the customer's needs and our contractual obligations'

(From Olivetti UK Quality Policy)

Olivetti UK now have their major Account Directors actually residing as close to the customer as possible, often on their premises. Says Paolo Tosi:

Account Directors co-ordinate the work of quite a large spectrum of skills which are specifically devoted to the customer. For example, it used to be that the Account Manager only dealt with the commercial problems of that customer. When technical issues arose they were dealt with by any other manager, as of course would be any other problem. Now we have built all these factors into the one role – an Account Director who has total responsibility for all the servicing of a customer's account, whether it be delivery, sales support, software developments, projects or service. As co-ordinator of all activities, this one Account Director acts as a single interface to our customer. This brings total unity into the account. Now both Olivetti and the customer know that if there is something which does not run to order we can go immediately to the same person for action. This offers our customer a very immediate problem-solving facility. Also, as the Account Director is in the customer's premises everyday, we are able to see everything that happens there and, more important, anticipate what might happen. We therefore anticipate our customer needs. This has not really meant a re-organisation for Olivetti UK – more of an uplift, improvement or progression. In other words, more evolution than revolution.

As Paolo Tosi further explains:

Today there are so many business aspects, and so much technology which we have to co-ordinate for our customers. For instance, until two years ago, from a technological point of view, we could have two or three people handling one account. Today it would be 20 people. To integrate all the different technologies, and to give the immediacy required today by our customers, we must have global co-ordination in order to give total customer service.

Sustaining Customer Service

As we have seen, in the quest for greater market share a positive customer referral network is the best selling aid that an organisation can have. Olivetti UK see efficient customer service as the key, as Paolo Tosi points out:

> *It has always been our profile not to be a very aggressive company. More than anything else we have always been able to sell by our referrals and references. It has been our strong point to try to build those references – in fact, we have always been better than perceived. And we want to pursue this ethos. There are very good organisations in this industry, so we have got to be better. We have got to be better in terms of efficiency, in terms of price and performance, and in sustaining customer service.*

Paolo Tosi measures Olivetti UK's success in terms both of the growth of business and of the acknowledgement of quality coming from market research. Twice a year the company run a comprehensive customer care survey of all their accounts to try to tune their service even better. Another measure of worth is simply in the permanence of customers. There are so many options open to customers today, so much choice, that companies who are going to keep their customer, and increase their customer base, must be good. Olivetti UK have lost almost no accounts in the last six years, whilst simultaneously growing considerably in both the UK and in Europe as a whole.

Internally, the customer service message is constantly being reinforced to all Olivetti UK employees. Already the service section of their company conforms to BS 5750. But consistency of customer service across all departments, not just attaining a quality standard, is their priority task. To help achieve this, twice a month senior management have a marketing meeting. This, says Paolo Tosi, is:

> *Just to tune the co-ordination of services, and all our divisions, to understand that they are part of the same company. It is a focused fortnightly meeting specifically looking at quality and service issues.*

Every time we find something wrong, or something which can be improved, we immediately implement that improvement.

What is vital is that it is an *action* meeting. For example, Paolo Tosi highlights the action emanating from one such recent meeting.

One of the issues we discussed related to customer care. We recently created a new 'customer care desk' different from our established helplines. The task of this new desk is to re-route, within the company, people who do not know to which point they should address a particular query. If someone calls us and does not know which kind of problem they have got, we have discovered that they cannot be re-routed to the helplines. Now, they will be directed to our customer care desk. This has an interviewer who will understand the customer's total problem, and can then steer them to the right department in the company. This approach was agreed at the meeting, and was operational the following week.

In Olivetti UK, as in other excellence organisations, it is boardroom drive which steers the sustaining of customer service. And, of course, such meetings would be worthless without the insistence on immediate action. So, keeping the account director as close to the customer as possible, doing regular customer surveys to anticipate problems, and having fortnightly boardroom briefings specifically on quality and service issues are all routes helping Olivetti UK retain their competitive edge.

To sustain customer service over a period of time is a challenge, and one constantly stressed by the board. Without that continual commitment, complacency would set in and culminate in customer conflict. It is a striking fact that Olivetti have not lost a corporate customer for some six years. More than any other measurement this record reinforces the message that they are a service company with which their customers enjoy doing business.

16. Kwik-Fit

'Wha's like us – dam' few and they a' deid.'

Anonymous Scottish Poet

There are 22.5 million licenced cars and light vans on Britain's roads today – 25 per cent more than a decade ago. Eighty-one per cent of these are more than two years old, which means that Kwik-Fit, as the best-known UK car service organisation, are ideally placed to take advantage of the replacement market that must service this growth. Despite the recent slow down in new UK car sales, industry estimates suggest there will be nearly 29 million cars in use by the year 2000. The cars purchased in the 1988-9 boom years have passed MOT age and will soon need increased repair and maintenance work. This, together with the changes in tyre legislation introduced in 1992, will continue to increase the momentum behind Kwik-Fit's sales growth.

Currently, Kwik-Fit serve over four million customers a year. The company was founded in 1971 by the current Chairman and Chief Executive, Tom Farmer CBE, and the first Kwik-Fit centre was opened in Edinburgh, Scotland. For the last two years their group strategy has been to curtail expansion and strengthen core business. This co-ordinated approach to business has helped to achieve consistent growth over the years, and should enable the group to meet its objective of maximising profits by increasing market share. The year 1992 was another of substantial growth, for example:

- Turnover up 17 per cent to £254 million.

- Pre-tax profit up 66 per cent to £32.1 million.
- Operating profit up 51 per cent to £34.5 million.
- Group borrowing eliminated compared with £19.1 million the previous year.

Figure 16.1   The Kwik-Fit Code of Practice

Our aim is 100% Customer Delight

The Staff of this Centre will:

- Always treat your vehicle with care and always fit protective seat covers.
- Ensure that your vehicle is inspected by a technically qualified staff member.
- Ensure that the initial diagnosis is confirmed by another technically qualified staff member prior to work commencing.
- Examine your vehicle with you and give an honest appraisal of the work required.
- Give a binding quotation which includes all associated charges prior to work commencing.
- Ensure that you are aware that any non-exchange part or component removed from your vehicle is available for you to take away.
- Ensure that all work is carried out in accordance with the company's laid down procedures.
- Inform you immediately of any complications or delays.
- Ensure that all completed work is checked by a technically qualified staff member.
- Offer to inspect the finished work with you at the time of delivery.

Should you ever have any concerns about our products or our service, please speak to the Centre Manager or call our **Free 24-hour, 7-day Customer Helpline on 0800 269 866** and immediate action will be taken.

Specialising in products that are essential to motorists, such as the repair and replacement of tyres, exhausts, brakes, batteries, radiators, suspension parts and in-car safety items, the group operates through some 600 fitting centres in the United Kingdom, Eire, Holland and Belgium. Centres are conveniently sited on main traffic routes and nearly all of them are open 363 days a year and offer a 'drive-in, while-you-wait' service.

Kwik-Fit Fleet is a business unit specifically set up to meet the needs of the important business sector of the market. A successful fleet operation must provide quality service, seven days a week, nationwide. It is estimated that almost 60 per cent of all new car purchases are registered under company names, and some 20 per cent of all cars on Britain's roads are company-owned. The Kwik-Fit Fleet service is designed to reduce significantly their customers' costs, and the administrative workload, in maintaining a company fleet of cars and light vans. A team of 25 specialist account managers has responsibility for the personal contact and administration of some 8,000 Fleet accounts throughout the UK, and they are supported by the Fleet Management Centre, based in St Albans in Hertfordshire. Kwik-Fit Fleet's customers, including such household names as Avis, BTR, Sainsbury, GEC and Customs & Excise, are together responsible for over 1.6 million vehicles and depend every bit as much on high standards of service as the private motorist.

In recognition of their service to fleet users, Kwik-Fit have won three awards. Last year, for the second year running, they were awarded the Fleet News Award for the 'best fast-fit company in the UK' and also the Award of Excellence from the Institute of Transport Management. The third award was from Fleet News for the best overall service given in the automotive industry.

AIMING FOR 100 PER CENT CUSTOMER DELIGHT

Today's motorists increasingly demand value for money from the company to which they entrust their car's repair and parts replacement requirements. Kwik-Fit Group has strengthened its leading position in the European market for automotive repair and parts' replacement by meeting these needs and sustaining the high standards of service their customers demand. Over the last 21 years, the group has developed a strong identity, which customers know guarantees quality service, professionalism and convenience. During the past year over four million customers benefited from Kwik-Fit services. Kwik-Fit are supported by local and national advertising campaigns which are high-profile and distinctive. On-site stocking, and direct delivery 'just in time' replenishment by suppliers, ensures that customers' needs are met. Sophisticated computer systems not only improve efficiency and profitability, but are also used to enhance customer service. During 1992, for example, point-of-sale computer terminals were installed in the Eire centres and linked to the group's mainframe computer in Edinburgh. As in the UK, this has enabled the centre managers to benefit from reduced administration and increased customer care and attention. It also enables management to focus quickly on the key areas that affect sales and profitability. As John McKillen, General Manager of Kwik-Fit Eire's DC Tyres and Exhausts, says, 'In Eire, we are determined to sustain the high standards of customer service and quality which are the keys to Kwik-Fit's Code of Practice and our success.'

Kwik-Fit also simplify the customer's life with their 'fleet recorded electronic data' system – known as FRED. FRED gives fleet operators greater control over the work carried out on their vehicles. Specific requirements for individual accounts, such as preferred tyre brands, can be programmed into the central computer and the information called up electronically by any Kwik-Fit centre. Point-of-sale systems in each centre allow detailed invoices to be sent out within two days. Alternatively, customers with suitable electronic data interchange technology can receive invoices instantly 'over the wire'.

Kwik-Fit's longstanding aim of '100 per cent customer satisfaction' has now been replaced by the aim of '100 per cent customer delight'. Reflecting this, the entire organisation is geared towards the customer. Says Tom Farmer,

> Kwik-Fit are always striving to improve customer service in all our centres. To help achieve this, we have strengthened our customer service team who continually monitor service reports and follow up customer contacts. We have also engaged the services of the Automobile Association (AA), and their technical engineers are monitoring and providing independent reports on the standards of workmanship and good housekeeping in all Kwik-Fit centres throughout the UK. We have our own Code of Practice, prominently displayed in every Kwik-Fit centre, which tells our customers about – and reminds our people of – the high standards the customer has a right to expect from us.

It was in 1972 that Tom Farmer introduced the innovative Kwik-Fit Code of Practice, which became, and still is, a cornerstone of their policies and procedures. As Peter Holmes, Director of Marketing says:

> The Kwik-Fit Code of Practice reinforces the message that the customer

has a right to expect the highest of standards when they come to us for work carried out on their cars. There are ten points on the Kwik-Fit Code of Practice and they go through the various procedures which should be carried out when work is required on the customer's car.

In using the services of a Kwik-Fit centre, customers have the advantage of dealing with a local business that is backed by the resources of a national company, with all the related benefits of bulk-buying, staff training, centrally co-ordinated advertising, well-equipped centres and nationwide guarantees. Apart from their Code of Practice, at the heart of the operational structure is Kwik-Fit's Partners in Progress scheme, whereby motivated and skilled people from the centres are appointed 'Kwik-Fit Master Managers'. They are responsible for running their centre and receive a share of its profits in addition to their salary. Furthermore, groups of three centres are placed under 'Kwik-Fit Partners', i.e. Master Managers who have achieved consistent growth for their centres and shown outstanding leadership qualities. In return for monitoring operations, standards of service and keeping a tight control on costs, Partners share in the profits of the three centres within their partnership.

Through a lean management structure, Partners, the Master Managers and the teams of fitters are supported by Divisional and Central Services personnel who are organised to provide the necessary back-up to ensure the efficiency and continued profitability of each centre. All Kwik-Fit staff in the field, and in the support functions, participate in profit sharing. Through the Employee Share Scheme, 1,193 Kwik-Fit people are shareholders in the company. In addition, the company's Sharesave Scheme enables those staff who have been with the company for six months or more to buy Kwik-Fit ordinary shares on special terms, with money saved under a savings contract operated by the Yorkshire Building Society. A new Profit-Related Pay Plan has also recently been introduced which allows staff to benefit from new government pay schemes and to reduce their income tax payments, linking a proportion of their earnings to the profitability of the group.

The weekly newspaper Kwik-News, now in its eleventh year, keeps all staff informed and provides a forum for news, views and information about events in all parts of the group. In addition, an annual report, drawn from the Group's Annual Report, is distributed to all employees.

COMPLACENCY CAN BREED SERVICE CONTEMPT

Kwik-Fit's Code of Practice has been in existence for a long time, but has had to be further strengthened recently, supplemented by intensified training programmes. The reason for this was a rather damning report on the 'fast-fit' industry by the Consumers' Association magazine *Which?* This survey came as a surprise to Tom Farmer, to put it mildly, because it reported that Kwik-Fit centres were not the icons of customer service he had thought they were. He had spent many years rigorously enforcing his Code of Practice among his managers and fitters, and had made Kwik-Fit the premier brand in replacement parts in the UK. Added to this, the company had received thousands of letters from customers praising the standards of workmanship, courtesy and helpfulness of the staff. There was, in fact, no hint that anything was wrong until the *Which?* inspectors found that an above-average number of Kwik-Fit centres surveyed had advised customers to have parts fitted that they thought were unnecessary. This was particularly surprising to Kwik-Fit, as the company had been asked by *Which?* to advise it on how best to carry out the survey – and had happily done just that. Much bad press followed, so Kwik-Fit had to act.

As Peter Holmes explains:

We did not necessarily change things. Which? *published their survey results in January 1992, but we knew well in advance, in September 1991, what the results were. It became clear from their survey that in 11 of the 42 centres they had visited our people had given an inaccurate diagnosis. We immediately held meetings with every individual in every single centre that we operate in the UK, and stressed the importance of adhering to the company procedures in the Kwik-Fit Code of Practice.*

At the same time, the company newspaper spearheaded a fresh campaign on the customer service standards expected of staff, and Tom Farmer himself embarked on a nationwide tour, calling meetings at which he spoke to small groups of fitters and supervisors. In total he saw 2,500 staff. Large posters were immediately erected in all Kwik-Fit outlets re-emphasising to customers the standards they should expect, and particularly that no work was to be carried out on their car until the fitter's initial recommendations had been checked by the supervisor. New procedures were introduced whereby every customer could request a written diagnostic report on any work required. A free Customer Helpline service was also installed to allow customers to seek advice and register their attitudes to Kwik-Fit standards of service. In addition, Tom Farmer commissioned the AA themselves to make unannounced spot checks on Kwik-Fit garages up and down the country and to report on the quality of the advice and service given to customers. This information, together with other regular market research, was used to identify where further improvements could be made. Kwik-Fit customers also continued to have the reassurance that all Kwik-Fit centres have 'AA-approved' status, and that the company's own Centaur Supreme range of products has the AA Seal of Approval.

Having outside independent arbitrators monitoring product and services is a very brave commitment to customer satisfaction. Even now, Kwik-Fit cannot fully explain where its Code of Practice went wrong in practice. The company had been entirely happy that its carefully-stipulated operating procedures would prevent any of the incidents reported by *Which?* magazine. However, Kwik-Fit now openly admit that management were to blame for not ensuring that these procedures were followed. After so many years of living with the Code, some bad habits had inevitably crept in, despite striving to keep customer satisfaction at the top of the priority list.

To its credit, Kwik-Fit has learned its lesson. Since the *Which?*

report, every aspect of the Code of Practice is meticulously monitored. As Tom Farmer says, 'Simply satisfying our customers is not enough. We want them to be delighted with the service we provide.'

SUSTAINING CUSTOMER SERVICE

There are other major initiatives that Kwik-Fit have adopted to sustain their service levels, and to reassure customers that they are an 'excellence' company. The promotion of car passenger safety is among their highest priorities. Last July, in partnership with the Department of Transport, Kwik-Fit launched a national 'Belt-up-in-the-back' campaign to increase awareness of new legislation making it compulsory to wear rear seat belts where fitted. Also, supported by the Department of Transport and the Royal Society for the Prevention of Accidents, Kwik-Fit is involved in a number of excellence efforts such as the Child Safety Scheme, which encourages parents to buy and fit child safety seats by giving a full refund once the seat is outgrown. Explains Peter Holmes:

> The basis of this scheme is to supply and fit for around £35. Once a child has outgrown the seat, if they return it to us, then we will refund the purchase price in full. The child seats are suitable for children aged about nine months to five years of age. We ask them to keep their receipts and they are also required to register under this particular scheme. At the time of purchase they are given a customer registration card, which they complete and send back to us here, which we log on our database. So, we have a record of all the child seats that have been sold to these parents, and on that registration card we also ask them to put the name of their child and their age. That enables us to verify, if they should claim for a refund down the line, that everything is in order. Given this information, one of the things we do with that database is to send the children a birthday card every year. Bearing in mind this scheme has been going since 1987, we have sent out hundreds and thousands of birthday cards every year!

Clearly, in 15 years' time Kwik-Fit will have a remarkable database of young drivers who could become their customers.

The marketing policy for sustaining customer service is therefore simple, direct and practical. It is to build consumer confidence by offering good service and value for money, backed by high standards of workmanship, quality components and reliable guarantees. It is summed up in the promise 'You can't get better than a Kwik-Fit fitter', one of Britain's most successful and best-liked TV advertising campaigns, now in its sixth series. They regularly take large advertisements in papers to reassure their customers, and to reinforce the message of the AA's independent audits on the quality of their workmanship.

The company also has a 24-hours, seven-days-a-week Freephone number, which registers the attitudes and concerns of customers, and also reminds Kwik-Fit of how well they are sustaining customer service. As Peter Holmes states:

> *We constantly examine all areas of our business in order to identify where we can make meaningful improvements. We encourage our customers to comment on the service they receive and our free Customer Helpline Service has been specifically installed to allow customers to seek advice and register their attitudes towards our standards of service. Should any customer register any concerns, we insist they are contacted by return and that every effort is made to put the matter right. That customer will then be contacted again to make sure they are happy with the way the matter was handled.*

In addition to their ongoing programmes which review the general efficiency and operating procedures, Kwik-Fit have BS 5750/ISO 9000 accreditation and recognition under the Government-sponsored Investors in People initiative. It is one of the group's prime objectives to increase the opportunities for the development of all its staff – to encourage promotion from within wherever possible, and to provide security of employment with proper financial reward for effort. As demands on their staff are high, the group considers it important to have human resource objectives as clearly defined as sales and profit objectives. Being an investor in people, therefore, has become an integral part of their business planning, and internal customer service commitment. Kwik-Fit believe that their ongoing staff training and career development are pre-requisites of attaining the group's business and service goals. Even in a recession they have not reduced their training budget. Modular training programmes provide their people with a thorough and detailed understanding of all the main areas of the group's activities, including customer service, sales, technical skills, administration and management development.

Kwik-Fit fitters and Master Managers are trained in their centres by mobile Technical Service Field Trainers, at the group's Training and Development Centres. This high quality of training has been acknowledged by the City and Guilds Institute, which gives all trainees the opportunity to achieve nationally-recognised qualificataions. During 1992, in response to the changes taking place in the UK labour market, the Kwik-Fit Apprenticeship Scheme was introduced, to provide up to 100 school leavers a year with the opportunity to start a career which is one of the most attractive in the auto repair industry. A graduate recruitment programme has also been successfully launched, providing the expanding group with a greater pool of talented young people.

DELIGHTING THE COMMUNITY

As an organisation that provides a local service, Kwik-Fit is keen to contribute to the development of their customers' community and to support the needs of local people. In addition to providing financial support, staff provide training, expertise and time for a wide variety of projects and initiatives. During 1992, some 106 charities and other organisations were helped in this way. They have worked closely with schools, colleges and universities to give young people a better chance of understanding the industry and the opportunities that Kwik-Fit provides for their careers. Kwik-Fit staff have also enthusiastically helped those less fortunate than themselves in many ways. For example, around the country their staff collected over

5,000 blankets for Britain's homeless in the Operation Blanket Coverage campaign last winter. It is another constant in excellence companies that they service their local communities and support people who are not necessarily their direct customers.

The Kwik-Fit Child Safety Scheme, mentioned earlier, has played a major part in making it safer for young children to travel in cars and has enabled the group to put something back into the community. They reguarlly donate child safety seats, child cycle helmets and rear seat belts to organisations and individuals with special needs. Kwik-Fit has sponsored a Young Enterprise company, giving teenage entrepreneurs guidance on business development and marketing. They are a supporter of the Prince's Scottish Youth Business Trust, whose aim is to provide finance and professional support to young people, whoever they are and wherever they come from, in order that they can set up and run their own businesses. During 1992 Kwik-Fit was invited to participate in the Prince's Trust Volunteer programme to help young people develop their full potential. It was also one of the ten leading companies that spearheaded the 'Charter for Business', which aims – over a five-year period – to encourage 100,000 young people in industry to participate in the Duke of Edinburgh Award Scheme.

Kwik-Fit is an impressive organisation. It 'feels' like an excellence company and there is a buzz about whenever you visit their centres. They are also an honest company, openly admitting their mistakes. Their efforts to improve have paid off. Surveys for this book, of Kwik-Fit centres, including two in Eire, showed exemplary, energetic and enthusiastic customer attention. As one of their sales and training team said, 'In Kwik-Fit we have a policy of caring – caring for our customers, because they know this company cares for them.' Today, as a company, they are a pleasure to do business with.

17. Metropolitan Police Service

'A state without the means of change is without the means of its conservation.'

Edmund Burke (1727–1797)

In recent years the Police Service has received increased resources, however the demands made on it have also increased, quite considerably. Against this background, Sir John Woodcock, Her Majesty's Chief Inspector of Constabulary, says:

> *We must open the Service to the consumer. We must create structures which will enable the public to set priorities with us. We must admit the limits of our powers. British policing is undertaken with public consent, which does not mean acquiescence but a broad tolerance, indicating a satisfaction with both the helping and enforcement roles of policing.*

Sir John agrees that genuine consultation has to exist between UK Police Forces and their customers. In the course of Force inspections, the nature and frequency of this community consultation has been examined by the Inspectorate. Consultative groups now exist in all Forces, enabling a dialogue to take place between local police and their customers, i.e. the members of the community they serve. Both Sir John and the Metropolitan Police Commissioner agree that effective consultation is essential if the police are to provide a quality service in keeping with the priorities and expectations of their customers. They both appreciate that there is no 'quick fix' in quality of service and that the success of current initiatives will only be witnessed over time.

'Value for money' is often seen as an exercise solely to reduce costs, but both Sir John and the Commissioner regard financial discipline as a part of customer service quality. There can be an impression that the two militate against each other, but this is not so. As many organisations in this book will confirm, quality of service does not depend on large budgets. It does, however, demand a clear understanding of the type of performance being sought, and a commitment to allocate resources accordingly. As Sir John says:

Police Forces need to develop long-term, corporate plans to assist them to make rational decisions concerning resource allocation and organisational development. While a number of forces have strategic plans and actively use them as management tools, others see little merit in them. So these Forces are being encouraged to develop strategic corporate planning and to incorporate quality of service targets within their planning cycles.

In all the organisations studied in this book, mistakes are seen as opportunities, and complaints as a tool for measuring customer confidence and performance. The Police Service is no exception. It must seek to reduce public complaints, principally through quality of service initiatives. Some Forces, such as the Metropolitan Police Service, are succeeding. Says Sir John, 'I believe this to be directly attributable to the effort that has been made at all levels to provide a service which seeks to meet the requirements of local people through co-operation and consultation.'

However, research for this book indicates that concern is still being expressed by customers about the length of time taken to investigate police complaints. To speed it up, many Forces have developed computer software packages for managing the administration of complaints, and processing the information obtained. Sir John agrees that the Police Service must make every effort to cut out avoidable delays, but points out that in many cases the sheer volume of investigative work makes the early resolution of a complaint difficult. It has been agreed that the Police Service will run a pilot scheme, the aim of which will be to complete complaint investigations within 120 calendar days, and the Chief Inspector of Constabulary will monitor the scheme closely. For the complainant, however, the unexplained, and often ludicrous, length of an investigation will do little to increase confidence in the present system in the short term.

If customer service is to be sustained, the public have a right to expect not only the highest standards of behaviour from police officers but also that complaints, when made, are thoroughly investigated and are seen to be dealt with firmly and fairly. This is fundamental to the confidence that the community has in its Police Service and is absolutely essential to the delivery of quality policing. But how do senior police officers feel that much-publicised complaint cases affect the drive for an improved quality of service within their Service?

Many believe that, from time to time, they have to live with the decisions of other people. They also regret, and are very disappointed and saddened, when some police officers behave unacceptably. When policemen are overtly rude, arrogant, offensive, sexist, racist, or whatever, that is totally unacceptable to most officers I have talked to, and they will say so. The process by which police performance is dealt with is often somewhat subjective, prescribed by legislation and police regulations, etc. In the past this has not always allowed as much flexibility to deal with complaints as many senior police officers would, themselves, wish. The Police Service must be conscious of the full implications of all the actions they take and the way they behave. Everybody in the organisation has got to be responsible for their own actions, for the implications of what they do and what they say, and the effect it can have on the community, on public confidence, on the esteem and reputation of the Service.

In an open society the media will, quite rightly, examine and question the police and take them to task on critical issues. Most senior officers I talked to for this study believe that it is right for them to do so; they want a debate, and for the Service, if found wanting, to be exposed. Many want to learn from such experiences, which may be extremely painful but at least are open. Appreciating this, London's Metropolitan Police Service (MPS) have drawn up a 'mission' Statement of Our Common Purpose and Values (see Figure 17.1). This states that the MPS must always respond openly and properly to fair criticism.

Over the five years of my involvement with the MPS I have noticed an awakening of concern about public perception of what they say and do. It matters to them. At all levels of the organisation there is a more genuine commitment to improve service to the public and to one another. I see attitudinal change evident in a number of people, not only new recruits but also the more experienced officers. Nevertheless, there is a long way to go yet, and the realists in the Service will not deny that.

For the MPS the size of the problem is daunting. The task they face in London every day is to co-ordinate 28,000 police officers and 16,000 civil staff to police 800 square miles. Policing has never been more demanding or challenging than it is today. As the largest Police Service in the country, the MPS is, understandably, being asked to provide ever-more assistance and to respond more rapidly and effectively on an ever-widening front. The philosophy of policing

---

Figure 17.1 MPS: Statement of our Common Purpose and Values

- The purpose of the Metropolitan Police Service is to uphold the law fairly and firmly; to prevent crime; to pursue and bring to justice those who break the law; to keep the Queen's Peace; to protect, help and reassure people in London; and to be seen to do all this with integrity, common sense and sound judgement
- We must be compassionate, courteous and patient, acting without fear or favour or prejudice to the rights of others. We need to be professional, calm and restrained in the face of violence and apply only that force which is necessary to accomplish our lawful duty
- We must strive to reduce the fears of the public and, so far as we can, to reflect their priorities in the action we take. We must respond to well-founded criticism with a willingness to change

from the earliest days has had as its cornerstone the concept, indeed the reality, of working with the support of the public. The MPS frankly admit that crime is too important a matter to be left entirely to the police. Without the support of the majority, the Police Service would be unable to function. The partnership between police and those they are endeavouring to serve is vital if they are to succeed in combating and preventing crime. It cuts across every aspect of policing today.

Today there does exist a more open and positive attitude to change within the MPS. Their customer-centred quality of service programme, PLUS, has ensured that change is focused towards one end – putting their Statement of Common Purpose and Values into action. In that way they seek to deliver and sustain a high-quality service to the public, one which reflects their customers' needs and priorities. In the words of the outgoing Commissioner of the Metropolitan Police, Sir Peter Imbert:

I would like to think, and I do believe, that after I leave this Service, if any member of my family has need of the Police Service, or is in anyway involved with it, or may be apprehended by a member of the Police Service, they would be dealt with firmly, but fairly and in a friendly way. That is what I would like to leave behind me: a Service which one can trust, one which has plenty of integrity and one of which all within it can be suitably proud.

Sir Peter Imbert retired in early 1993, having served as Metropolitan Police Commissioner for over five years. After being appointed in 1987, he was responsible for positive changes in attitudes on service to the public in the MPS and for carrying forward organisational changes made by his predecessor. The Statement of Common Purpose and Values was part of his customer-centred PLUS programme and has been an important element in restating the concept of service which is fundamental to policing in the community.

As Home Secretary Kenneth Clarke says:

Sir Peter Imbert has focused the attention of the Metropolitan Police Service on the need to provide a high standard of service and to maintain the trust which must exist between the police and community. His successor, Paul Condon, who was Chief Constable of Kent, will I think prove to be a forceful successor to a very distinguished Commissioner. Paul Condon has shown his commitment to similar ideals in his management of the Kent Constabulary and I believe that under this leadership the Metropolitan Police Service will continue to make significant improvements in its relationships with the public, and in its effectiveness in meeting the ever-rising demands placed upon it.

MAKING CUSTOMER SERVICE HAPPEN

The MPS is huge. It has 44,000 employees and carries out a wide variety of duties; ranging from the obvious areas of public order and crime prevention to royalty and diplomatic protection, traffic management, lost property and taxi cab regulation. The 16,000 civil staff who support 28,000 police officers perform a similarly bewildering range of tasks. They include cooks, cleaners, forensic scientists, engineers, mechanics, press officers, administrative staff, typists, welfare officers, trainers, photographers and technicians.

In 1988 the MPS set about a review of every aspect of their Service, in particular of how they delivered that service to the people of London. This systematic review resulted in a wide variety of recommendations, which became known as the PLUS programme. The MPS looked at their command and policy-making structures at the way their front-line policing was delivered, and who actually delivered it; the means they used to reward their 44,000 workforce; how they sanctioned poor performance; how they communicated with each other and the public; how to streamline paperwork and bureaucracy; how to improve the physical image of the MPS.

PLUS aimed to bring about nothing less than a change in culture. Its core aim was to turn the Metropolitan Police Force (as it was then called) into the Metropolitan Police Service. The MPS wanted to put the 'customer', i.e. the public, at the forefront of their planning and resourcing. It wanted to bring the Service closer to the community it actually served, and to build a Service whose workforce more accurately reflected in its own composition, the community it was policing.

The popular perception of the police service is of a conservative, bureaucratic body which is traditionally resistant to change. However, the experience of police officers' daily working lives does not support this view. They are used to dealing with change and never know what is going to happen next. In the course of a 30-year career, officers will have worked in a wide variety of posts with a continual flow of colleagues and senior officers. They will have seen constant changes in legislation, with some actions being decriminalised and others brought within the control of the law. Change for the police is part of their job, but they are realistic enough to appreciate that any police service is a mirror or microcosm of society at large.

The Common Purpose and Values Statement, which was drawn up after extensive consultation within and outside the Service, states clearly what the MPS are in business for. Framed copies are prominently displayed in every building in the MPS area, but words on a wall mean nothing unless they are read, understood and translated into action. Mission statements may remind people of the need for customer service but, of themselves, do nothing to sustain it. It was for this reason that the MPS embarked upon a series of seminars which brought everyone, from messenger to chief superintendent, together at one of eight centres where they spent a day discussing the Statement's meaning. Says Peter Winship, MPS Assistant Commissioner:

It took 65 weeks to reach 97 per cent of the organisation, and the programme was not without pain. The role of senior management in this process was vital. Initially, every seminar was merely opened and closed by a senior manager. However, experience showed that their presence throughout the day was beneficial. Where possible they stayed to answer any queries that arose, to participate and to demonstrate their commitment to the customer-centred PLUS ethos.

For the first book in this series on customer service I talked to more than 400 members of the MPS, police and civilian. Many said that, subsequent to the seminars, they were not seriously convinced about the commitment from the senior management towards the PLUS ethos. The outgoing Commissioner, Sir Peter Imbert, is emphatic in his response:

My commitment is total. PLUS is not a gimmick, it is not just going to last for my term of office, it is going to be enduring. The Statement of Common Purpose and Values is the first time since 1829 that we have brought up to date our philosophy of policing and it is a philosophy of policing for the 21st century, not just to the end of the 20th century.

MAKING CUSTOMER SERVICE STICK

One of the problems with any customer service philosphy is moving on from the 'making it happen' stage to 'making it stick' at the grass roots level. A major grievance from that level in the MPS has been that PLUS fell a bit flat and that there has been little follow-up to the initial PLUS seminar razzamatazz. Another constant theme of criticism was of poor management and lack of leadership. Peter Winship comments:

This was due, in part, to a lack of understanding about what senior managers actually did, highlighting a further problem – communications within the Service itself. Part of the problem was that nowhere was it set out exactly what was expected of leaders. There was a great deal of discussion about what made a good leader and arguments about whether good leaders are born or whether the skills can be taught, but no-one had taken the trouble to write down the qualities that went to make up the 'ideal'.

The MPS took the problem to their workforce. In a series of discussions with representative sample groups from all over the Service they asked people to identify what qualities separated the best person they had ever worked for from the worst. The result was a list of 127 practical qualities – for instance, knowing your job, talking to staff, trusting people, being receptive to ideas and treating people fairly. Subsequently these criteria have been set out in a document which is the basis of the new 'leadership standards' of the MPS. This standard is being actively progressed throughout the MPS organisation by senior managers who have been given the task of ensuring that all those with leadership responsibilities are familiar with the contents and have identified ways to apply them in practice.

Peter Winship says:

New standards of leadership have been introduced, and responsibility firmly placed on local management to ensure the standards are actively promoted and applied in their areas of responsibility. This is further backed up by the creation of a Leadership Development Forum, headed by a Deputy Assistant Commissioner, which is calling on all our Divisions to present their plans for ensuring that these standards are applied. Also the way we choose our leaders of the future has changed. Greater importance is attached to their display of the identified leadership qualities and its practical assessment.

This ethos is built into the MPS appraisal system. Notes Peter Winship:

The actions and values which form the new leadership standard have become the benchmark against which all leaders are now being judged, and have been written into new staff appraisal systems. With a greater emphasis on personal objective setting, developing leadership qualities will become a prerequisite for promotion. This links closely into our new promotion selection system, which will put an emphasis on practical assessment where leadership qualities will be tested. The one-day seminars, involving all our workforce, were the catalyst for change. The leadership aspects are a vital tool to make that change stick.

We cannot expect our staff who work closely with the public, sometimes in difficult and dangerous circumstances, to constantly improve their standards if they feel that they are the only ones being asked to do so. PLUS is a quality customer service contract between the police service and the public but it is also a contract between senior management and those who deliver that service direct. Part of the deal must be to improve working conditions for them. The Statement of Common Purpose and Values uses a number of words – integrity, compassion, fairness, honesty and professionalism – which should apply no less to the way we treat our staff, than they do the way we treat members of the public.

SUSTAINING CUSTOMER SERVICE

Another initiative permeating the MPS consists of 'quality of service' team–based discussions building on the individual experience of the PLUS seminars with a view to identifying ways of putting the Statement of Common Purpose and Values into action in the workplace. Says the Commissioner:

> *There has to be a commitment by leaders at all levels to build into our normal working schedule, discussions with the teams we lead, and an obligation to put into practice the actions agreed. For example, a group of police officers in a police station, whether it be Hackney, Stoke Newington, Bromley or Wimbledon, would come together to discuss 'quality of service' issues. What are we doing in order to pursue the concept of PLUS to increase our quality of customer service, to enhance and sustain that quality? These are the questions we must ask ourselves, and having gone through the mixed seminars we are now going through the team-based workplace discussions to ensure that we do that. These quality of service groups really will hammer home the message. What I find gratifying is that people are not complaining that they have got to take part.*

The 'quality of service' discussions demand that all managers get their team together, identify who their customers are (both internal and external), establish what services are presently provided, canvass customers to find out the service they actually require and then devise strategies to bring supply in line with demand. This must become part of their normal working practice. The police service is public property – on their quality of service depends our quality of life. For this reason, the whole style of policing in London is changing. The MPS have moved from a time-based style – where an area is policed by an equal number of officers throughout the 24-hour period – to a more geographically-based style – where small teams of officers will be responsible for policing a much smaller community area than is presently the case.

Says Peter Winship:

This new style will return us to much closer contact with the communities we serve and will enable us to build a more equal partnership with the public. With this change of style comes a greater awareness of quality of service, placing an emphasis on finding out what the customer needs rather than assuming that we always know what is best for them. We are determined to create a more efficient, more responsive police service which accurately reflects the needs and priorities of the community we serve. This involves a wide variety of changes, some simple and easy to achieve, some complex and slow to bring to fruition.

A constant theme of the MPS programme for change has been consultation with the ground floor: helping them gain an awareness of the need for change and giving them the opportunity to identify practical ways of putting theory into practice. All of this, according to Peter Winship, has been reinforced by management, locally and centrally:

Their responsibility is to ensure that once such practical measures are identified, there are sufficient resources to make change happen. There may remain some who have not committed themselves to change, viewing the customer-centred PLUS ethos as merely a 'flavour of the month'. But I can assure you that they must acknowledge that PLUS, and the change it represents, is here to stay. It is the MPS way of life for the 1990s.

How these major challenges are being steered in the MPS to

enable them to sustain service and develop their customer partnership is the subject of the next section of this study.

SELLING THE SERVICE MESSAGE

As indicated earlier, everyone in the MPS attended the customer-centred PLUS seminars. Following on from that, 'quality of service' discussion groups are initiated to reinforce the message of PLUS and to carry it through into day-to-day policing and into relations with internal customers.

The important aspect of the 'quality of service' seminars is that they are 'action' encounters, or 'doing' discussions. Quite frankly, there is no point having a team meeting on a regular basis involving customers if you do not improve service as a result. Also important is belief in the value of holding such a discussion. It is no use if a superior simply orders that a 'quality of service' meeting should be held because it is now mandated by the 'mahogany corridor' in head office. Participants must genuinely want to come together as a team to focus on issues which will improve quality of service and performance. The climate must be conducive to encourage such encounters and senior management must give total commitment to the team's endeavours; especially if a solution requires a change of policy, budget reallocations or other support from senior management to those at the service delivery level.

Detective Chief Inspector (DCI) Heather Penna is responsible for the Criminal Investigation Department (CID) and its 60 staff, at Paddington Green Police Station, a major division within 8 Area of the MPS. It is one of Heather Penna's teams that are reviewed in this section, as they live through their 'quality of service' exercise.

DCI Penna explains:

Just as partnership between the police service and the public and other agencies is the future of policing which gives our customers ownership in policing problems, so must there be ownership in solving those problems, and in delivering a service. The days have gone of a rigid perception of a problem, met by an unbending and unvarying solution which was often inappropriate. The officers in regular close contact with the public are usually best placed both to identify problems and design solutions. If they are to take pride in themselves, and their work, they must be given every opportunity to identify and take responsibility for problems, and suggest solutions. My role is to create a climate where initiative can be encouraged, created and tested.

Detective Sergeant David Hills was a 'team leader' at Paddington Green Police Station. His team comprised a number of people who work with one another, although not necessarily on a day-to-day basis. Encouraged by DCI Penna, his team launched 'quality of service' team-based discussions at the workplace, the first time they had been held in 8 Area. As a team leader, with line responsibility for the initiative, how did David Hills get things underway? He explains:

I think it is important to establish at an early stage what these meetings are about, and what is actually going to come out of them. Otherwise it's 'meetings for meetings' sake' with nothing in sight, nor produced. They have to be seen as valuable, and worthwhile, otherwise they will deteriorate into gripe and grievance sessions. I wanted my meeting to be shorter rather than longer, because I was conscious of the fact that this was the first of the 'quality of service' discussions in Paddington Green Division, and I needed to create a good precedent. I did not want it to become yet another slog. I set a reasonable time limit which, encouragingly, has always been exceeded. So, rather than insist that there is a meeting between 6.00pm and 8.00pm, I have tended to suggest, for example, 6.00pm to 6.45pm which, in practice, has gone on until 8.00pm because the team themselves wanted it to.

In that the police often work unsocial hours, the bringing together of DS Hills's team posed problems. He agrees that the logistics of regular team-based discussions can be a liability.

It is very difficult getting everybody together at the one time, even on day one, although everyone knew the time, venue and the reason for our meeting. Through operational duties I lost two to Crown Court and they never made it. Okay, certain problems can be overcome, but to get seven or eight people together at a given time, and from different departments within the police station, creates difficulties.

He also acknowledges, however, that if he 'sells' the concept right this may well encourage his team to want to be there. 'I wanted to get the team there voluntarily, and genuinely interested in the content, but it had to be more than just talk, there had to be an action list which would make it all worthwhile.'

A team leader has a major responsibility as 'facilitator', certainly in the earlier stages of such exercises. David Hills says that he found it easier than he had anticipated to 'sell' to his team the importance of sustaining and improving quality of service.

I had anticipated, but did not receive, many hints of cynicism. It was important for me to establish that people could say exactly what they liked, provided it was constructive. . . . Not having been a facilitator or a team leader before in this type of discussion, I wanted to sell myself, and how I felt about things, without imposing my views on the others.

David Hills realises with hindsight that there were many things he did not ask his team, and a number of issues he should have come back on.

I should have been more of a devil's advocate. I was so wrapped up with getting my bit right: for example, working issues through in a logical order, ensuring that the team each have an input and, if the enthusiasm waned a little, introducing something else. In fact, the normal problems of running a meeting without aimless waffle. Through being concerned about getting my bit right I did miss much of the content.

To me, running a 'quality of service' group discussion is a skilled art. You have to control the meeting, keep team members motivated and interested, whilst still letting people have their say. Remember, I'm also trying to keep within some sort of structure as outlined in the MPS brief.

All those things were occupying my time, and I believe rightly so. However, from being a divisional detective to managing workplace, team-based discussions is a big leap without any training at all, except for a few bullet points in a leaflet I was given for guidance. There is certainly a definite need for us to receive training in how to do it well.

SUSTAINING THE SERVICE MESSAGE

When I attended one of the meetings at 8 Area, David Hills asked for suggestions on how the team could improve its quality of service. Initially, people were suggesting what *other* people could do, or should do. It took a while for him to ask 'OK, but what can we do *ourselves* to improve our service tomorrow?' It was that question, which completely changed the direction of the meeting. As he explains:

Maybe what I should have said was 'What can we do to improve our service quality today?' Anyway, I did notice the change in the meeting at that point. I don't know if that is because most of us, rightly or wrongly, feel that we already provide a good service, so when we talk about the deficiencies we are talking about someone else's shortcomings, not our own. I would like to think that everything the MPS customer service PLUS programme has highlighted, everything we are doing for the public, we have always done. That may sound an arrogant statement but it simply never occurred to us that we were not getting it right.

You will speak to a lot of policemen who will look at the PLUS programme and say: 'It's not for me, it's for someone else – I have always provided a good service.' It is not until you ask the question 'Well, how can you do it better then?' that positive, constructive discussion begins. For example, at the meeting I said 'Alright, 90 per cent of the time you do a terrific job, but can anybody hold up their hands and say "I do 100 per cent", or even "91 per cent?"'. 'No' was the simple answer. Given that response, the next stage becomes clearer: 'What can you do to improve?' Responding to that question started to change their minds towards improving our customer service, and doing just that little bit extra for the public, victims, and for one another.

Because David Hills's team had different backgrounds, needs and job roles, everyone on it was in reality a customer of someone else in the Service. During the discussion, therefore, they reviewed ways of improving the quality of service internally as well as externally. Interestingly, DS Hills did not think the group members thought of themselves, before they actually talked about it, as 'customers'.

Whilst being aware that we all worked with each other, and that we have to perform different roles and tasks to provide the complete picture, it is not until you split the internal/external customer relationship that the group say 'Yes of course, we are all customers of each other'. Working together is nothing new, but it is the word 'customer' that is new to them. Identifying our external customers was easier.

At one of the meetings his team discussed the view that their customers, the general public, possibly expect too much of the Police Service. The team unanimously thought that was true! The answer for DS Hills lay in improved communications with the public: 'It is important that our customers understand why we sometimes get it wrong and make mistakes. It is not because we don't care, or that we cannot be bothered, rather that there can be genuine problems we face in day-to-day policing.'

This is where David Hills still believes the 'partnership' approach is vital.

If our customers can appreciate some of our problems, together we might be able to resolve them. This is why our divisional customers' forum – the Police/Community Consultative Group – is so important. It gives me a chance to discuss such issues with a cross-section of our local community. Sometimes as many as 50 representatives come along every two months, and it really is a customer clinic.

It used to be customary that senior officers would attend this type of meeting. Now, in keeping with Heather Penna's earlier comments relating to ownership at the level of service deliverers, Paddington Green include Sector Inspectors and Sergeants at these meetings. As David Hills explains:

> *It is very important for us at grass-roots level to see how the representatives of the public respond to us; likewise, we can tell them what our problems are. At the Consultative Group meeting last month, I had good reactions from community representatives, who said 'I didn't appreciate you have all those problems'. Exchanging that kind of information is important, and resolving where we can improve our quality of service is what these discussions are all about.*

SERVICE IN ACTION

The success of the 'quality of service' initiative, and the team-based discussions which promote it, will not be measured by the number of discussion groups held, but rather by what has come out of them: what problems they have identified; what has been done to narrow the gap between what is provided and what customers expect.

For Paddington Green Police Station, St Mary's Hospital is the biggest customer. Approximately 2,000 staff work in this major central London teaching hospital; its Accident and Emergency department sees more than 60,000 casualties per year; and outpatients number annually more than 308,000. At the local Police Community Division Group it had been highlighted that working relationships between Paddington Green and the Hospital were at times poor, and that considerable support was required if customer service was to be improved.

The 'quality of service' initiative was considered the ideal vehicle to steer such change, enabling David Hills's team and others to meet with service deliverers at St Mary's Hospital to discuss issues of concern. This allowed the team to see the problems as perceived by the customer, not what the police believed the problems to be. The meetings proved invaluable, in part due to being 'action' or 'doing' encounters. There is no point in having such round-table talks if nothing happens as a result. (See Figure 17.2.)

David Hills and his colleagues firmly believe this sort of partnership approach is the only way forward, because the MPS has got to win Londoners' support. They can't skirt around the issues. The population of London is around eight million people. What is their impression of the police service when they see high-profile cases on the news where convictions have been overturned and quashed because of police malpractice? When a police officer comes knocking on their front door people may well be thinking: 'Have I got one of *those* kind of policemen?' The MPS is going to have to work very hard to turn it all around. David Hills is keen to point out: 'We have also got to be realistic. If things have been going gradually wrong for a number of years it is not going to be made right over night. So we have got to work at it and work at it hard.'

David Hills admits that peer pressure has a strong role to play in changing the culture. What, then, would happen if he had on his team a person who was not committed to the 'quality of service' exercise and thought it a load of rubbish? 'There would be no place for them', he says. 'I personally do not work with anyone like that. I do not honestly think there is anyone like that in our office. I would say that in the current climate they would become ostracised pretty quickly and they would probably, out of sheer embarrassment, want to come on board.'

The MPS flagship station at Paddington Green has clearly made progress towards recognising that true quality of customer service has to be the priority for the Police Service. All I talked with believe that the team discussions have been very beneficial in creating greater understanding and awareness. David Hills sums up:

If we pull together with the Service we can make inroads on the enormous task of providing that quality of service. There is no doubt in my mind that the more we understand one another's problems and needs, the better we can offer the quality of service our customers now demand and, since they pay the bill, deserve. There simply is no other way ahead.

Figure 17.2 Discussion and Action Plans

'QUALITY OF SERVICE' TEAM ACTION PLAN ST MARY'S HOSPITAL – PADDINGTON, LONDON W2 AND PADDINGTON GREEN DIVISION POLICE – CID

In attendance – CID/Sector Inspector/Head of Hospital Security, Queen Mary's Hospital/ Senior Sister A&E/Business Manager A&E/ Chairman Divisional Police/Community Group. Meeting Held 24 July 1992

What were the issues discussed with the customer?	What was the problem as perceived by the customer?	What steps are we taking to improve the standard of service to the customer?
Doctors' fees in relation to the making of statements in crime cases	Frequently, fees are not being paid to Doctors for completion of Medical Evidence Statements. Therefore, there may exist a certain reluctance on the Doctor's part, to comply expeditiously with future requests.	i) Detective Sergeant (Det Sgt) David Hills (DH) CID to liaise with Detective Chief Inspector and Hospital Medical Secretary to establish whether a previously agreed system of payment to doctors is still in operation. ii) If yes, to examine methods of improvement. iii) If no, to adopt a system in consultation with the customer
The admittance of escorted prisoners to a ward.	On occasions escorted prisoners admitted to the ward without the knowledge of a Ward Sister or Hospital Security.	Memorandum to come from Chief Superintendent to custody officers to ensure both Hospital Security and Ward Sisters are informed *in all cases* prior to the arrival of a prisoner.
The arrest of persons for crime within the hospital.	Breakdown in communication, lack of information and feedback in relation to the result.	i) Sector Inspector Paul Holmes (PH) to appoint a liaison officer. ii) Copy of Sector Officers' shift pattern to Hospital Security staff. iii) Telephone number of Sector 'dedicated answerphone' given to Security staff.
The completion of administrative forms in cases of Road Traffic Accidents.	Lack of information to Hospital reception in relation to victims of Road Traffic Accidents.	Inspector PH to review current Road Traffic Accident forms and, if required, consider the possibility of the form being re-designed.

Figure 17.2 Discussion and Action Plans (continued)

'QUALITY OF SERVICE' TEAM ACTION PLAN ST MARY'S HOSPITAL – PADDINGTON, LONDON W2 AND PADDINGTON GREEN DIVISION POLICE – CID

Meeting Held on 24 July 1992

What were the issues discussed with the customer?	What was the problem as perceived by the customer?	What steps are we taking to improve the standard of service to the customer?
A.T.L.S. (Advanced Trauma Life Support).	Lack of vital information by police to Accident and Emergency (A+E) staff in relation to victims suffering multiple injuries as a result of a Road Traffic Accident. Action taken by *medical staff* within the "golden hour" of arriving in A+E normally dictates whether the patient survives. Examples of vital information would be – was the victim inside or outside the vehicle/if inside, speed of vehicle/ position in vehicle/type of impact eg another vehicle, lampost etc?	i) On a Service level, Chairman of Paddington Green Police Committee to research feasibility of inclusion in recruit/driver training at Hendon Police College, when next visiting the College. ii) On an Area level, PH to appraise Traffic Patrol officers. iii) On a local level, DH to liaise with Divisional Training Unit for inclusion in officers' training days.
Section 136 Mental Health Act 1983.	Who is responsible for Mental Health Patients. Police or Hospitals?	Long term problem which requires close co-operation between Police and Hospital staff. No immediate answer to the problem. May require legislative changes.
Information to police from Doctors in A & E in relation to victims of crime.	The 'badgering' of Doctors by Police when dealing with seriously injured victims of crime.	The Nursing Sisters run A+E. They are in the best position to provide the information police require. Memo to come from Chief Superintendent advising all officers to consult Nursing Sisters, wherever possible.
Liaison with hospital security departments and officers.	Through poor communication, failure to appreciate the problems of hospital security.	DH to liaise with the Divisional Training Unit, and if feasible, for them to include in officer training days, an attachment to the Hospital Security, to appreciate one anothers job role and work problems.

ACTION = Further "getting to know you" meeting between Hospital Security and Sector Inspector. NEXT full meeting 3rd Sept 1992, 1600hrs.

Figure 17.2 Discussion and Action Plans (continued)

'QUALITY OF SERVICE' TEAM ACTION PLAN ST MARY'S HOSPITAL – PADDINGTON, LONDON W2 AND PADDINGTON GREEN DIVISION POLICE – CID

In attendance – CID/Sector Inspector/Head of Hospital Security, St Mary's Hospital/ Senior Sister A&E/Business Manager A&E/Chairman Divisional Police/Community Group.   Meeting Held 3rd Sept 1992

What were the issues discussed with the customer?	What was the problem as perceived by the customer?	What steps are we taking to improve the standard of service to the customer?
Doctors' fees in relation to the making of statements in crime cases	Frequently, fees are not being paid to Doctors for completion of Medical Evidence Statements. Therefore, there may exist a certain reluctance on the Doctor's part, to comply expeditiously with future requests.	i) There is a system in existence. However, when the Medical Evidence Statements (MESs) are not collected by the individual Police Officers in Charge, the system at St Mary's can become blocked. It was agreed that there should be a 2 month trial period when a designated Officer from Paddington Green Division would collect twice weekly from the Medical Secretary at St Mary's all the MESs and their accompanying documents, ie Medical Authority, Statement and Expense Forms. The actual individual selected to collect these documents would be agreed in consultation with the Detective Chief Inspector (DCI) as the officer may be from Sector/Crime Desk or Crime Support Group. It was hoped this approach would help unblock the system. ii) Further discussion was required with the DCI and the Sector Inspector/Crime Desk re the system to be adopted at Paddington Green Police Station to administer and improve the transfer to the Pay Branch of the Expense Forms in relation to the MESs in order that the Doctors can then be paid. It was agreed that all the above documents should remain together as one item on their submission to Paddington Green. Separating them, as at present, was contributing to the delays occurring in the payment of the fees to the Doctors.
The admittance of escorted prisoners to a ward.	On occasions escorted prisoners admitted to the ward without the knowledge of a Ward Sister or Hospital Security.	See Ref MPS 9 – Letter from Ch. Supt Gerry McBride.
The arrest of persons for crime within the hospital.	Breakdown in communication, lack of information and feedback in relation to the result.	After consultation between Sector Inspector and St Mary's Head of Security, no specific liaison officer at this stage should be appointed. Rather the six sector team Sergeants are to be available for direct contact between Police and St Mary's. Points (i) and (iii) from July meeting have been actioned and implemented, and matters relating to the problem of crime within St Mary's has been addressed in the Chief Supt's letter at Ref MPS 9.
The completion of administrative forms in cases of Road Traffic Accidents.	Lack of information to Hospital reception in relation to victims of Road Traffic Accidents.	The administration forms relating to the Road Traffic Accident (RTA) require further discussion between management at St Mary's and Paddington Green Police. The current RTA form is standard throughout the MPS and it was agreed that the method of communication and information required via the form should be further debated with relevent expert opinion within the MPS.

Figure 17.2 Discussion and Action Plans (continued)

'QUALITY OF SERVICE' TEAM ACTION PLAN ST MARY'S HOSPITAL – PADDINGTON, LONDON W2 AND PADDINGTON GREEN DIVISION POLICE – CID

In attendance – CID/Sector Inspector/Head of Hospital Security, Queen Mary's Hospital/ Senior Sister A&E/Business Manager A&E/ Chairman Divisional Police/Community Group.   Meeting Held 3 Sept 1992

What were the issues discussed with the customer?	What was the problem as perceived by the customer?	What steps are we taking to improve the standard of service to the customer?
A.T.L.S. (Advanced Trauma Life Support).	Lack of vital information by police to Accident and Emergency (A+E) staff in relation to victims suffering multiple injuries as a result of a Road Traffic Accident. Action taken by *medical staff* within the "golden hour" or arriving in A+E normally dictates whether the patient survives. Examples of vital information would be – was the victim inside or outside the vehicle/if inside, speed of vehicle/type of impact eg another vehicle, lampost etc.	Regarding points (ii) and (iii) from July meeting, and relating to the Advanced Trauma Life Support (ATLS) issue, it was agreed that a dedicated officer from the Sector team at Paddington Green Police Division, an Area Traffic Division officer and, if feasible, a member from the Divisional Training Unit would attend a briefing at St Mary's given by the Senior Sister on ATLS. Information on ATLS could then be disseminated to all via The Training Unit/Sector teams/Traffic patrol. When above is up and running, the feedback could reinforce any action to be taken at point (i) from the July meeting – in that the matter could be raised with Hendon Police College to consider its incorporation within MPS wide training. Consideration is also to be given to the issuing of a laminated card to Police Officers which would provide a reader-friendly check list of information required by Accident and Emergency on their arrival with a serious Road Traffic Accident.
Section 136 Mental Health Act 1983.	Who is responsible for Mental Health Patients. Police or Hospitals?	It was agreed that parts of Section 136 Mental Health Act 1983 were ill conceived, and this constituted a long term problem within the community itself. A meeting was considered between Police/A&E and the Patterson Wing (for Mental Health Patients) of St Mary's. However, after discussion, many meetings had been previously held with nothing achieved for the benefit of Mental Health Patients. Consideration is to be given to a letter being sent from the Chief Supt. via the Divisional Community Group and the 106 Westminster-side Consultative Group re this problem. This issue was felt to be one of much wider significance, therefore, it should be handled at MPS/Local Authority and District Health Authority levels.
Information to police from Doctors in A&E in relation to victims of crime.	The 'badgering' of Doctors by Police when dealing with seriously injured victims of crime.	This matter was all agreed and being implemented. See Ref MPS 9, the memo from Chief Supt. at Paddington Green to help alleviate this problem.
Liaison with hospital security departments and officers.	Through poor communication, failure to appreciate the problems of hospital security.	Improved liaison could occur by having one officer from each of the six Sector teams, when on day duty, to be attached to Hospital Security between 0800 and 1600 hrs. Sector Inspector agreed to implement this liaise directly with St Mary's Head of Security. At this stage there was no requirement to involve the Divisional Training Unit.

ACTION = Next full meeting 22nd Oct 1992, 1645 hrs. To explore other initiatives with the Hospital other than above, for example, involving CRIMESTOPPERS to work alongside Head of Hospital Security to ascertain whether a joint approach could increase staff awareness of crime prevention. Sector Inspector to pursue during coming months.

Figure 17.2 Discussion and Action Plans (continued)

METROPOLITAN POLICE

MEMORANDUM   4th September 1992

To	From
Superintendent	Chief Superintendent H G McBRIDE
Chief Inspectors	
Inspectors	
Custody Suite	
Parade Books and File	(Police Network)

ST MARY'S HOSPITAL

Following a recent meeting with the Chief Security Officer at St Mary's Hospital, the following instructions are now to be followed:

1. Whenever a prisoner is transferred under escort to the hospital and is to remain under police guard, whether awaiting minor treatment in the Accident & Emergency Department or admission to a ward, the relevant ward or department Sister and a member of the hospital security staff should be informed *prior* to arrival of the prisoner and escort.

2. Where officers require information concerning a patient currently undergoing treatment at St Mary's (whether a prisoner or victim), the first point of reference will be the ward or department Sister, *NOT* the doctor concerned. The Sister will be in a better position to provide police with the required information. Where it is necessary to refer to the doctor, this will be arranged with the Sister on duty. (Requests for statements, etc, from doctors will continue to be arranged through the medical secretary in the normal way and are not affected by this instruction.)

3. The level of reported crime at St Mary's remains high and in many cases these crimes are linked. Therefore, whenever persons are arrested within the grounds/premises of St Mary's Hospital for offences of dishonesty (whether staff or not), the arresting officer should liaise with a member of the security staff and consideration should be given to searching the home address of the prisoner.

These developments have arisen following consultation with the security and Accident & Emergency Department staff at St Mary's Hospital and it is hoped that this increased level of consultation will enable both sides to have a better understanding of the other's role and problems.

Signed
Chief Superintendent
Paddington Green Division
METROPOLITAN POLICE SERVICE
London

LEADERSHIP FOR SUSTAINING CUSTOMER SERVICE

Excellence organisations all recognise that training is the major foundation upon which quality of service is sustained, particularly for the team leaders designated to spearhead the exercise. Many of the letters received as a result of the first book in this series asked for more information on the training for these team leaders, who have to 'sell' the concept of change down the line and ensure that styles of behaviour are geared to the new culture. This can be a difficult role. Unless team leaders are given the necessary skills they will seldom have the confidence to undertake their task effectively.

Experience distilled in this book illustrates that the style of leadership in an organisation geared to service is open and visible. David Kendrick, Commander Operations of MPS 2 Area, is an energetic enthusiast for the visible style of management, although he appreciates that there can be problems arising from different management styles. He says that one of the things he is constantly learning, and being reminded of, is that it is possible to communicate in a variety of ways.

> *Whilst I am an advocate of the 'walkabout', making yourself available, and the 'being approachable' style of management, it is no good walking about if you don't have the other qualities that go with it. 'Management by walkabout' is all to do with making yourself available, being prepared to listen, and being honest in feedback. It is then about actually doing something about a problem in a balanced and constructive way, and giving feedback as to what you can or cannot do about it.*

The 'message' on the 'quality of service' initiative was distributed throughout the MPS in a booklet. In some MPS divisions every effort was made to ensure that it was read and understood, although it was widely felt that not enough explanation was provided to support the written word. This view was endorsed when team leaders had to run group discussions on the concept. Acknowledging this situation, 2 Area decided to provide comprehensive training for all their team leaders – of the type that David Hills said he would have benefitted from before leading his sessions at Paddington Green. 2 Area also recognised that there were wide variations in the methods of progressing the 'quality of service' and associated leadership initiatives, whereas it was clearly important to achieve consistency across the organisation.

TRAINING FOR QUALITY OF SERVICE LEADERSHIP

Against this background, one of David Kendrick's Superintendents, Gary Miller, was asked to make recommendations for the further progression of the 'quality of service' discussions in 2 Area. He set up a small team of four people with a particular interest in customer service issues. The result was an innovative and far-sighted five-phase training programme for some 600 potential team leaders in 2 Area, developed by Chief Superintendent Peter Twist, Chief Inspector Bob Anthony and Sergeants Nick Osborn and Peter Clarke of 2 Area's Training Unit at Wapping Police Station.

Under the 2 Area programme, two staff members from each division received appropriate training and became 'team advisors' in a two-day module for the team leaders. Bob Anthony says:

> We wanted the course to concentrate on three main aspects: to make sure that everybody understands why 'leadership' is a vital component in management; the importance of team-building or sector policing; and the need to equip team leaders to run the 'quality of service' discussions.

Each Division and area nominated its own team advisors, and each nominee had to undergo a gruelling assessment day before being accepted. A two-week foundation course was created, by the end of which each pair of advisors were equipped to design and deliver their own two-day module. (For more detail on the specific phases of the programme, see Appendix 17.1.) The team advisors' responsibilities for the training of the team leaders were considerable, and the foundation course proved quite punishing for the first group in 1992. Some very lively debates and discussions were generated. Inevitably, the new sector policing initiative, described later in this chapter, featured prominently, and the special needs of the operational team leaders were acknowledged. Nevertheless, energy and enthusiasm were apparent by the end of the course, when comments by participants were overwhelmingly positive.

David Kendrick has attended this two-day training programme; in fact, every manager from executive officer and sergeant upwards, including the 2 Area Commanders, and all ranks in between, are on the programme. It is a conscious policy to mix up the ranks on each course, as Kendrick explains:

We do not have a separate Area Head Office course, where we are remote or distinct from our division. I and my colleagues will go for a two-day session with a group at a particular division or unit, where we will be talking through issues such as leadership, team building, how we do business together and our customer service priorities. This training is vital, right the way down the line. For example, sector policing has the Sector Inspector, who is the operational leader of the sector. He will be, in effect, the Community Liaison Officer, and the overall police Commander for that area. We need to prepare that individual for that role. Then there are the sergeants who will be the team leaders for six or seven constables or detectives on an ongoing permanent basis, which they've never had to do before in such a precise way.

Says Nick Osborn:

From our point of view in the Training Unit, we must avoid complacency. The task we have set the team advisors is far from easy in the cultural climate that exists in our Service. We have asked our advisors to steel and prepare themselves for some negativity and cynicism. A positive approach is, of course, essential but they almost consider themselves apostles. They can expect and permit a limited amount of complaint and 'dumping' – all the usual organisational moans and groans will manifest themselves. Providing these can be aired briskly they can build the platform from which team leaders can seek remedies for poor performance, lack of motivation and to use their workforce to help the organisation seek improvements in the quality of service delivered to the public, our customers.

David Kendrick explains further:

The emphasis in the 'quality of service' training is on building and valuing people. It is also on developing in people a greater awareness that they have a personal responsibility for their own development, rather than the culture of the police service which tends to spoon feed, through formal training courses. We must accept part responsibility for our own training and development – making sure we update ourselves on new legislation, procedures or approaches, but also ensuring that we allocated our own private time to our own development professionally. Individuals can no longer expect all their training to be provided in job time. So, although we will give supportive formal training, I expect all team managers to give their own time as well as police time to self-development.

THE SERVICE WAY FORWARD

There is an open line of senior management support for this major service training initiative, in which the most senior MPS officers are participants. Nick Osborn says:

The training is vital and valuable, but some battles still have to be fought with old ideas. I feel sure there are still bastions of support for the 'old order', but at least we have made a start! Old practices are being openly challenged and there appear to be sincere attempts to change for the better within our Service. Caring for the individual both within and outside the organisation is now an established and largely accepted concept in the MPS.

What David Kendrick is trying to get over in the training process are the qualities of leadership needed in police officers taking on board the 'quality of service' message:

I don't mean to be glib, but in leadership ranks, from Sergeant up to Commissioner, the thing which overrides everything else is 'the role model bit' – what I say and what I do. I see that as being so powerful, because the higher you go in an organisation the more people listen, watch and hear. They don't miss a trick. If you, as their role model, aren't right – in what you say, what you do, how you conduct yourself, what your values are – then the police service internally can be a very cruel culture.

From my own experience 'credibility' is critical in the police culture. In fact, it is an extremely powerful word. David Kendrick agrees:

Unless you are credible, even more so now, and actually practise what you preach, you are lost. Remember, action is so much more powerful than words. We've actually got to put into action and practice everything that we are talking about in customer quality service. It's about talking to people, listening to people – by reinforcing good practice, valuing people and endorsing it. It's also about condemning bad practice and unacceptable behaviour – in other words, thinking quality of service in everything we say and do. Quality is pride as far as I am concerned.

But what happens with those who do not think like David Kendrick? 'First of all I have to identify that problem', he responds. 'I have to give a lot of time and care to identifying their motivation, their values, etc., and to do everything I can by example, encouragement, training and support to deal with their problem, once it is identified. If, after that, they don't come on board, then I must give the appropriate actions, warnings or advice. If that fails, they will have to leave the organisation.'

SUSTAINING SERVICE AT THE POINT OF CONTACT: SECTOR POLICING

Sector policing is the most fundamental change in the history of the MPS, having taken place across every Division and became fully

---

Figure 17.3   Carter Street MPS Operating Principles

1. Consultation with the public and their views taken into account
2. Consultation with staff and their views taken into account
3. Balance sustained between response to emergencies and ownership in the resolution of policing problems, with decisions being taken at the lowest appropriate level and with flexibility built in
4. Adequate resources to meet demands
5. Enhanced policing performance where possible
6. Welfare and development of staff taken into account
7. Involvement in change of those affected
8. Consistency of policy as change occurs

---

operational in 1993. Sector policing is all about managing change. Ever since the creation of the Metropolitan Police in 1839 discussion has continued about the critical role of the 'bobby on the beat'. Reams have been written and volumes spoken about the uniformed constable on the beat being at the heart of the MPS organisation. Much of it was so much hot air, because little was done about the question in the way of new strategy or tactics. Now there is a fundamental difference, turning some 150 years of history on its head. This is that the public, the customers who ultimately pay for the Police Service, have insisted that they want their coppers back on the beat.

Inspector Paul Holmes is the Inspector for Bayswater Sector at Paddington Green Police Station, part of MPS 8 Area. His philosophy is quite simple: 'If you are paying the bill, you are entitled to a say in how the customer service is delivered. I don't see how anybody on any basis can object to that concept.' That may be an over-simplification of what is a very complicated equation, but as a basic thesis it must be right. The MPS, indeed any police force or service, can only police by consent. The concept of sector policing is really only an extension of that.

A good example of the new approach is to be found in the Carter Street Division of MPS 3 Area, to the south of the Thames, where all the familiar problems of inner city decay, social deprivation and crime are in evidence. Carter Street have at the head of their 1993 Divisional objectives a 'Quality of Service Action Plan' focusing on 'adapting policing style to a more community-based approach'. The 'mission' philosophy behind this objective specifies that Carter Street Division will 'strive for the provision of a better policing service to the people who live and work in our area and the improvement of working conditions of the staff who provide that service'. To this end Carter Street have evolved an eight-point list of principles within which they operate (see Figure 17.3).

Under sector policing the key role is taken by the Sector Inspector – a completely new role in the MPS. A Sector Inspector may have more than 50 individuals in his or her sector team, so that it is a more managerial role as opposed to 'hands-on', out in the streets with the constables. This does not particularly endear it to inspectors such as Paul Holmes who have often enjoyed being out and about on the ground in 'hands-on' situations. That being said, he thinks the role description for the job must be a managerial one in terms of more direct overseeing of the teams themselves, and guiding them in the direction that he, his senior management and indeed his customers, expect them to go.

To Paul Holmes, this new role is a very exciting one because:

I believe in the concept of sector policing. I'm enjoying the extra responsibilities of having a lot more officers, the various personnel problems that come up and the welfare problems. I'm directing six smaller teams in a much more focused way, and watching the teams start to grow. It's satisfying to see the teams realise that they can play with the new ball they have been given, and watch them develop their own tactics and plans, as the ethos of sector policing permeates down to the constables and out to the customer.

It is rather too early to say how Paul Holmes's role will eventually progress. For example, he has yet to fully develop a liaison team (local working party) in terms of a direct feedback as to what the community wants:

I'm looking forward to doing that, as we can then develop on the one or two little vignettes that I have already had experience of in relation to local complaints from residents via their Paddington Green Police/ Community Group discussions. Hopefully that will just be the start of it and we can develop it to much more powerful and potent levels.

On the philosophy of sector policing, Paul Holmes believes that provided the police do their job properly there will not be a question of winning the hearts and minds of the local community. 'Hopefully', he says, 'they will see a great deal of improvement in any event, maybe not in terms of how we impact on our levels of crime or whatever, but certainly in terms of feeling a lot more cared for. They will receive a far higher level of service because we have got local contact and we do take their problems seriously.'

The biggest worry for many managers is the customer ending up with false expectations of what they can actually deliver. Says Paul Holmes:

The team I have got are working very, very hard. They fully embrace both the concept of sector policing and the new shift system that has been developed for it which is a great advance on what they have worked with for many years. . . . I don't necessarily see customer service under the umbrella of sector policing as a new concept. When I first joined the police, customer service used to be a big thing anyway, because courtesy and civility and looking after our customers was always a prime consideration.

He believes that dealing with people with courtesy and promptitude and civility

. . . has just got lost somewhere between the 1960s and the 1990s. Whereas I was brought up on the 'Dixon of Dock Green' sort of ethos, a lot of the kids that came in the 1970s and beyond were brought up on Jack Regan and the 'Sweeney'. We have only just come to realise the gigantic gulf that has developed between the police and the public that we serve.

There are more complicated arguments, about police racing around in panda cars rather than on walkabout, but at the end of the day does it really matter how the police officer gets about? It is surely what they do, and the service given, that are important. Paul Holmes believes that, whatever the job, his people are committed to the philosophy of customer service. As he endorses, 'I find, as a rule, that the majority of ordinary police officers have a desire to do well and want to give a proper service to the customer. So really all we have done is refocus them on that and convince them that there is a future to this new sector police system – that it is not a fad, and that we can do an awful lot with it.'

A major difficulty that many sector inspectors have experienced in the initial stages of this customer-centred change process is that, by its very nature, police work tends to make one cynical and suspicious. For this reason it often takes the best part of six months for those at the sharp end to realise that there are no gimmicks or catches. Says Paul Holmes:

It has been very illuminating and rewarding for me to see the first buds of sector policing develop, with the various stages of meetings and conversations in our sector office. Suddenly, your officers, instead of saying 'We have to pass this up the line', are saying 'Never mind about anybody else, it is our problem, we'll go and deal with it'. An example would be drugs addresses on estates where there are nice folk living in the blocks. Previously, before sector policing, this was passed to the central drugs squad, or possibly to a crime squad; now it is ours, it is local, they are our customers. We will get a warrant and we will start making enquiries ourselves and give the customer service. Obviously if we need resources or backup we know where to find them, but it is very rewarding for me now to see the officers not only realising that they can play with the ball, but seeing just how far they can kick it if they want to.

Provided the MPS keep reinforcing this 'ownership' message, sector policing will take them from strength to strength. Of course, it will take a long time to bed in, because places like Carter Street are standing 150 years of police practice on its head. However, the majority of managers I have interviewed believe that once those at the front line understand the parameters of sector policing, and how far they can go, all kinds of developments will come out of it – in particular that officers will take 'ownership' of local problems.

SUSTAINING CUSTOMER SERVICE AT ALL TIMES

As indicated earlier, sector leaders often discover that what their sector can achieve is limited by lack of resources, principally in terms of manpower. It is not so much non-manpower resources they may be lacking, because management can always box and cox on those sort of problems and scrape their way by. As regards manpower, many areas across the MPS have very busy sectors and heavy workloads, not least in maintaining station records. Clearly, a shortage of manpower can impact upon the quality of service which the police can give.

There are a number of improvements that may be feasible, but they are really no more than fine-tuning an engine that is missing a cylinder. For example, duties could be rearranged, to allow dedicated officers longer at the scene of a burglary to do the necessary follow-up. The problem remains, however, that no matter how much fine-tuning is possible, MPS managers are always likely to lose manpower to various extraneous duties such as policing demonstrations.

Such factors are always going to impact upon sector policing in terms of how much constant service the local police can provide. Like everyone else in this country, and all the organisations is this book, the Police Service has got to work within available resources. Perhaps customers should be as aware of that as they are of paying the police bill. Showing faith and goodwill, customers will usually run with the service deliverer, providing they are honest and open as to what they can and cannot do. Obviously there will be times of friction when, for various operational or judicial reasons, the police cannot be as open as they would wish to be. Even then, if they can convince those sharing their service partnership of their bonafides, in the fullness of time, the police believe they can sustain customer service and support.

Most sector teams know they cannot achieve all that is expected of them, and that is a bald fact. Providing, however, the Police Service are open, and explain to their customers why they cannot achieve everything, then there will be fewer problems with customers. Certainly most of the sector teams that I have researched for this book are working flat out. Although many will admit that it is taking time for change to be accepted, most believe in sector policing and say they are happier being closer to their public.

Members of the public are usually satisfied with service received if they think they have been treated fairly, with courtesy and the right attitude. Even if the first two are present, without the third a member of the public would be left feeling aggrieved. This is one of the major problems the Police Service has, and there is no easy way to overcome it. The Community Liaison Officer at Paddington Green Division, Paul Ramsay, comments:

Sector policing goes some way to combat this problem, by giving officers the ownership of the area they police. If they want to improve the quality of service and sustain the relationship with the public, then it is in their interest to deal with individuals properly in the first place, because the chances of them being called back, or meeting that individual again, is much greater now than in the past.

In common with many others I talked to for this chapter, Paul Ramsay insists that: 'The public, too, must realise that the police cannot deliver everything the customers want. It is up to us to find time to explain to them why we cannot do certain things they rightly or wrongly think we can.' There is no doubt that this has been a major failing of the MPS in the past, which is only now being slowly corrected, primarily through better sharing and understanding of their problems and the exchange of information on a one-to-one basis with customers. At the end of the day, however, it is only through service deliverers appreciating what customers want that the partnership approach so earnestly wished for by police and community will go forward.

As the new Metropolitan Police Commissioner, Paul Condon, told me:

> *You must define your core business. This is reinforced by a regime of tight performance standards in relation to the core business. These key performance indicators then become strict criteria against which our customer service is judged. Our duty, values, priorities and aims are the foundations upon which all our services are built.*

Like other chief executives of customer-centred organisations featured in this book, Paul Condon, as MPS Commissioner, can expect to preside over constant re-evaluation of business priorities and reappraisal of customer demands and standards of service performance. There is simply no point in having values and a policy style if they are not giving the customer what they want. That is why Commissioner Paul Condon believes strict performance measures are critical to sustaining customer service.

Paul Condon is right. For the Metropolitan Police Service and their public, as with all the organisations I have looked at in this book, there really is no alternative.

I have reiterated throughout this book that sustaining customer service is a journey *not* a destination. All the organisations will admit it is one that is never ending and tough. I personally wish them all 'bon voyage' and every success as they travel towards excellence.

APPENDIX 17.1

THE AIM OF LEADERSHIP TRAINING IN 2 AREA, METROPOLITAN POLICE

The aim of the Leadership Training initiative in 2 Area is to progress the 'PLUS' generated initiatives of 'Leadership' and team-based 'Quality of Service' discussions and to provide training and support for Team Leaders engaged, for example, in the introduction of the Sector Policing programme. Its purpose is to identify two 'Team Advisors' per Division and to provide them with a comprehensive training package. It is the responsibility of these 'Advisors' to deliver a two–day module for all Team Leaders specifically covering aspects of: Leadership; Team Building; Quality of Service.

SELECTION OF FACILITATORS

It was important to ensure that those nominated to receive training and undertake the role of 'Team Advisors' were of the highest calibre and possessing the necessary qualities and potential. To this end, Chief Inspectors were provided with a draft job description and a guide of positive personality characteristics and experience that their nominees should ideally conform to. To assist this process, and to ensure that the appropriate personnel were nominated, a one day Assessment was held approximately two weeks prior to the commencement of the 'Advisors' Foundation Course. (Details of the Selection Guide for this Assessment Day are at the end of this Appendix.)

SELECTION GUIDE FOR TEAM ADVISORS

This outlines the job requirements and candidate qualifications.

The Job
The post of 'Team Advisor' is intended to provide Divisions with a further local training resource with specific responsibilities in progressing both the 'Leadership' and 'Quality of Service' issues. After appropriate training, 'Team Advisors' will return to the Division being required to run a two-day module for *all* 'Team Leaders'. The administration and servicing of these courses will be the sole responsibility of nominated 'Advisors'. In addition, they will provide guidance and advice for all supervisors in running their initial team-based seminars with particular attention to personnel involved in Sector Policing. As Divisional members, they will remain a constant and easily available source of counselling and support.

Qualities
Each Division is being asked to nominate two 'Advisors' who will be required to work amicably as a pair. A blend of individuals with different skills and leadership experience would be ideal. These individuals will need to be self-motivated and capable of dealing with the wide variety of groups and their managers, from Police Sergeant/ Administration Officer to Chief Superintendent rank/grade. Individuals should be able to liaise with their Chief Inspector and, after instruction, be confident in providing a presentation to their Divisional Management Team. Some experience of training or working with groups would be of value but full training will be provided in the areas of group dynamics, module construction, presentation and facilitation. The 'Advisors' will receive comprehensive training in the specific areas of: Leadership, Team Building, Facilitation, 'Quality of Service' and Equal Opportunities. It is anticipated that for their initial training role on Division, a period of *dedicated* duty (or posting) will be required to effectively service all of the teams on Division and nominees should be aware

and agreeable to this. It is necessary to emphasise that selection of each nominee must be based on the suitability and the potential competence of the individual. Gender, rank/grade, service and current role/duty is not a qualification (or disqualification) for this important training post.

Course Requirements

Suitable nominations must be able to attend the Initial Training Course for the full 2 week period. It is essential that each Division/Department provides two students for assessment and training on the appropriate dates as only one course per Division will be available.

Assessment Day

Before deciding on your nomination, please bear in mind:

- the commitment to provide 2 day modules may last for several months, so choose people who will be around and available;
- do consider civil staff colleagues possessed of the necessary energy and charisma;
- rank is unimportant, it's the personality that counts;
- if your nominees don't pass the assessment day, you'll need to have a re-think, so make your selection carefully;
- some of this training may be adventurous, unusual and challenging, so choose people whose brains and bodies are in gear;
- finally, remember each trainer acts as a role model – chose only people who match up to the highest professional standards.

There were 4 Assessors and 5 Assessment days that had to be run to ensure suitable clients were selected. Some nominees did fail as the letter at the end of this Appendix indicates.

ASSESSMENT DAY

The Assessment Day is held on the 19th and 21st May at Wapping Training Unit. All nominated Area delegates will be assessed and evaluated to ensure their eligibility to attend the 2-week training courses on Leadership. Ideally, nominated pairs will attend together and their working and personal relationship will be taken into consideration in the overall assessment.

FORMAT

The day will be divided into three stages (given in this Appendix) although observation and evaluation will take place throughout the proceedings in both the formal exercises and informal gatherings. The day will commence at 9am for tea and reception, and the observers will be present. At 9.30am there will be a briefing for the delegates on the day's schedule and the formal proceedings will commence at about 9.40am. At the earliest time it should be ascertained whether the delegates are attending 'of their own free will'.

THE THREE STAGES ARE:

Stage I – Leaderless Group Discussion (30–40 minutes)

The delegates will be equally divided into two syndicates and this exercise will be run simultaneously with the two groups but in different rooms. Two observers per group will be employed. This exercise requires no preparation from the delegates prior to the briefing and will be run as a very low level evaluation. The delegates will be seated in a circle, with the observers included, and participants should be briefed to join in a discussion on one of the following:

'Money and the Police'	'What does fairness mean'
'Morale in a large organisation'	'Sector Policing'
'What's in a team'	'Corporacy'
'A good Governor is . . .'	'A unified Europe'

As in the Extended Interview Assessments the delegates will be informed that they will commence their discussion immediately after being told the subject heading. They should also be advised that, without notice, their discussion will be terminated and a new subject will be provided. Essentially the assessment is restricted to the individual's ability to communicate in an articulate and balanced way. How much they are willing, and able, to contribute and whether they exercise any level of control, or dominance, over the group. As potential facilitators it is essential that they are willing to listen to others' views and to acknowledge the points and issues raised by others. Each subject may be changed at the discretion of the assessor and it is suggested that during this exercise at least three variations are provided.

Stage II – Chaired Discussion Exercise (75 minutes)

The delegates will remain in their two respective groups and venues. This time, the briefing will state that for each group member no further information should be provided. An arbitrary running order may be followed and each 'Chairperson' will have to lead the discussion for about 10 minutes. The subject for discussion may be chosen from the following list:

Europe	Arms	Law	Reasonable
Fascism	Art	Liberty	Sexism
God	Bullshit	Morality	Truth
Happiness	Capitalism	Nationalism	Wisdom
Honesty	Discipline	Power	Youth

Time keeping needs to be quite strict for this exercise and initially this is the responsibility of the 'chair'. However, in the event of a likely over-run, the assessors must guillotine the proceedings and move the 'chair' on.

The individuals are to be assessed on their ability to control and facilitate a group. It will be necessary to observe the quieter and more dominant members of the group and see whether any element of control or encouragement was exercised. The delegates interpretation of the position of 'chairperson' will also be evident and will provide interesting evidence of their potential competence in a training/facilitation role. The subject headings should be deliberately obtuse in order to encourage a limited explanation and sense of direction from the 'chair'. A summary of the discussion would also prove of value. A brief outline of the 'Chairperson's' role will be provided in the exercise briefing.

Stage III – Presentations (90 minutes)

The delegates will remain in their respective groups and venues. Each individual will deliver a 10 minute presentation to the rest of the group. These presentations will be pre-prepared and on a subject of the delegates own choosing. It must be a verbal presentation, unsupported by overhead projection or video, however, a white board, flipchart and stand, together with a collection of coloured pens, will be available. The assessment will be on the demonstration of each individual. An evaluation can be made of the apparent preparation and confidence displayed by the delegates. Observer sheets, to act as aide memoirs, will be used by each assessor. Polished peformances are unlikely and should not be expected. Training in presentation and facilitation will be provided – this exercise merely provides the assessors with a change to observe the delegates 'potential' and to provide a reasonable indication of existing confidence levels and diction.

Debriefing

At the end of the presentations, delegates should be invited to get refreshment and assemble as one group. A debriefing will follow and delegates will be advised that their results will be forwarded direct to respective Chief Inspectors the following day. Failed candidates will be personally contacted and invited to reattend for counselling. (An example of such a letter is shown below.) Questions should be invited following a brief resumé of the proposed 2 week course.

Example of feedback letter

2 Area Training Unit, Wapping Police Station, 98 High Street, London E1 9NE

Date

Dear (personalised greeting)

LEADERSHIP TRAINING
ASSESSMENT DAY ON 19TH MAY

Thank you very much for coming along yesterday and participating in the Assessemnt Day for Team Advisors. On this occasion you were not selected and I hope that this does not cause you too much disappointment.

As I emphasised at the commencement of the assessment yesterday, this should not be viewed as a failure. The absence of characteristics we considered necessary for 'Advisors' in no way reflects upon your acknowledged competence as a police officer and a manager.

I would welcome the opportunity of providing you with detailed feedback on your performance and this can be easily arranged for a mutually convenient date. We have spoken with Chief Inspector (personalised) of our decision today, but have declined to provide detailed reasons as we consider our assessments to be of a confidential nature. My telephone extension at Wapping is 5015 and I look foward to hearing from you.

Yours sincerely,

Nick OSBORN
(Facilitator)

Index